Praise for *100 Places in Greece Every Woman Should Go*

"OH MY GODS! Amanda Summer lights up the country with magic, history, power, and mystery. Do not go to Greece without this book.... though you will definitely be there as you read. She lures you in with sparkling waters, caves, temples, sculptures, foods...and her lively prose and passion will bring you into lives and loves, healings, and an underworld that feels as real as the temples you can touch. Greek mythology, as she passionately and powerfully describes it, is alive and well and still hovering."

—Rita Golden Gelman
Author of *Tales of a Female Nomad, Living at Large in the World*

"This book makes a perfect traveling companion for any woman discovering Greece, whether she's exploring its ancient ruins or modern life. Pull it out of your bag, open up to your location, and get ready for a fresh perspective, interesting insight or useful information—everything you'd want from a buddy joining you on your odyssey."

—Eleni Gage
Author of *North of Ithaka, The Ladies of Managua* and *Other Waters*

"A captivating account of thousands of years of female experience in one of the most enchanting places of the world. Amanda Summer, an archaeologist with an intricate and profound knowledge of Greece, masterfully combines the hard facts of history with the romance and mystery of Greek culture. Her lively, powerful, and intimate writing brings to life not only the ruins, the landscape, and the culture of Greece, but also the connection between the past and the present. The author manages to captur   ess, and *joie de vivre* that define Gree.   y."

los
Author of *Bronze Age E*   *ries*

100 Places in Greece
Every Woman Should Go

AMANDA SUMMER

TRAVELERS' TALES
AN IMPRINT OF SOLAS HOUSE, INC.
PALO ALTO

For Phil

Travelers' Tales and Solas House are trademarks of Solas House, Inc. 2320 Bowdoin Street, Palo Alto, California 94306. www.travelerstales.com

Art Direction: Kimberly Nelson Coombs
Cover Design: Kimberly Nelson Coombs
Interior Design and Page Layout: Howie Severson/Fortuitous Publishing
Author Photo: Philip Slavin
Production Director: Susan Brady

Library of Congress Cataloging-in-Publication Data

Names: Summer, Amanda, author.
Title: 100 places in Greece every woman should go / Amanda Summer.
Other titles: Hundred places in Greece every woman should go | One hundred
   places in Greece every woman should go
Description: First edition. | Palo Alto : Travelers' Tales, an imprint of
   Solas House, Inc., 2016.
Identifiers: LCCN 2015041532 | ISBN 9781609521073 (paperback)
Subjects: LCSH: Greece--Description and travel. | Women--Travel--Greece. |
   Greece--History, Local. | Historic sites--Greece. | Historic
   buildings--Greece. | Sacred space--Greece. | BISAC: TRAVEL / Reference.
Classification: LCC DF728 .S86 2016 | DDC 919.49504/76--dc23
LC record available at http://lccn.loc.gov/2015041532

First Edition
Printed in the United States
10 9 8 7 6 5 4 3 2 1

Table of Contents

II. Goddesses of Cinema, History, and the Arts

III. The Blessed Virgin Mary, Saints, Sinners, and Mysterious Places of Healing

VIII. A GREAT SCENIC DRIVE

Introduction

THE FIRST TIME I SET FOOT on Greek soil, I was an eleven-year-old child on a family vacation. I can still remember the fierceness of the sun, the surreal turquoise sea, and the smell of pines marinating an atmosphere that seemed infused with mystery. I can also remember being mesmerized by the cute Greek waiter who flirted with my older sister at a seaside family dinner one night, and recall that, even at an early age, the tumbled column drums and foundation stones of ancient temples really did seem to speak to me.

As a college student, years later, I felt compelled to return to Greece on a study abroad program. After living in rural Crete with a family to learn the language, I returned to Athens and had an experience one afternoon in a restaurant basement that changed my life. After imbibing my share of golden retsina with a group of girlfriends, I inquired as to the location of the ladies room, and was directed down a spiral staircase that seemed to penetrate the earth itself. Wandering down a dark passageway, my hands fumbling along the damp stone walls for purchase, I heard a voice in the distance. "Do you want to see something interesting?" it asked. As I drew nearer I saw a figure looming in the distance; upon closer inspection I could make out that it was our waiter. "Uh, sure," I answered, not sure at all. In fact, I felt like Persephone, perched at the edge of an abyss, about to be abducted by a real life Hades into the Underworld. "You will like it," he grinned, his teeth shining white in the darkness. "Come and see," he said, grabbing my hand and pulling me deeper into the cellar. A riot of emotions surged through my body: just as I felt I was about to be kidnapped and no one would know where to find me, we entered into a clearing. My Hades raised his arm and pointed—there in the distance, a slender, white rectangle of marble erupted from the earth. Upon closer inspection, I could see inscriptions engraved onto the face of the stone. Hades spoke, his teeth once again gleaming through the flannel light. "You see," he said in a hushed and reverent tone, "that is a grave." He paused for a moment, and then released a sentence with the veneration of a priest giving an Easter Sunday benediction, "and we are standing in a cemetery."

I stood, silent and awestruck. Hades waited a few moments before interrupting my reverie. "You like?" he asked, innocently, wondering if my silence meant I was disappointed. Here I was, thirty feet below the modern Athenian street level, cars and buses rumbling above me, knocking dust off the rafters that floated onto my hair in a gritty benediction. "Did I like?" I was standing in an ancient Roman graveyard! Somewhere in this hazy intersection between ancient and modern, past and present, lay my future. Right then and there, I made up my mind: I wanted to become an archaeologist. Hades was no abductor; in fact, I had to thank him, for he had unlocked the key to my future. I took in a breath and gave him my answer. "I like," I said quietly, "I like very much."

Ever since that transformational moment in an Athenian restaurant basement, I have been mesmerized, maddened and emboldened by the ancient landscape of Greece. Every time I return, I find a way to channel my inner goddesses. Feeling independent? Artemis is your gal. Ready to take on the big boys and own your feminine power? Let the supremacy of Athena course through your blood. In a sexy mood? Aphrodite is never far away in this sensual and passionate country. Ready to take a plunge into the depths? Allow Persephone, Queen of the Underworld, to guide your way. Remember, the world's most potent modern divas were born with Greek fire in their blood: Maria Callas, Melina Mercouri, and Irene Papas, and other screen goddesses have tested their artistic chops on this magnificent soil: Meryl Streep, Pauline Collins, Daryl Hannah, Alexis Bledel, and Jacqueline Bisset to name a few. Yet another famous Jacqueline—Jackie O—put Greece on the map after marrying the country's richest and most infamous shipping tycoon, Aristotle Onassis.

There is a sense of chaos (a Greek word!) and dirt-under-the-fingernails quality to this country that makes it real. Greeks say what they feel, don't hide their emotions and live life to the max. They will gladly give you everything they have, for the obligation to *filotimo*—respect for oneself and others—is a real and undeniable one. Because they want to please, Greeks will give you directions, even if they don't know the way, for not to offer you something is considered rude. Greeks love to help, love it when you try to speak their language, and will tell you stories with a zest, passion, and *kefi* worthy of Homer. Aphrodite lives in their soul, for Greeks worship beauty. You will find it in the line of the columns of the Parthenon, on every beach where the sea caresses the pine-laden shore, in the precise placement of cloves burrowed into diamonds of rich, flaky baklava, and in the wrapping of gifts you bring home to loved ones, painstakingly and lovingly cradled in tissue, bagged or boxed, and tied with an exquisite medallion or bow.

Alexandra Fiada in her book, *The Xenophobe's Guide to the Greeks*, accurately captures the boundlessly passionate essence of the Greek sensibility, "Self-control—although invented by the ancient Spartans—is not only unknown but also incomprehensible to the modern Greek. They are eager in everything: their joys, their sorrows, have no moderation. They shout, they yell, they rant and rave for important and unimportant issues alike, in happiness and in sorrow. No emotion is considered private enough to remain unexpressed and their excitement knows no bounds."

I will leave you with another quote, from Lawrence Durrell's *Prospero's Cell*, a memoir of the author's life on the Ionian island of Corfu. In my humble opinion, Durrell managed to sum up the joyous and mysterious nature of his adopted homeland when he wrote: "Other countries may offer you discoveries in manners or lore or landscape; Greece offers you something harder—the discovery of yourself."

May the following pages offer you a peek into this powerful and ancient place, and the opportunity to discover many things about its manners, lore, landscape, and sites, both ancient and modern. But more evocatively, as you explore this collection of beloved, handpicked places dedicated to the feminine, may you ultimately unearth the most cherished treasure of all: your inner goddess!

AMANDA SUMMER
SAINT LOUIS, MISSOURI

I

Goddesses of Mythology and Antiquity

1 The Acropolis

THE PARTHENON, ERECHTHEION, AND
THE TEMPLE OF ATHENA NIKE

When I arrived in Athens to live in Greece my junior year of college, I was in a state of shock. Racing past row upon row of concrete apartment buildings and traffic-clogged streets, I remembered thinking: this isn't what I expected. What I was expecting were temples with pristine white marble columns decorated with statues of gods and goddesses. The garish billboards lining the highway emblazoned with bold Greek letters did nothing to help; in fact, they made me feel even more disoriented. In short, it was an assault on the senses.

Then I saw it. Just as the taxi rounded a corner I looked up: sitting on top of a huge stone outcropping was the Parthenon—the temple of Athena, reflecting the midday sun in a white-hot illumination that almost burned my eyes. In spite of the miles of concrete canyons I had just passed through, if Athens holds something as gorgeous as this at its core, I thought, this is indeed a beautiful place.

If you choose to stroll the city by foot, you'll enjoy getting lost in the marketplaces and stumbling upon ancient architecture that seems to appear around every corner. However, to make the most of your visit to the city of a goddess, it's best to hire a guide or take a tour bus to make sure you don't miss important sites. But above all, don't miss the most important one: the hilltop of the Acropolis not only dominates the Athenian skyline, it holds a collection of exquisite buildings, all of which are dedicated to the city's goddess. Come with me as we explore this celebration of the Divine Feminine at her most divine.

The Parthenon

Imagine you are entering a darkened room. A hush falls all around you, you are aware of a few other people nearby, but for the moment you feel completely alone. You notice a glimmering in the shadows and are suddenly aware of something towering above you. As your eyes adjust, you realize an enormous statue made of ivory and gold stands before you, soaring thirty feet in the air, almost scraping the ceiling. It's 430 B.C. in the  ancient city of Athens. You have come a long way to visit the most important temple of your time period, and you are not disappointed.

Known by its traditional name, The Parthenon (which means temple of the virgin) is the temple dedicated to the goddess after whom Athens is named: Athena, goddess of war and wisdom. This nearly architecturally perfect building was constructed from 447–438 B.C. and Athena dominated the temple in the form of a huge gold and ivory statue. At one time looming over worshippers in the darkness of the temple's interior, this priceless treasure has been lost to looting over the intervening millennia.

The story of the mythological beginnings of the city of Athens is embedded on the eastern and western ends of the temple known as the pediment. The sculptures within this triangular structure, many of which are now housed in the newly opened Acropolis Museum, tell the story of the Birth of Athena on the eastern end and the Battle between Athena and Poseidon for the city on the western end. Obviously, Athena won! Mythology tells us that Athena sprang fully formed from the forehead of her father, Zeus, and for a country that is largely focused on machismo-heavy values, it is fascinating that the major city of Greece is dedicated to the feminine. Athena is often thought of as one of the more cerebral goddesses, less emotional than her Olympian counterparts, such as Aphrodite. As the goddess of war and wisdom, she is always the embodiment of stoicism as she rallies Odysseus to the Trojan War, or gently guides him back home to Ithaka.

You can no longer go inside the temple, but enjoy a long stroll around the exterior of this remarkable building and imagine the enormous gold and ivory sculpture that once stood within its interior, dwarfing the worshippers who came to pay their respects to this powerful goddess. Note that the temple was once covered in a continuous sculptural frieze depicting the citizens of Athens in sacred procession, with teams of Lipizzaner-like prancing horses and wheeled chariots holding the gods and goddesses. Imagine that the building was once vividly painted in blue and red pigment and the friezes were festooned with an almost garish assemblage of metal attachments depicting spears, reins, and other trimmings. Marble panels, known as metopes, also decorated the exterior and depicted battles of Lapiths and Centaurs, Amazon invasions and the Trojan War. Much of this sculpture is currently in the British Museum, having been brutally hacked away by Lord Elgin and taken back to Britain in the early 19th century. During the Ottoman period it was used as an arsenal, and sadly, in 1687 a Venetian attack made a direct hit on the structure, destroying much of the building, particularly its southern flank.

Pay special attention to the base of the structure, known as the sty-lobate. The architects, Ictinus and Kallikrates, wanted the building to appear to spring up from its foundation, so they installed the plat-form on a curve. Theoretically the columns, all slightly tilted towards one another, would eventually converge several miles into space.

The Erechtheion

The porch of the Erechtheion is held up by no fewer than six female figures, each balancing the weight of the world on her head. If this isn't a place for women to admire their ancestors, I don't know what is. Erected between 421 and 406 B.C. to honor both Athena and Poseidon, this structure was uniquely constructed to accommodate the uneven surface beneath and contains a number of porches that extend out from the main cella. Designed by the master sculptor Phidias, this elegant building stands atop the site of an earlier temple dedicated to Athena Polias, or "old temple." The most famous portico, the Porch of the Maidens, contains the renowned columns in the form of women known as Caryatids, pos-sibly named after women from Karyes of Laconia, who danced in honor of the goddess of the hunt, Artemis.

Due to deterioration from excessive pollution in the 1970s, the ladies were removed and placed in the old Acropolis museum; since then they have been moved to the spanking new Acropolis Museum where you can see them up close in all their glory. There you can admire every detail of the pleats and folds of the fabric, the impassive yet knowing gazes of their faces and the elaborate, thickly braided hairstyles that served a dual purpose: as well as indicating the style of the day, the additional density of marble helped to reinforce the delicate neck portion of the column, adding stability to the structure.

Within its foundations was thought to live a sacred snake of Athena Polias, who was fed honey cakes by the goddess's priestesses. Bad omens were predicted if the snake did not eat the cakes. In later times, the temple was converted into a church, and then during the Turkish occupation it became a harem, perhaps not too surprising a choice considering there are six gorgeous women outside the building, holding up the weight of the world and inviting all to enter.

Temple of Athena Nike

Completed in 420 B.C., this tiny temple balanced precariously at the southern flank of the Acropolis is dedicated to the aspect of Athena as a goddess of victory. From ancient accounts we know a wooden statue of the goddess occupied its interior, holding a helmet in one hand and a pomegranate in the other. Most Nike statues (the word means victory in Greek) have wings, but this one did not. As such, it was said the "wingless" statue could never leave Athens. The temple's graceful Ionic columns create a lovely foil to the Parthenon's more severe Doric style, balancing the graceful trio of temples on the top of this sacred mount.

My suggestion is to visit the Acropolis monuments first thing in the morning. During the heat of the Athenian summer, the light bouncing off the glossy marble can be blisteringly hot. Rest assured you will be in good company; no matter how early you arrive you will be accompanied by legions of visitors winding up the serpentine pathway to the Propylaia, the massive gateway to the site, along with tour guides hoisting their colored flags aloft and describing the site in polyglot tongues.

❊ www.acropolisofathens.gr/aoa/the-acropolis/monument

Be sure to wear sturdy footwear and not flip-flops, as you will be sliding all over these centuries-worn stones that are as slippery as river rock. Not that you would consider it, but note that spiked heels are banned at all archaeological sites in Greece. And if you want to put on Santa Claus hats for that holiday photo op, think again: the Parthenon police will shrill their whistles and come running. All structures atop the Acropolis mount are considered sacred sites, so any behavior that smacks of the slightest disrespect is forbidden.

Before leaving, pause at the southern edge of the Acropolis hill. You can admire the theaters of Herod Atticus and Dionysus on the slopes below, as well as pick out the new Acropolis Museum in the densely packed Makriyanni neighborhood. The Hill of the Pnyx looms to the southwest and the sensual outlines of four major peaks surrounding Athens punctuate the turquoise sky: Mount Hymettos to the east, Mount Penteli to the northeast, Mount Parnitha to the north and Mount Aegaleo to the west. Just beyond the Pnyx Hill you can see the Mediterranean in the distance and the evanescent outlines of islands in the Saronic Gulf, its cerulean waters glittering beyond the vast Athenian plain.

♣

2
Hills of the Muses, the Pnyx and the Nymphs

DAUGHTERS OF THE ARTS DWELL AMIDST THE FATHERS OF DEMOCRACY

The city of Athens is ostensibly an immense crater filled with concrete rivers of buildings surrounded by the Pentelic mountains to the east and the shimmering Saronic Gulf to the west. Take away the buildings and you'd immediately discern several remarkable outcroppings of stone rising above the vast plain, most notably the Acropolis, Lykavittos, and the bare marble rock of Mars Hill, also known as the Areopagus. But above the chaos of the city loom three lesser-known hills filled with places where you can find peace: the Pnyx, the Hill of the Nymphs, and the Hill of the Muses.

The hills are connected and you can easily explore them all through a series of serpentine pathways. These stark outcroppings of marble reign prominently on the Athenian horizon, most significantly the Mouseion, named after Mousaios, an ancient poet and disciple of Orpheus who was believed to have lived here and was buried at this site. Atop it, soaring above the pine-encrusted rock that reflects the sun like a smooth, balding pate, stands the Philopappos Monument in a commanding position just across from the Acropolis.

A climb of almost five hundred feet, a trip to the top is well worth it for the spectacular views of the Parthenon, the city itself and the Saronic Gulf in the distance. The monument is dedicated to C. Julius Antiochus Philoppapos, a famous Roman senator who admired Greek culture. Exiled from his own country, he was an important benefactor of Athens and wanted his funeral monument to be in a prominent place. At a height of forty feet and constructed entirely of glimmering Pentelic marble, the senator's memorial certainly achieved his lofty posthumous goal.

During ancient times, the Mousaion was thought to be the home of the nine muses. Daughters of the god Zeus and Mnemosyne, the goddess of memory, these deities are responsible for inspiring all aspects of the arts. Originally hailing from central Greece, the Mouseion is thought to be where these sister goddesses came to roost in Athens.

The muse Clio is named for the ancient word, *kleos*, or heroic acts, which has the same root as the English word "glory." She is credited with the invention of both history and the guitar, and holds a book in her left hand and a clarion in her right. Calliope, muse of epic poetry, holds a tablet and is surely whom Homer was summoning when writing *The Odyssey* and *The Iliad*. Erato, as her name implies, is the muse of love poetry and plays a lyre. Muse of music, Euterpe, holds a flute and her sister Melpomene, the muse of tragedy, is depicted wearing a tragic mask; even the word tragedy comes from the Greek, meaning "song of the goat." In antiquity, people dressed in goatskins to perform songs during the festivals of Dionysus, which were held in the wilderness during the 6th to the early 5th centuries B.C.

Polymnia is the muse of sacred poetry (I know, there is a theme here with all this poetry!), whereas Terpsichore is the muse of dance. Like sister Erato, she too holds a lyre. Thalia is the muse of comedy and wears the comic mask, and Urania as muse of astronomy holds a globe.

Homer invokes them in the opening lines of his epic poem, *The Odyssey*:

Sing to me of the man, Muse, the man of twists and turns . . .
. . . Launch out on his story, Muse, daughter of Zeus,
Start from where you will—sing for our time, too.

While these girls were historically unmarried, they are credited for giving birth to a number of famous characters of mythology, such as Orpheus, the hero endowed with a superhuman gift of music. These lovely ladies decorated many a Greek pot, and hallways were a favorite placement for statues to bring on the creative juices of the muses.

Their cousins, the nymphs, have a more diluted genesis. As opposed to the muses, who represented the art of humans, the nymphs were representations of nature. While not considered equal to the gods, they were allowed to attend their gatherings on Mount Olympus. They too found their human form in the guise of beautiful young women and were sought after as the lovers of gods and heroes; Apollo famously chased one known as Daphne, who was transformed into a laurel tree by her father, a river god, to avoid being caught.

As nature spirits, they represent groups rather than individuals. There are nymphs for all parts of nature, forests (Dryads), the sea, (Nereids), springs and rivers (Naiads), lakes and swamps (Limniads) and valleys (Napaea—ring any famous valley bells?) Today the modern national observatory sits atop this hill, and I'd like to think sister muse Urania flew over specifically to be the inspiration for that.

Around the corner is the Pnyx, considered the birthplace of democracy in 508 B.C. This semicircular terrace, where Athenian leaders assembled ten times a year, was man-made but terminates in a perpendicular wall of living rock. At the center is a bema, or stage, where famous leaders such as Pericles, Themistocles, and Demosthenes orated to an audience of up to 10,000. A niched wall nearby once held tablets, known as ex-votos, consisting of offerings made by women during the Roman period to the god Zeus Hypsistos.

As you wander back down the hill, you will pass the church of Agios Dimitrios. Dedicated to Saint Dimitri, the church is unusual in that it is fabricated out of wood and, along with the nearby teahouse, it appears to blend seamlessly into the trees. If mass is being offered, you can hear the drone of the priest chanting the liturgy and catch a fragrant trace of incense mixing in the pine-scented air.

My favorite time to visit the hills of these lovely ladies is after a morning run around the Acropolis. I detour off the paved pedestrian walkway of Dionysiou Areopagitou and Apostolou Pavlou, and, vaulting a series of marble steps that lead up to the Hill of the Muses, suddenly find myself in a haven of peace. Lying down in the lush grass and lacy ferns far above the traffic, noise, and millions of people, I feel connected with the ancient souls that still wander there. It's a marvel that, somewhere amidst these ancient ladies, democracy was born. But I often wonder, as I stare up at the deep blue sky and hear whispers in the wind, if it might not be just a little crowded on these ancient hills with all these women hanging around.

❧

3 *Lykavittos Hill*

ATHENA DROPS A ROCK

As you approach the vast, sprawling city of Athens (and that is usually in a taxi from the airport) likely the first prominent geological feature that will grab your attention will be the Parthenon: the temple dedicated to the Goddess Athena, standing proudly on the Acropolis rock. But as your eyes roam across this vast canyon

of concrete buildings, you will be wondering about the other landmark that rises above the Attic plain. It's an anomaly, a singular upthrusting of rock as the city slopes towards the sea. Considering the flatness of the surrounding landscape, the comparison to a woman's breast isn't far from the mind. Reaching a height of over nine hundred feet, Lykavittos is the highest point in Athens.

Legend has it that, flying over the city named in her honor, the goddess Athena was carrying an enormous rock to be installed in her temple on the Acropolis hill. While on her way, she accidentally dropped the boulder smack in the middle of Athens. Lykavittos is actually a small mountain dominating the city's skyline, topped by a church dedicated to St. George. The name comes from the Greek word "lykos," wolf, and means "hill of the wolves." But never fear, you won't encounter any wolves while climbing up the slopes of this natural wonder, only marvelous views that just get better the higher you go.

Located in the upscale neighborhood of Kolonaki, the summit is a popular destination with visitors as it offers a panoramic 360-degree view of the city. If you are feeling energetic, you can hike to the top on the zigzagging path that winds its way to the summit. Be sure to do this in the morning or early evening if you are visiting Athens during the summer months, as it will probably be too hot midday. Another alternative is to take a cab to the base of the hill to Ploutarchou Street. Ride the funicular to the top and suddenly you are above it all.

❋ www.athensinfoguide.com/wtslykavittos.htm

Athens can be overwhelming, but a visit to the top of Lykavittos offers an orientation to the city below. You might want to take a map and plot your itinerary from high above the busy streets. This serene aerie offers a view that extends for miles, from the mountains of Hymettos, Penteli, and Parnitha to the north and east all the way to the glittering Saronic Gulf. Telescopes ring the viewing platforms on the different levels, but it's easy to pick out all the major monuments with the naked eye, including the Parthenon and buildings of the Acropolis hill, the Hill of the Pnyx beyond, and Mars Rock. Scan around to see the Kalimarmaro or 1896 Olympic Stadium built into the rocky hillside of the Pangrati neighborhood, and the Lykavittos Theater, one of Athens's major amphitheaters used for music performances. Close to the main downtown square of Syntagma is the Temple of Olympian Zeus, whose remaining sixteen Corinthian columns grace the landscape near Hadrian's Arch.

Once I had the fortune to visit Lykavittos on the night of the full moon. I arrived at sunset just in time to see a women's spiritual tour group gather at the top. Folding into a tight circle, the women bound their arms around each other's backs and leaned into prayer. As their soft chants filled the violet evening air, a hush came over the other visitors. I watched, spellbound, as a full harvest moon rose, blushed with the sun's setting rays, scraping Mount Imitos to the east, while the sun's orange bulk melted over the Saronic Gulf to the west.

A restaurant and cafés are located at the top, but if you don't feel like paying for their overpriced drinks, just take a seat on the stone wall surrounding the small plaza outside the church and settle in to watch the sun set and the moon rise. Once you've exhausted yourself from the views, be sure to step into the church of St. George. Erected on the site of an older church from the Byzantine period dedicated to the Prophet Elijah, the sanctuary is a cool respite from the midday heat. After admiring the ornate wood paneling and exquisite hammered silver portrait of St. George, one of my favorite things to do is stand by the door and marvel at the near-aerial view of the city below. Before you leave, you might choose to light a candle in honor of St. George. If so, don't forget to light one for Athena too, and thank her for dropping that rock.

4 Tower of the Winds

AN ANCIENT WATER CLOCK IN ATHENS'S ROMAN AGORA

As you wander through the Plaka neighborhood of Athens, you will eventually turn a corner and come across an ancient, four-story, eight-sided edifice that will immediately capture your attention. Not a temple or a statue base, this elegant, octagonal structure will stop you in your tracks with its sheer beauty and make you wonder, what was it used for? Located in the Roman Agora, this creamy white marble confection was properly known as the *horologion Andronikus*—but more simply, it is a clock. Today we rely upon our watches, or more likely our smart phones, to tell the time, but in ancient Greece, shoppers, politicians, and all Athenian citizens used this splendid timepiece.

Made with the same Pentelic marble that fashioned the Parthenon, this elegant structure was designed by the Greek astronomer Andronikus of Cyrrhus in 50 B.C. The octagonal tower stands on a base of three steps and has a pyramidal roof made of marble slabs fixed with a circular keystone.

Standing forty-two feet high and twenty-six feet in diameter, each of the structure's eight faces is decorated with a frieze depicting the winds that blow from that direction. Boreas, or north, blows into a twisted shell and wears a sleeved coat with billowing folds;

Kaikias, northeast, carries a shield full of hailstones. Apeliotes, or east, is shown as a young man bearing flowers and fruit; Evros, or southeast, is an old man wrapped tightly in a coat fending off a hurricane. Notos, or south, is a man emptying an urn and producing a shower of water, while Lips, southwest, is depicted as a boy driving the stern of a ship and promising good sailing weather. Zephyros, or west, is a youth throwing a lapful of flowers into the air, whereas Skiron, or northwest, shows a bearded man carrying a bronze vessel of charcoal in his hands, which he uses to dry up rivers.

While all the wind gods are male, known as *anemoi*, the *aurai*, or winged nymphs of the breezes, are feminine. Romans believed the direction that the wind was blowing could foretell the future and the *aurai* often brought news from far away. From Quintus Smyrnaeus's *Fall of Troy*,

> *The Breezes brought Ares news of the death of his daughter Penthesilea in the war of Troy: For the Aurai, Boreas's fleet-winged daughters, bare to him, as through the wide halls of the sky he strode.*

The Tower was a multi-tasking feat of engineering, offering the triple information of being a sundial, a weather vane, and a clock. A sundial was used to tell the time during daylights hours, but to mark the time at night a water clock was employed; known as a clepsydra, it functioned with water that flowed down from the Acropolis hill. The Roman architect, Vitruvius, who visited Athens in the Ist century B.C., described a revolving bronze weather vane atop the building, depicting Triton holding a wand, which pointed to the corresponding face of the prevailing wind.

Vitruvius was so captivated by the tower that he drew the structure, influencing later architects such as Christopher Wren in the 17th century, who designed St. Paul's Cathedral in London. The structure has inspired designs of other similar clock towers around the world, including Sevastopol, Russia and Livorno, Italy.

The Tower was not only replicated throughout the world, its space was used by a variety of different cultures and purposes throughout the ages. The Christians converted the building into a bell tower for a Byzantine church. During the Ottoman period when the city was under Turkish domination, the building was used as a *tekke*, or spiritual lodge for Sufi worshippers. The interior space became a meeting space and venue for the famous whirling dervishes to perform their sacred dance.

As you stand and look at this delicate, yet enduring edifice, recall the layers of history this small building has seen. Conceived as a scientific tool, it's fascinating to imagine its transformation from functional object into a Christian house of worship and later a place for Sufi rituals. The light streaming in through the cuts in the walls has shone upon the golden age of rationality, gold crucifixes of Byzantium, and ultimately, mystical Sufi priests in their flowing gowns and white turbans, performing their sacred whirling dance to a frenzied mix of voices and drums.

❧

5 Hadrian's Library

STATUE OF NIKE

I am embarrassed to say that, after more than thirty years of traveling to Greece, I had never before seen this exquisite statue. But there is a reason for that: before 1988 it lay, still buried, beneath the Athenian streets, awaiting her mysterious discovery. There are Nike statues, and then there are Nike statues, and this one is a queen among her kind.

Smack dab in the middle of the Roman agora of Athens sits Hadrian's Library. As you wind your way down Adrianou Street in the Plaka district, past t-shirt shops and walls of gauzy Greek goddess dresses fluttering in the Athenian afternoon breeze, suddenly a row of columns will appear. Fluted, tall, and magnificent, they line the front of a building that has long since disappeared, but its grandeur can still be felt.

Hadrian's Library was constructed in 132 A.D., during the Roman occupation of Athens. Filled with reading rooms, alcoves, outdoor courtyards used as discussion rooms and even serene pools, this gigantic structure housed thousands of papyrus scrolls stored in niches throughout the building. The remnants of this magnificent building have been incorporated into later walls surrounding the city, not to mention a church, and what is left today is a series of restored columns, several flanking an end wall and four freestanding, allowing a peek into the cavernous space beyond.

✳ www.greeka.com/attica/athens/athens-excursions
/library-hadrian.htm

Sequestered behind the dusty remains of what was the central space of the library is a small museum housing one of the most lyrically lovely statues in Athens. Carved from a single block of Pentelic marble, this unforgettable lady was found at the bottom of an Ottoman era cistern. Sadly, now wingless and armless, her gravity-defying nature is still evident as she is portrayed just at the moment when her feet touched the earth. Balanced exquisitely on a globe, her composition is unique among Nike statues.

Standing more than three meters high, this impressive lady makes it hard to avert your gaze. After resting underground for so many centuries, she appears ready to soar once more, her elegant feet pressing upwards from the globe, her shapely legs visible through a froth of gauzy fabric, collecting in unctuous rolls at her ankles. The figure springs to life, the pull of the gown lifting upward with the outstretched arms, and you can just imagine how the wings would have fanned out in an awe-inspiring revelation, with the face registering the triumphant expression that her name implies.

As with most statues of Nike figures in ancient Greece, her creation was meant to commemorate a man's battle, in this case a victory of the emperor Augustus. Her undoing was likely during the Barbarian invasion, where her lovely form was unwittingly incorporated into a wall, and then later found its way to the bottom of a well. But we all love a tale of survival, and that is certainly hers. This Nike has seen it all, sculpted and prominently displayed in a grand setting and surviving the fall of Rome only to be mutilated, smashed, and buried with the invasion of various tribes.

An eternal embodiment of the divine feminine archetype, she rises once again, her indelible beauty intact despite missing a head, wings, and arms,. Buildings rose and fell around her, battles were fought, won and lost, and civilizations were erected and tumbled. But she, the quintessence of victory and endurance, remains untrammeled. So on your visit to Athens, don't do what I have done for the past twenty years and pass Hadrian's Library without wending your way into a nondescript building hidden behind the ancient ruins. You will be amply rewarded.

%

6 *Mighty Aphrodite— Paphos, Cyprus*

PETRA TOU ROMIOU: BIRTHPLACE OF
THE GODDESS OF LOVE AND BEAUTY

Foam, sea, fertility. The aquamarine, sea-caressed coastline of the Mediterranean island of Cyprus is where Aphrodite, or Venus as the Romans refer to her, has been worshipped for the past 3,000 years. The Mycenaeans erected a temple in her honor, and shrines dedicated to fertility goddesses have been found here dating to the Neolithic period. Clearly, this entire region of Cyprus has long since been thought of as a place of love, beauty, and sensuality...just like our resident goddess.

Near Paphos, on the southwestern coast of Cyprus, lies a series of gigantic stone formations along a beach known as Aphrodite's Rock. These huge sea stacks jut out of the water, creating a striking, almost phallic landscape that is fitting for the goddess of love. The approach to the beach is as dramatic as the beach itself. Visitors must pass through a long and narrow stone passageway, much like a birth canal, that leads down the hill to the water. Just a few steps ahead, you see the light glinting off the sea and hear the waves crashing; all of a sudden you are released, like a birth, onto this resplendent seashore. Take note of those bushes outside the passageway; Aphrodite worshippers leave offerings of tissues tied to them, asking the goddess for divine intervention into their love lives and to bring healing to their hearts.

As the goddess of love, beauty, sensuality, and sexuality, Aphrodite's star shines brightly in the Olympic pantheon. But her birth had unfortunate consequences for her father. When the Titan Cronus castrated Uranus and threw his testicles into the sea, Aphrodite was born from the foam that gathered on the water's surface. Many accounts say she washed ashore on the island of Cyprus on this very beach near Paphos, called Petra tou Romiou, or Rock of the Greek. Apparently it wasn't just her sheer beauty that drew in admirers; Aphrodite also wore a magic girdle that had the effect of making everyone she encountered desire her. And desire her they did. Aphrodite's lovers read like a who's who of Greek mythology. The goddess married the lame smith-god Hephaestus, and their relationship got off to a great start, only to falter when she cheated on him with Ares, the god of war. As Virgil in his *Aeneid* states,

> *Venus [Aphrodite]…spoke to her husband, Volcanos [Hephaistos], as they lay in their golden bed-chamber, breathing into the words all her divine allurement [persuading him to forge armour for her son Aeneas in Latium]…Since Volcanos [Hephaistos] complied not at once, the goddess softly embraced him in snowdrift arms, caressing him here and there. Of a sudden he caught the familiar spark and felt the old warmth darting into his marrow, coursing right though his body, melting him; just as it often happens a thunderclap starts a flaming rent which ladders the dark cloud, a quivering streak of fire. Pleased with her wiles and aware of her beauty, Venus [Aphrodite] could feel them taking effect. Volcanus [Hephaistos], in love's undying thrall [conceded to her requests]…Thus saying, he gave his wife the love he was aching to give her; then he sank into soothing sleep, relaxed upon her breast."*

Unfortunately, things went south after this lovely interlude, and Hephaestus divorced her. She went on to bear five children with Ares: Eros, Anteros, Deimos (Panic), Phobos (Fear), and a daughter with a name more fitting to a love goddess: Harmonia. Aphrodite had a brief affair with the god of wine, Dionysus, but the jealous goddess Hera cursed her with the deformed child Priapus, who possessed the famously oversized penis. Curiously, when Aphrodite hooked up with Hermes, the messenger god, the child that was born of their union was, naturally, Hermaphrodite!

The most celebrated of myths is the story of Aphrodite and Adonis, a cautionary tale the ancient Greeks loved the most: when a god falls in love with a mortal, catastrophe results. Adonis, as the name implies, was a gorgeous young man who was fond of hunting. Besotted with his looks, Aphrodite fell head over heels in love with him and, fearing for his safety, warned him of the dangers of the bloodsport. Naturally, he ignored her and was gored by a boar (actually Aphrodite's enraged husband Ares, the god of war, who had conveniently shape shifted for the deed). As he fell into a grieving Aphrodite's lap and died, droplets of his blood fell onto the earth, transforming into anemones. Allegorically, the myth recounts the cathartic power of the goddess as the Great Mother, who oversees the great cycles of death and regeneration.

You've seen the famous painting by Botticelli of Aphrodite, or Venus as she is referred to in Roman times, emerging from the water on a seashell, coyly clasping her hand to her chest while covering her genitals with a lock of reddish, flowing hair in the other. On her left, the winds, symbolized by cherubic *putti*, blow on her, gently caressing her with the breeze, while on the right her handmaid, Ora, waits to dress her mistress. This Neoplatonic version of the myth comes out of the 15th century, when it was popular to blend pagan mythology with Christian thought, therefore homogenizing the more sexual aspects of the myth and converting them into idealized versions of the birth of love and spiritual beauty.

Aphrodite has her more carnal versions as well, in the form of sculptors who idealized her physical form and sensual aspects. The Venus Kallipygos (literally Venus with the Beautiful Butt) at the National Archaeological Museum in Naples, twists her body and gazes admiringly at her own rear end—a far cry from the more demure and prudish Botticelli version. And don't forget the famous painting by Titian in the Metropolitan Museum, which captures Venus in all her fleshy glory, hanging on to a bemused Adonis for dear life, hoping to prevent him from taking off for the hunt and his ill-fated death.

If you come to Paphos, be sure to spend some time on the beach, where acolytes swear they feel the goddess's energy. Plan to make a side trip to visit Palea Paphos, the sanctuary of Aphrodite, located in Kouklia, about fourteen kilometers from Paphos. Fertility idols have been found in the region dating to 3800 B.C., but the cult was officially established in 1500 B.C., when a temple was erected on a hilltop. As at Corinth, the cult involved ritual prostitution, and at least once in her life, every maiden made her pilgrimage to the site to make love with a stranger. Upon meeting her lover, the man would throw money at her feet and utter the sacred words, "I invoke the goddess upon you." The cult of Aphrodite flourished at Palea Paphos until the 4th century A.D., when the Christian Emperor Theodosius outlawed the rituals as pagan. Virtually none of the sanctuary's structures survived the damage of time and intentional destruction, yet the presence of Aphrodite is palpable. After all, when a goddess has the gifts of the powerful and eternal attributes of love, fertility, and procreation, there is no question that her allure continues to permeate the landscape with an ethos of sensuality.

✣

7 *Eleusis*

WHERE PERSEPHONE DESCENDED
INTO THE UNDERWORLD

Imagine a rite so clandestine that you would be put to death if you divulged its secret with someone outside the cult. If you were an initiate living in 5th century B.C. Greece, this would be your reality. Now imagine that you are part of a group that will begin its pilgrimage from the Parthenon, and walk along a path known as the Sacred Way to a sanctuary some fourteen miles in the distance. At this moment in time Athens is a major metropolis, the Parthenon temple sits gleaming atop the Acropolis hill, the waters of the Middle Earth shining in the distance. Sandals shuffling along a dusty road, you pass over the Ilissos River and follow the coast of the sea. At the front of the contingent a group holds baskets known as *kistai*, containing mysterious and sacred objects that will be shown to initiates later in the proceedings. Suddenly, in the distance, you see your final destination come into view: the gleaming marble courtway, gates, and brightly colored temples of a sacred grove known as the sanctuary of Eleusis.

For those of you who are enamored of the myth of Persephone, the maiden taken away from her mother, the grain goddess Demeter, and abducted into the Underworld by the god of Hell, Hades, this place is ground zero. As the goddess of agriculture,

Demeter was worshipped for the abundance of the annual harvest, but during Persephone's abduction into the underworld, Demeter lamented and nothing grew. Desperate worshippers petitioned the gods to let Persephone free so they could grow their crops again. When Hades was finally forced by Zeus to return Demeter's daughter, he did so, on one condition: that she eat a few seeds of the pomegranate, the food of the dead. Upon hearing her daughter ate

three seeds of the fruit of the dead, she grieved, knowing her daughter would have to return annually to the underworld, one month for every seed eaten. During this time she continues to let nothing grow in her daughter's absence, a time period we more modern folk refer to as winter.

Founded almost four thousand years ago, and lasting more than eighteen centuries until 392 A.D. when it was banned by the Christian Church, Eleusis is the birthplace of one of the world's oldest and most continuous religious cults. The settlement, erected on the slope of a hillside, was where the cult of Demeter was developed, and its longevity is underscored by the sheer amount of buildings erected over many periods, well into the Roman era. While the word cult has earned a negative connotation in modern times, the term mystery cult is distinctive. As Michael Cosmopoulos, professor of archaeology at the University of Missouri, St. Louis, explains, "Mystery cults represent the spiritual attempts of the ancient Greeks to deal with their mortality. As these cults had to do with the individual's inner self, privacy was paramount and was secured by an initiation ceremony, a personal ritual that established a close bond with the individual and the gods. Once initiated, the individual was liberated from the fear of death by sharing the eternal truth, known only to the immortals. Because of the oath of silence taken by the initiates, a thick veil of secrecy cover those cults and archaeology has become our main tool in deciphering their meaning."

As you stroll through the ancient marbles of Eleusis, try to imagine the majesty of the annual sacred rites. Thousands of initiates are pouring into the sanctuary, all wearing their white *himation*, the ancient Greek garment, tied with a belt. Once the melon-colored sun melted into the sea and torches were lit, the pilgrims would be seated in the huge square temple known as the Telesterion and drink from a *kykeion*, a sacred vessel. Some recent theorists believe this potion, given to all initiates, contained a hallucinogenic agent derived from a fungus grown on wheat and barley, which helped to bring on the necessary psychological state to witness the evening's sacred proceedings.

The celebration took place over nine days each autumn. The initial four days involved assemblies, races, and state sacrifices and the *Pompe,* or great procession, began on the fifth. The night after day six signified the *Telete*, or secret ceremony, which consisted of *dromena*, or pageant, *legomena*, words spoken, and *deiknymena*, things shown. The night after day seven, the *epopteia*, or revelation of sacred objects, was the holy of the holies, when the secrets of the cult were divulged to a spellbound audience. The final two days consisted of offering libations to the deceased and the return to Athens.

As you stand next to the Telesterion, take in the grandeur of the sanctuary: vast, daunting, and once surrounded by a thicket of tall pines, to keep uninvited onlookers from spying on the proceedings. We know from ancient accounts that initiates were exposed to fearsome lights and sounds, and if they were imbibing a special concoction meant to induce hallucinations, then the experience must have been terrifying. However the cult's ultimate purpose was to enhance the sense of joy for a better life by decreasing the fear of death. What we do know of the ceremony's finale is that a participant playing the role of Persephone returns to the upper world, accompanied by an explosion of blazing torches used in her search, and all rejoice in the mother-daughter reunion.

The site's most significant structures include The Sacred Court, a gathering place located at the end of the Sacred Way. Walk up the steps to the remains of the Greater Propylaea, a gate built in the Doric order in the 2nd century A.D. to resemble the Athenian Parthenon. The Lesser Propylaea, erected in 54 B.C. by a Roman consul, acted as a smaller gate to the inner sanctuary and had sculptures of two massive Caryatids, female figures holding *kistai*, the containers of the sacred object, on their heads. The Triumphal Arches are Roman reproductions of Hadrian's Arch, built after 129 A.D. The original Mycenaean Megaron, consisting of the remains of a rectangular temple with two columns, was built at the site's genesis in the 12th century B.C. The most massive structure, the Telesterion, an almost square-shaped building used as a stadium for the initiates, had six entrances with eight tiers of seating and, as all temples in ancient Greece, would have been brightly decorated in intense red and blue pigments.

The most curious feature is the Ploutonion. Dedicated to the god Pluto (the Roman version of Hades), this is as close as a temple to a god of death the Greeks came. In actuality, it is a retaining wall around a cave, which the initiates believed was the entrance to the underworld. Since this is Persephone's realm, make sure to take a peek into the cave and picture the goddess's triumphant return to the above world, upon which initiates waved their torches, spinning like fireflies in the night sky, while her overjoyed mother, Demeter, waited to embrace her so that spring could once again return to the earth.

꒜

8 *Samos*

BIRTHPLACE OF HERA

Pythagoras, Epicurus, Aesop...do any of these names ring a bell? What all these illustrious figures have in common is the island of Samos. Tucked between its fellow islands of Patmos and Chios, this mid-sized, vineyard-cloaked island lies tantalizingly close to the mainland of Turkey. It is the birthplace of the ancient Greek mathematician, Pythagoras, after which the Pythagorean theorem is named, and the philosopher Epicurus, whose three hundred written works espouse the goals of *ataraxia* and *aponia*—freedom from fear and pain—in order to attain a joyful and happy life. The fabulist Aesop spent a portion of his life as a slave on this island, where as a personal secretary to his master, he enjoyed a great deal of freedom to observe the animals of the natural world that figure so prominently in his fantastic tales.

Yet it is a woman for whom this island is most known; none other than the queen of the pantheon herself, the great goddess Hera. According to the ancient travel writer Pausanias, Hera was born on Samos, on the banks of a river underneath a Lygos willow tree:

> Some say that the sanctuary of Hera in Samos was established by those who sailed in the Argo, and that these brought the image from Argos. But the Samians themselves hold that the goddess was born in the island by the side of the river Imbrasos under the willow that even in my time grew in the Heraion.

29

There are many construction phases of a temple built in honor of Hera, which the ancient historian Herodotus claimed was the largest of its day. One of the original buildings was constructed in the Ionic order by the architects Rhoikos and Theodoros, and was 320 feet long by 160 feet wide with a mind-boggling 160 columns in all, resulting in the effect of a marble forest. Built in 570-550 B.C., it only stood for a few years before its destruction by either fire or an earthquake in 525 B.C. Many of its parts were used to construct a successive sanctuary, which had the largest known floor plan of any Greek temple. Built under the ruler Polykrates, this temple was never completed due to economic collapse, but visitors can gauge its massiveness by the size of the colossal statues that were erected in its interior, one of which is on display in the Samos Archaeological Museum. Sadly, the building was used as a quarry in the Byzantine period, and was dismantled over successive centuries, leaving only the lone column that stands today.

The reason these temples were constructed on marshy earth surrounding the mouth of the Imbrasos River instead of on more stable land, is likely due to the fact that evidence of a Mycenaean era cult to Hera, such as small ritual bowls dating to the second millennium B.C., were found on the same site. As wife of Zeus, Hera is considered to be a major deity of the Greek pantheon. She is often depicted, like her sister Demeter, wearing a polos, or high cylindrical crown, that is the symbol of the great goddesses. These female deities predate the classical Greek era, and there are indications that a Neolithic fertility goddess that celebrated the feminine aspects of motherhood, fertility, and the earth was also worshipped at this site. Today the tradition continues, as the 5th-century Christians built a basilica dedicated to the Virgin Mary on the temple grounds.

Prior to the first millennium B.C. a simple wooden board served as Hera's object of worship, which was later enhanced with a copper statue of the goddess. In a strange annual rite, the statue was brought to the mouth of the Imbrasos River on a litter of willow branches, bathed in seawater and decorated with gifts. In another yearly rite in memory of Hera's marriage to Zeus, the Heraia, the copper statue was dressed in ceremonial wedding dress and paraded at athletic contests in honor of the goddess.

Images of the goddess, flanked by willow trees and accompanied by her sacred animal, the peacock, are stamped on Samian coins of the Roman era.

✳ www.visitgreece.gr/en/greek_islands/
   northeastern_aegean_islands/samos

Driving around this lush island it's easy to see why the ancient historian Herodotus, who once lived here, described Samos, the center of Ionian civilization, as first among all Greek cities. The island's proximity to the coast of Asia Minor also makes it a bridge between cultures. Two mountains dominate the island's interior and the westernmost, Mount Kerkis, rising forbiddingly above the sea, is the second highest peak in the Aegean. Today two monasteries occupy Kerkis, but strange stories abound about this summit, whose caves were occupied by religious hermits during the Byzantine era. Sailors reported seeing glowing lights in the mouths of the caves, which they believed were the souls of departed saints. Fishermen state this same strange light guides them during storms, and some believe the light may be the spirit of Pythagoras.

After a trip up Mount Kerkis, make a stop on the way down at Karlovassi. Waterfalls at this area form two crystalline lakes, ideal for swimming, and offer a change of pace from the usual Greek beach!

Samos is thickly latticed with olive groves and vineyards, and Samian wine was celebrated in antiquity and still is today. Known for its Muscat grapes, the island produces a number of vintages from this legendarily sweet fruit, particularly dessert wines that pair well with traditional honeyed Greek treats such as *baklava* and *karidopita* (walnut cake). If you're on Samos in August, be sure to attend the annual wine festival that takes place the first ten days of the month. Buy one glass, as the brochure says, and refill it as many times as you want...or can handle!

Be sure to stop by the island's main towns of Vathy and Pythagorio. As the capital, Vathy, also called Samos town, is built amphitheatrically around a deep and generous harbor. Lined with shops, restaurants, and cafés, the area bustles with fishermen bringing in their catch and a tourist bazaar. Its old quarter, Ano Vathy, first settled in the 1600s, recalls an earlier era of the island with its steep, narrow cobblestoned lanes and crimson-tiled rooftops. Be sure to make a stop at the island's archaeological museum, which contains artifacts from the sanctuary of Hera, including the massive statue of a Kouros, or boy, the largest standing in existence. Pebbled and quaint, little Gagos Beach lies nearby if you want a workout for your feet!

On the opposite side of the island lies the small town of Pythagorion, named in 1955 after the island's most famous mathematician. Sitting on the site of the ancient settlement, ruins from the sanctuary of Hera are incorporated into houses of the modern village. The area is also known for a tunnel constructed by Eupanlinus, an ancient feat of engineering genius, and its harbor mole, or ancient pier. This sleepy, red-tiled village, embracing an implausibly cerulean harbor, is where my friend Mary Carpenter lived for many years.

"I used to love going out to the end of the mole in Pythagorion and look at the sky and Turkey at night," she recalls. "The mole is made of parts of the ancient walls built by the tyrant Polykrates. It was easy to understand how Pythagoras was inspired to think the great thoughts he did in this exact place."

I asked her, as a long-term resident of Samos, what she loved most about the island.

"That it's only about half a mile to Turkey. It's as close as you can get to East meeting West. In ancient times, the area was Ionia, the melting pot of all civilization at the time."

This dangerously close flirtation with the Turkish coastline does give Samos an added allure. If you're looking to explore the mother of all goddesses' birthplaces as well as a Greek island within shouting distance of Asia Minor, then take a cue from Epicurus. Spending a few days on Samos will unquestionably contribute to a joyful and happy life!

౾ఒ

9 *Mycenae*

IPHIGENIA AND THE FACE THAT LAUNCHED A THOUSAND SHIPS: HELEN OF TROY

Mycenae. The name may not conjure up many images—until I mention a certain notorious lady of history: Helen of Troy. Helen, daughter of Zeus and Leda, whose face "launched a thousand ships," was single-handedly responsible for one of the most epic battles of history: the Trojan War...and Mycenae is the place where all the drama began.

Long before you arrive, you see it, a mesa-like plateau, rising above the dun-colored earth spackled with low-lying scrub. It seems like this is the harshest environment in Greece—how could anyone live on this hot, arid plain? In antiquity, as today, this is known as the Argolid. The road from Athens takes you across the Corinth Canal, then plunges deep into the Peloponnese. Driving over the winding roads, you enter a part of Greece unlike the tourist posters portraying cubist whitewashed houses and turquoise shores. This part of Greece is a wide-open, virtually desert-like setting, and you can almost imagine the tales of faraway battles, deception, and sacrifice that took place on these sacred grounds.

Approaching the front entrance to the settlement, you will see two headless lions—or perhaps griffins—guarding the opening. A huge architectural accomplishment, the ancient builders constructed two supporting pillars for a massive, eighteen-ton lintel on top of which is a carving of two lions standing on an altar and flanking a column. Probably inspired by similar heraldic patterns of animals from the Middle East, the animals' now missing heads were fashioned from another substance, possibly metal. The Mycenaeans, whose civilization reached its height in the 13th century B.C., built many royal settlements, including Tiryns, Thebes, the Palace of Nestor at Pylos in southwestern Greece, and ancient Ithaka, home of the hero Odysseus. As the inventors of the Linear B script, and creators of timeless art, including lyrical frescoes of everyday palace life, magnificent ceramics and sculptures, this culture's achievements pre-date the Golden Age of Greece by eight centuries.

Once you enter, note the circular area to your right, known as Grave Circle A. You may recall the story of a peculiar man named Heinrich Schliemann. Born in Germany, Schliemann taught himself ancient Greek by reading *The Odyssey* and *The Iliad* in their original. Fascinated by the ancient sites he read about, Schliemann set out to find these storied kingdoms, and succeeded in locating ancient Troy (in modern-day Turkey) and Mycenae, which is known today, thanks to Schliemann's findings, as "Rich in Gold." Grave Circle A contained the burials of nineteen bodies, and some of the artifacts he uncovered in this double walled enclosure include the so-called gold Death Mask of Agamemnon. Incorrectly attributed by Schliemann, the mask pre-dates the Homeric age he was hoping to find, yet the name has managed to stick, after an excited Schliemann, upon uncovering the mask, cabled the Greek King, "I have gazed upon the face of Agamemnon." Schliemann's team also excavated four other gold death masks in the royal burials as well as gold cups in the form of bulls' heads, golden diadems, rings, swords, and richly inlaid daggers all attesting to the wealth of the civilization.

Head outside, downhill from the citadel, and you will reach Grave Circle B. Here the remains of twenty-three people, including two children, were uncovered. Predating those in Grave

Circle A by some decades, these individuals were possibly from a less sophisticated culture. However, important grave goods were unearthed here as well, including ceramic remains, swords, a boar's tusk helmet, and an elegant rock crystal vase in the shape of a duck.

Tragic tales, as oppressive as the heat of an Argolid summer afternoon, hang over this site, and the most storied is that of Agamemnon's eldest daughter, Iphigenia. Hunting one day in the grove of Artemis, goddess of the hunt, Agamemnon killed a stag, sacred to the goddess, and then boasted about his accomplishment, saying his skills were equal to the goddess's. Bad idea, as we all well know—taunting the gods in ancient Greece was a sure way to bring on punishment. And punishment she did in spades; Artemis ordered his eldest daughter to be sacrificed, else the Greek fleet would not sail.

Many versions of the story exist. In one, Iphigenia is lured under the precept she is to be married to the hero Achilles, but when the sacrifice is imminent she is miraculously transported to a city by the Black Sea and a deer is sent in her place. Another tale tells that, upon hearing that the seer, Calchas, has prophesized that all Greek women will be raped and murdered if the Greek fleet cannot sail and defeat the Trojan army, Iphigenia willingly offers herself as the ultimate sacrifice to protect her fellow women.

Clearly the most celebrated female figure of Mycenae was Helen, the wife of Menelaus, the brother of Agamemnon, the king of Mycenae. When the prince of Troy, Paris, came to visit, he fell in love with Helen and the feeling was mutual, for Paris whisked her onto the ship and took her back to Troy. When Paris's father realized his son's action, he knew what horror was to come. Agamemnon would not stand for such an embarrassment, and retribution was ensured. Mycenae launched a fleet and sailed to Troy, taking with them the famed soldier Achilles. An epic battle ensued, and in order to breach Troy's impenetrable walls, the wily

Mycenaeans came up with a plan not to outmuscle but outsmart. They built a huge horse of wood and brought it to the gates as a peace offering. Accepting the gift, the king of Troy opened the city gates and let the horse be pulled in.

That night when the city was asleep, the Mycenaeans unleashed their plan. They had stowed their army inside the hollow wooden horse, and when the moment arrived they escaped and unleashed their army on the city, burning it to the ground. Thousands of years later, the story of the Trojan horse endures as a classic brain versus brawn method of conquering one's enemy.

A gorgeous new museum has been built near the site and is well worth a visit. The modern, low-profiled building lies snugged beneath a ridge in these scrub-coated hills. Softly lit cases with muted displays tell the tale of this magnificent civilization through a parade of ornately decorated terracotta vases with the distinctive geometric patterns, exquisitely fashioned, often witty animal figurines and brightly painted frescoes portraying ladies of the court in all their royal finery. Be sure to make a stop at the imposing Treasury of Atreus, a beehive style tomb whose soaring interior was the supposed burial site of King Agamemnon.

Before you leave, do what I like to do. Climb to the top of the fortress and look out across the Argolid Plain. As the sun bores relentlessly down on this arid region, remember the reason the Mycenaeans built here in the first place: because they felt safe. And then remember that these walls, as strong as they were, could not protect the king from being robbed of his most precious prize. Deception, betrayal, and illicit love: although it may appear serene, Mycenae possesses all the ingredients for the ultimate Greek tragedy.

❦

10 *Mad for Leros*

ISLAND OF THE MOON GODDESS
AND A NOTORIOUS ASYLUM

I squeezed the button on my watch and a poisonous green glow ignited the dial: 3 A.M. Standing on the deck of a ferryboat in the middle of the Aegean Sea, I shivered, not only from the chilly night air, but in trepidation, as I watched the distant shoreline draw closer. I was about to arrive at a place that, until recently, people didn't come to voluntarily—they were sent here. Since the Greek government opened a psychiatric hospital on this remote island decades ago, Leros has primarily been a destination for the insane.

The song, "Crazy," by the singer Seal, cued up on my headphones, and I laughed at the coincidence, secretly questioning my own sanity in coming here. Since I began working as an archaeologist in Greece some twenty years ago, I had heard many horror stories about this notorious island gulag: over the years, the psychiatric hospital had become not only a residence for the mentally ill, but a depository for all of society's castoffs and undesirables. Considering the island's reputation, it seemed fitting that the ferry, headed toward its last stop from the mainland, was arriving in the middle of the night.

A little known story from Greek mythology had also lured me to this forbidden place: Leros was the ancient birthplace of Artemis.

Celebrated primarily as the goddess of the hunt, independent, tomboyish Artemis has always appealed to me because of her other attribute—goddess of the moon. Anyone with a little Latin under her belt could tell you that moon is the root of the word lunatic, so I asked myself, could this be a complete fluke?

Whereas Aphrodite was more interested in issues of love and beauty, and Athena war and wisdom, Artemis spent her time wandering in nature, roaming the woods with her pet dogs and deer. If a mortal or god ever took an erotic interest in her, he was quickly dispatched by her utter disinterest, as Artemis preferred to return to the solitude of the forest and the company of her companion animals. She was known for her curative abilities, particularly with women and young girls, and offered assistance in recovery from illness. While other Greek islands in Greece claim to be the birthplace of Artemis as well, none share such an inexplicable and extraordinary connection with the moon.

Another of Artemis's distinctions was as the guardian of animals. My pet Airedale, Mia, was scheduled for surgery back home in a few weeks, and I had brought a photo of her along. Since I was visiting the temple anyway, I figured it wouldn't hurt to ask for some divine protection. The ferry docked and I crowded into one of three taxis waiting on the darkened pier. After a harrowing ride through narrow streets and winding alleyways, we arrived in front of a small pension near the top of a hill. Clearly, Artemis had been spinning some madness of her own; the building's terrace, suspended directly over the sea, was drenched in the light of a full moon.

The next morning, my hostess, Maria Pantelides, laughed at my question as to whether the island was crowded. "Any tourists have left," she said, setting down a tray of magma-thick yogurt spangled with walnuts, homemade *koulourakia*, and chamomile tea. She gestured over the edge of the whitewashed terrace wall, revealing a blindingly sapphire sea being sliced by the wake of a sluggish fishing boat. "Enjoy," she called over her shoulder on her way back to her kitchen. "You've got this place all to yourself. Peace and quiet."

Leros's history as a penitentiary started during World War II, when Mussolini opened a military prison on the island, and the facility became a psychiatric hospital in the years following the Italian occupation. Curious to explore this modern-day gulag, I set out the first day in a tinny rental car. Unlike the typically stark, whitewashed islands portrayed in Greek postcards, Leros is scrubbily wooded, with rolling hills and deeply recessed bays that explain its occasional misrepresentation as an island of lakes. As I drove along deserted roads lined with overgrown rosemary bushes the size of washing machines, it soon became clear that Leros's most enticing feature was its delayed development, thanks to decades of near-avoidance by tourists. I'd heard that the island's tarnished reputation was so deeply imbedded in the Greek psyche that mothers tell misbehaving children, "If you don't behave you will be sent to Leros!"—and even the word *lera* means filth.

After lunch in the village of Pantelis, I set out to locate the asylum that had garnered so much notoriety. The main road passed by houses with arched doorways and engaged columns profiled against pastel hues, showing evidence of the Italian occupation. In the small village of Agia Marina, with its distinct lack of Internet cafés, dive shops, and jet ski rentals, only a fisherman sat on the wharf, mending his nets in the suffused light. As I traced the road south, a white structure came into view, looming in the distance and hidden amidst a grove of spindly pines. I parked the car in a gravel lot and walked across the road toward the entrance; a uniformed young man leaned back on his chair in a guard booth, half-heartedly glancing up once in a while at the nondescript stucco building.

Walking up to a ridge ringed in razor wire, I looked down over a compound of tidy, Eucalyptus-shaded patient housing. After a few minutes, an elderly inmate suddenly appeared in a door; he shuffled, barefoot, onto the cracked concrete courtyard and stooped down, throwing scraps of food to eager cats that congregated around the doorway.

Making my way back to the entrance, I looked through the chain-link fence into the dusty courtyard; a scattering of red pine needles carpeted the pavement. The asylum was now almost empty, but after so many years, its ghosts were still here; it felt as though I was trespassing on sacred ground. Slowly, I walked back to my car and pulled out onto the road, watching for a long time until the chipped and graffitied structure disappeared like a mirage from my rear view mirror.

Driving through the town of Lakki, it was easy to see why the main port, with its wide but empty streets and phallic war memorials, served as an Italian naval base during World War II: Leros's deep main harbor was an ideal place to hide warships. Imposing art-deco buildings left behind by the Fascist occupation, like the abandoned Hotel Leros with its echelon of porthole windows, and the curved cinema Albergo, absurdly dominated the landscape.

That evening I joined my hosts, Maria and Panagos Pantelides, on the pension's terrace for a pre-dinner ouzo. Telling them about my day, I admitted my ambivalence about visiting the asylum, and wondered what they saw in the island's future.

"I worked at the hospital for almost thirty years," Maria said, her face reflecting pain as she spoke.

"But we needed to do something different, something new," Panagos added, "to support our family. That's when we decided to open up a hotel." Although their hand-built pension had only a few rooms, they were especially proud of the rooftop restaurant, with its unobstructed views of the Aegean.

Even though they had seen many decades of darkness on her native island, their optimism for a better future was clear. "The other islands have been built up, like Rhodes and Kos," Maria said, filling my wineglass and leaving me with a final thought, "but Leros hasn't been spoiled."

I ordered the evening's specialty—lamb, slow roasted overnight and served in a lemon sauce—and toasted the moon, rising like a bruised peach over the coastline of Asia.

With the moon goddess on my mind, I saved a visit to Artemis's temple for my last day. Parking my car in an olive grove, I forced open a rusted gate and waded up the hill through a field of lilies, thrusting upwards like pink knives from the underworld. Just a single row of foundation stones remained on the plateau, affording views of the sea in the distance, bisected by the single runway of the airport below. One can appreciate why the ancients would choose this spot to erect a temple to the goddess of the hunt and moon. From this height, the coastline of Turkey floats, an amethyst haze in the distance, and the scattering of nearby islands of the Dodecanese chain—slumbering giants in the mercury-colored waters—lie motionless, tantalizing with both their remoteness and mystery. Any goddess of the hunt would have had a clear view of her prey from atop this precipice to the valleys and hillsides beyond. But most of all, she would have had a clear and untrammeled view of her beloved orb, the moon, rising from the sea in the distance and ruling the night.

I was never able to establish a link between the goddess and the asylum, but my instincts tell me there's something more to this eerie correlation, just waiting to be uncovered. In the meantime, the absence of sightseers that afternoon provided a rare treat for an archaeologist: in all my years of excavating, I've never had a Greek temple all to myself. With Leros prying open a Pandora's box of tourism, it's just a matter of time before I'll have to share it with others. Taking the photo of Mia from my pocket, I found a chink between the smooth stones and wedged it in securely. Silently, I offered up a prayer.

꙳

11
Aegina

TEMPLE OF A VANISHING GODDESS

Most of the well-known Greek islands, such as Mykonos, Santorini, and Crete, are far flung from Athens, requiring a ferry or plane ride to access. But only a short hop away in the Saronic Gulf lie a handful of delightful islands, one in particular well worth a day trip. If you only have a few days and you're looking for a quickie Greek island experience with an amazing ancient temple to boot, then hop on a day cruise and make your way to Aegina. After meeting Aphaia and her temple, you won't be sorry.

The thirty-two Doric style columns aligned in a six-by-twelve format incline slightly to the center to give the building more stability and, even more important, like the Parthenon in Athens, a feeling of the structure springing to life. Built around 480 B.C., it was erected on the site of an earlier temple built around 570 B.C. but was later destroyed in a fire in 510 B.C. Possibly there was even another temple beneath this one (as the ancients were wont to do) and even beneath that there are remains found from the 14th century B.C. from the Minoan civilization.

More than three thousand years ago, the ancients worshipped a goddess named Aphaia on this holy site. Once again we have a tale, told over and over again in Greek mythology, of a young woman chased by a man with nefarious intent. In this case, the young woman in question was trying to evade sailors near this coastline. As the pursuing sailors watched her head up the hillside desperate to escape their clutches, she disappeared over the top of the hill and was never seen again.

Although she is known as a goddess of the mountain and hunting, Aphaia is strangely also known as the goddess who protects shipping. Just like a woman, she ends up protecting the very folks who were trying to harm her in the first place: behold the transcendent power of the divine feminine!

As myths go, there are often multiple versions. In another adaptation, a young half mortal named Vritomartis was born to the god Zeus and his lover Karmi. She loved hunting and became a favorite of the goddess Artemis. Along came a guy named Minoas who fell in love with Vritomartis and naturally, her first instinct, as an acolyte of the staunchly independent Artemis, was to run away. Falling into the sea, she got entangled in fishermen's nets and was taken up on their ship.

Once aboard, a sailor fell in love with Vritomartis, forcing her once again to flee. She jumped overboard and swam back to the island with the sailor in hot pursuit. As she made her way up the hill to the pine forests, a divine force interceded and she disappeared into the ethers. Her name then became Aphaia, from the Greek word *afandos*, which refers to one who has vanished into thin air.

The temple sits on a gorgeous plateau at the northern end of the island. Surrounded by lacy pines and within the lapping waves of the cerulean Saronic Gulf, it is actually a part of a complex of buildings. Ramps on either side of the temple lead to a large altar and are

(D) EAST ELEVATION

surrounded by four bases meant to hold statues. To the north is a cistern to collect rainwater from the roofs.

There is, as always, a story told by the frieze sculpture along the building. The temple's pediment sculpture shows battle scenes in which the heroes of Aegina fought against the empire of Troy to the east. Like the Parthenon in Athens, the temple's goddess is shown on both ends, center stage in the narrative. A wooden statue of Aphaia may have stood at a distance from the temple, but only its base remains. Unlike marble, wood doesn't survive the millennia of erosion and deterioration that occurs to these ancient sites across Greece. So even though her statue is gone, her temple complex allows us to imagine the life of a woman who was chased by sailors, ended up being their protector, and was rewarded with a gem of a temple whose columns shimmer like ivory stripes against a miasmic blue sky. As her name implies, Aphaia may have vanished, but she left behind a sacred site for the rest of us to contemplate and celebrate the sanctity and splendor of the tiny island she loved.

This pine-forested island, replete with citrus, almonds, and figs, is actually known for its abundant pistachio cultivation. Every September the Aegina Fistiki (pistachio) Festival is held over four days at the time of the harvest, and visitors are treated not only to a sampling of the delicious nuts, but to a celebration of dance, theater, and music. Like the nearby islet of Aggistri, Aegina has an abundance of beautiful beaches to choose from for a day in the sun, including the ethereal Moni beach island, reachable only by boat. Literary buffs may enjoy knowing that Aegina is the location where Nikos Kazantzakis wrote his epic novel, *Zorba the Greek*. While his former house is not open to the public, you can still gaze at the robin's egg blue gate and shutters from a distance and imagine the writer at work in this stunning seaside enclave.

If you have a clear day flying into Athens, take a look down at the landscape below; amongst the rumpled dun hills of the earth meeting the turquoise seas, try to pick out the sites of the three most intact temples of Attica, this southernmost region of Greece. From the air, the connection between the Temple of Apollo at Sounion, the Parthenon of Athens, and the Temple of Aphaia on Aegina are said to form a holy ancient triangle.

৯৫

12

Kos Nymphaeum

THE HOUSE OF EUROPA AND THE
BIRTHPLACE OF LETO

The way the light streams in from above, illuminating the interior courtyard outlined in lacy scalloped arches, makes you feel like you're in a fairyland. These delicate columns, holding up an arcade of intricate brickwork, remind you how much the Romans worshipped the idea of a good bath. And Kos is the perfect place for them to have erected one of the loveliest in the empire.

Sitting off the coast of Turkey, Kos is not on most travelers' itineraries. Yet the reason this comma-shaped island would house such an elaborate set of baths—called *thermidor* from the Latin—is because Kos is the birthplace of Hippocrates, the ancient physician who is known as the father of medicine. It's no surprise that modern medical conferences are regularly held on this idyllic and captivating island, close to perhaps the most famous of Greece's Asklepieia—ancient spas dedicated to healing. A majestic plane tree still exists where Hippocrates himself taught his students and examined patients, and at 2,500 years old, it is considered one of the most ancient trees in Europe.

This third largest island in the Dodecanese chain, Kos contains an imposing boulevard bordered with majestic palm trees near the city's medieval castle, and is peppered with all species of conifer as well as a thick forest of cedar trees. As you wander down a worn marble road, you find yourself approaching the Nymphaeum, a cluster of structures whose exterior resembles pixilated brick, which served as an ancient healing center. This included not just public baths of different temperatures, but a swimming pool, temples dedicated to the gods Hercules and Aphrodite, and a hippodrome for horse racing. Archaeologists originally named the site after nymphs because of the extensive baths, only later determining it was actually one of the most famous of the 300 Asklepieia that exist in Greece. In my humble opinion, the combination of nymphs and a healing sanctuary makes perfect sense!

Asklepieia were overseen by priests dedicated to the god Asklepios, and open to anyone looking for a cure. Kos's healing-spa had special facilities devoted just to athletes as well; one such area is called the Xysto, which means to scrape off the oil from the skin before an athletic event. Another area is known as the Xystos Dromos, which means Carved Street. To enable athletes to train regardless of rain or shine, the surface of the road was treated to prevent slipping and certain areas were covered to allow protection from the elements.

There are three levels of this combined temple and medical school, all linked by a staircase. The baths, dating to the 1st century B.C., are on the lowest level. The second tier is the site of the 2nd to 3rd century A.D. temple to Apollo. With its seven elegant restored columns topped with ornate Corinthian capitals, one can see how the massive temple once dominated the site. The third level is an older, Doric temple dedicated to Asklepios from the 2nd century B.C.

A visit to Kos wouldn't be complete without recognizing the resident goddess, Leto, whose birthplace is here. Leto is one of many goddesses associated with the moon and fertility who was first worshipped in Asia Minor (now modern Turkey) and then assimilated into ancient Greek culture. As Kos is very close to the

Turkish coast, it's not surprising that this magical island was chosen as her place of birth. Her sacred lineage is traced to her parents, the Titans Phoebe and Coeus, and she is mother to the divine twins Artemis and Apollo, sired by Zeus himself. Zeus's many trysts brought on the rage of his long-suffering wife, Hera, who chased Leto relentlessly during her pregnancy before she landed on the island of Delos to give birth to her sacred twins.

Another famous figure of mythology is also immortalized on Kos. In a house dating to the Roman period there is an exquisite mosaic depicting the abduction of Europa, yet another goddess who caught the roving eye of lascivious Zeus. One day she was tending to her father's herds when Zeus decided to shapeshift into a white bull and mix in with the crowd. While she was gathering flowers, she spied the white bull and decided to climb onto his back. Bad idea—crafty Zeus took advantage of this and swam out to sea with the lovely goddess, taking her to the island of Crete to ravish her there (a long swim by the way!). While there, she uncovered his real identity and she was made the first queen of Crete.

Take a moment to gaze at the hypnotic image of the lithe Europa, her naked behind and body seeming to float effortlessly atop the bull, who looks at her with intense interest. A small dolphin leaps in the ocean below the pair while the entire image is bordered by a roped design.

Before you leave the island, a popular excursion is to climb the hill above the sanctuary of Asklepios, ringed with thick pines, and stare out to the cerulean sea and catch a glimmer of the Turkish coast just beyond. Sit quietly and listen to the crickets and maybe you'll catch an owl's cry in the woods. Feel the balmy breeze on your skin and sense the peace, tranquility, and healing ethos that still permeates the air of this ancient sanctuary.

❧

13 *Delos*

LETO'S SACRED TWINS AND THE TEMPLE OF ISIS

One thing is for sure: if you're planning to have a baby, don't go to Delos. Incredible but true, the most fundamental of life transitions—births and deaths—are prohibited on this tiny island in the Aegean since the gods Apollo and Artemis were born here, rendering the whole island a sacred sanctuary. No one (except for a handful of government-employed guards) lives on Delos, but you can visit this spectacular island on a day pass. Departures leave throughout the day from nearby Mykonos, where a small boat will drop you on the island and make sure to pick you up again by sunset.

Delos is an archaeologist's heaven; in fact it is one of the most important archaeological sites in Greece. Greek mythology tells us that the goddess Leto, daughter of Titans Coeus and Phoebe, gave birth to Apollo and Artemis, twin gods of the sun and moon. Artemis was also supposedly born on Leros, an island several hundred miles to the east, near the coast of Turkey. With so many beautiful islands and so many gods and goddesses, it's not only hard to keep track of them all, it's no wonder every island wants to claim these Olympic deities for themselves!

A sacred lake in the center of the island, now dried up, is thought to be the birthplace of the sacred twins. When the Ionians arrived around 1000 B.C., Delos became a major religious center, and after a stroll around this massive archaeological complex, it is easy to see why. Surrounding the Sacred Lake is a series of imposing marble lions, mouths open and growling at visitors, ready to protect the sacred precinct. The lions' sinewy forms were sculpted of Naxian marble, and of the original nine, only five remain today at the site, safely within the confines of the island's museum. However, the reproductions faithfully represent how the beasts were depicted along this Sacred Way. Facing east, the lions lift off their front haunches and roar at the rising sun with the intent of inspiring awe and trembling in worshipers. Often compared to the Egyptian Avenue of the Sphinxes at Karnak, the original lions were carved in the late 6th century B.C. and ultimately were moved to the island's museum in 1999 after suffering erosion from the wind and sea.

In addition to being the birthplace of sacred twins, Delos was actually the home of two female figures normally not associated with Greece: Isis, the Egyptian goddess of health and marriage, patroness of magic and protector of children, and the infamous Cleopatra, the last pharaoh of ancient Egypt. You can visit the latter's house, in which two headless statues of the famous queen and her husband, Dioscourides, dating to the 2nd century B.C., stand in a magnificent restored marble colonnade. Nearby is the House of the Dolphins, which contains a gorgeous mosaic with intertwined dolphins surrounded by an intricate Greek key border design and waved edging.

✳ www.visitgreece.gr/en/greek_islands/cyclades/delos

An entire area is devoted to foreign gods, one of them Isis. With the marble façade at the end of the portion known as the cella, or holy of holies, is a statue of this mysterious goddess from across the sea. A perfume altar is installed nearby with marble in the shape of horns. Isis was thought to bring good health and fortune and also protected the fate of sailors. She is known to be part of a trio of gods including Serapis, also endowed with healing attributes, and Anubis, the jackal-headed god.

Because it is uninhabited, there is a purity and peacefulness to Delos that exists nowhere else in Greece. You are free to wander the day away, imagining how this sacred site must have functioned in ancient times. Sit on the edge of the Temple of Isis, look out towards the sea and picture travelers arriving by boat from faraway shores, having come all this way to pray for fortune and health from the gods.

If you're an archaeology junkie, or just here to take in the sheer beauty of this UNESCO world heritage site, you'll find the bone white lucidity of marble, unblinking sun and sapphire waters combine into a delectable cocktail. Far from traffic and crowds, you are free to stroll past a line of ferocious lions and gaze at the voluptuous forms of foreign women, or explore the House of Dionysus, a luxurious ancient private dwelling with columns piercing the pellucid air and a fabulous mosaic of the wine god riding a panther. And if that isn't enough to make your eyes pop, wander over to the Stoivadeion where a giant phallus was erected (sorry, couldn't resist the pun!) in 300 B.C. in honor of Dionysus.

Before you board the last boat back to Mykonos, stop to smell the wild sage and listen to the sweat bees hover in the honeyed air. The Sacred Lake may have been dry since 1926, according to Le Guide Bleu, but you can still, if you look closely, imagine Leto, in the grip of labor pains, grasping onto the sacred palm tree as she gave birth to her divine twins.

❧

14 *Naxos*

ISLAND OF STRAUSS'S *ARIADNE*, SEMELE'S *UNBORN CHILD*, AND AN UNFORGETTABLE SAINTS' DAY FESTIVAL

Naxos is an island of high drama, as my husband and I were to find a few years back. It was a hot, sticky Aegean evening, bouzoukis were whining their eerie sound, lambs were turning crispy on the spit, and children were being plied with Coca-Cola until the wee hours. As we settled into a night of celebration at a rural Greek island festival, there was no hint that something more preposterous than the usual entertainment—music and dancing—was on the menu.

We had just arrived on Naxos, a dreamy isle studded with khaki peaks, silvery olive orchards, verdant gardens, and mysterious valleys. I knew this Cycladic island was historically rich, but first things first: we had heard that a *panayuri*, or church festival, was to be held that evening in a village in the hills above the main port of Naxos town, and that meant an opportunity to sample some Naxian wine and *kitron*, a citron liqueur produced on the island.

As the moon rose, a pale pink lozenge over looming Mount Zas, the highest peak in the Cyclades, we paid for our tickets and searched for seats; locals and tourists alike crowded the outdoor tables scattered around a small dance floor strung with tiny white lights hovering like fireflies on a hot Midwestern summer night.

Soon after we settled into a pair of empty chairs, our table groaned beneath the weight of the local rose-tinted wine, platters of roast lamb, smoky grilled eggplant, and *horiatki* salads of fire engine red tomatoes, crisp cucumbers, and peppers sprinkled with oregano and feta.

We noted a burly, mustachioed gentleman, black hair sweatily matted about his head, move center stage. Shirt hanging out and lips boozily parted, he ceremoniously stooped to swat the floor with one hand. Grasping an overflowing tumbler of ouzo in the other, he slowly rose and began to sway, becoming engulfed in a ritual of Greek male machismo: the dance known as the *zeibekiko*.

Throughout the evening an aging waiter, his snow-white hair matching his apron, had been delivering trays of drinks to the crowd. After serving a few tables near the dance floor, he stepped onto the stage and, approaching the lone dancer, attempted to refill his ouzo glass. Without warning, instead of appreciating the free refill, the drunken dancer impulsively kicked the metal tray out of the waiter's hand and sent it spinning into the crowd. A hush came over the throng as the humiliated waiter scurried off into the darkness.

Ultimately the crowd recovered, and we treated ourselves to dessert: thick honeyed diamonds of baklava, shredded wheat rolls of *kataifi*, and the seemingly endless number of Greek confections to combine honey, nuts, and phyllo dough. Between sips of lava-thick Greek coffee, we watched the solitary performer, unsteadily commanding the stage against a backdrop of shadowy mountains etched upon a star-filled sky.

Suddenly, a familiar, silvery head reappeared in the throng. Moving ever closer to the dance floor, bottle of ouzo in hand, he stealthily approached the edge of the stage. As if watching a bad soap opera, we witnessed, mouths agape, the waiter crack the bottle on the dancer's head with full force, launching a cascade of ouzo over the shocked man's face. A moment later, the deed now done, the surprisingly nimble culprit sprinted like a track star back into the crowd and disappeared into the warm Aegean night.

With such a dramatic introduction, you'd think the rest of Naxos would pale in comparison. But Naxos did not disappoint; this densely valleyed island, replete with groves of pomegranate, fig, lemon, and orange trees is the largest and arguably most beautiful in the Cyclades. The ever-romantic Lord Byron loved it here, and if you think drunken feuds are hard acts to follow, try Richard Strauss on for size. This is the island featured in one of his most theatrical operas, *Ariadne auf Naxos*.

When Ariadne helps to rescue Theseus from the Minotaur in the famous labyrinth of her father, King Minos, the pair become lovers. Sailing from Crete, they stop at Naxos en route to Athens, where Ariadne falls asleep and is left behind. One version tells that Dionysus, the god of wine and festivity, spies her and makes her his wife. Another, less happy outcome has Ariadne pine for her lost love, ultimately leaping to her death from the cliffs near the village of Chora.

Another of the island's dramas involves the birth of Dionysus himself. When his mother, Semele, dies, his father, Zeus, takes the unborn child and sews him into his thigh. When the baby is born from Zeus's thigh on Naxos, he is attended to by a trio of nymphs: Philia, Coronida, and Clidi. In honor of the royal birth, the gods forever blessed Naxos, making it fertile and abundant in grapevines, the sacred plant of Dionysus.

The goddess of agriculture has a tie to this verdant isle. In the late 6th century B.C. a temple was built in honor of Demeter. The temple, near Sangri, was abandoned and disassembled, as were many sacred places of antiquity, during the Byzantine era when a church was erected on the site. Its recent partial reconstruction by German archaeologists recreates the temple's soaring, bone white

Doric style columns set starkly against the azure sky. Unlike most temples, which are rectangular in shape, this sanctuary was built in a rare square formation, making it all the more unique. The sanctuary has connections to the Eleusinian mysteries, an annual religious festival held outside Athens. Many gorgeous finds from the islands' excavations, such as sleek marble Cycladic figurines, gold jewelry, and a mosaic depicting a Nereid on a bull can be viewed in the island's tidy museum, which is located in an old Venetian mansion.

If you are lucky enough to attend one of Naxos's many summer saints' day festivals, be on the lookout for some potent entertainment on the dance floor, as this is the birthplace of the god of wine and merriment. But it won't be necessary to attend a panayuri if you are seeking drama and visual delights, for Naxos is filled with plenty of its own.

※

15 *Melissani and the Nymphs*

THE UNDERGROUND LAKE OF MELISSANI
AND DROGARATI CAVE

You descend deep into the ground, the smell of moss blooms in the dusky, heathered air, and you feel enveloped by the earth. Going deeper still, you see a lake: sapphire, sun-kissed waters eventually turning black in the distance, swallowed into the maw of a huge cavern. I've always loved the various ancient myths about going into the underworld, such as Orpheus and Eurydice, Charon and the ferryboat, and Persephone's abduction by Hades. Little did I know that there existed a place where you actually feel like you are descending into the underworld, and where a shadowy man stands ready to help you cross the River Styx.

But this isn't Persephone's lair or the River Styx; it is the Lake of the Nymphs. Just off the west coast of Greece's Peloponnesian peninsula is one of the largest islands in Greece. Formed millions of years ago, Kefalonia's subterranean core is laced with a network of underground rivers that have created some of the most spectacular caves and, in the case of Melissani, an underground lake. The walls are moist to the touch and the smell faintly sulfurous. You enter the darkness and there, in the distance, you see a glint of light reflecting off water. A ferryman awaits. As you settle into the boat, you look up and see the sky, framed by a ring of earth and trees, sprouting sideways off the cliffs. The oarsman paddles the diorite-colored water, which seems to descend to the center of the earth. The air is chillingly still, with the exception of the oars dipping into the murky depths and voices whispering from distant boats.

Discovered in 1951 by speleologist Yiannis Petrochilos after the cave's roof collapsed, the lake is a mixture of salt and fresh water, a product of the unusual geological formation of the area. When the sunlight hits the water at certain times of the day, it takes on an eerie shine and the black water turns to ultramarine, spreading a shimmering turquoise hue throughout the cave. In order to study the strange formations in 1959, geologists dumped food coloring into an underground aqueduct in a series of dye tracing experiments. Ten days later, the coloring appeared on the opposite side of the island, so don't let the calm surface fool you; the experiments proved that an underground river winds its way beneath this porous rock, constantly replenishing the lake's water supply.

In 1962, on a tiny islet in the middle of the lake, Greek archaeologist Spyridon Marinatos conducted excavations that turned up a number of artifacts, including oil lamps and votives to the nymph Melissanthi. Plates and other objects depict the god Pan, who was known to cavort with the nymphs around their favorite environs—water sources. Local lore tells us that Melissanthi was a shepherdess tending to her flock. Wandering the hills above, she accidently fell into the opening and met her death in the lake below.

Another tale is that the Nymph Melissani, spurned by the god Pan and mourning her rejection, committed suicide by jumping into the lake. The nymph supposedly used dolphins to carry messages to her love. After her death, they turned to stone, and locals believe their outlines are clearly visible in the stalactites found throughout the cave. Whichever tale is true, the lake's mythology is a sad one, with the echoes of a woman's loss reverberating between its massive walls.

Drogarati Cave, located only kilometers away, is an otherworldly space, its enormous stalactites and stalagmites spearing the interior like an armory of colossal amber javelins. The cave was discovered 300 years ago when the entrance was created in one of the many earthquakes that rattle this part of the world. The acoustics of this alien-looking interior are so favorable that orchestras stage performances in them several times a year. The largest chamber, formidably called the Chamber of Exaltation at 900 square meters, seats up to 500 people. Imagine listening to Maria Callas, who once expressed her interest in performing in this unusual venue, while admiring the prehistoric feel of the limestone interior. With its natural air conditioning and year round temperatures of seventy degrees, the space is a welcome relief to Kefalonia's sometimes wickedly hot summers.

If you're an archaeology buff, a cave enthusiast, or a lover of mythology, this spectacular area with its mysterious lake grotto offers a little something for everybody. Located just north of the island's main port of Same, it's an easy day's trip from anywhere on the island. Whether you're a spelunker, or you want to get a feel for what Persephone must have experienced when being pulled into the underworld, the trip to visit Melissani and her nymphs is well worth the drive.

❧

II

Goddesses of Cinema, History and the Arts

16 The Acropolis Museum, The Caryatids, and Melina Mercouri

WOMEN HOLDING UP THE WORLD

Until recently, the Acropolis Museum was housed in a tiny building next to the Parthenon. Priceless artifacts such as the Rampin Rider and the Kritios Boy were crammed into the small galleries, which visitors often shuffled quickly by on their way to catch a glimpse of the most famous statues of all, the Caryatids: a group of ladies I like to call the women holding up the world.

Sculpted by either Phidias or his student, Alkamenes, between 421 and 406 B.C., these six statues once held up the Porch of the Maidens, the portico of the Erechtheion atop the Acropolis hill. In the 1970s, due to increased erosion from Athens's pollution, the sculptures were removed and languished in the old museum until a light bulb went off in the head of a woman who envisioned a new home more fitting for these icons of power, grace, and endurance, a woman known as the last Greek goddess.

Enter Melina Mercouri, another icon of power, grace, and endurance and a force of nature unto herself. Born Amalia Maria Mercouri in Athens in 1920, Mercouri grew up in a political home, the daughter of a government minister and granddaughter of one of Athens's mayors. After attending drama school, Mercouri went on to star on stage and in film with her most notable role as a free-spirited prostitute in the movie *Never on Sunday*, which was directed by and co-starred her husband, Jules Dassin.

When a military junta took over the country in the late 1960s, Mercouri's political genes were ignited. After living abroad with her French husband, she returned to Greece in 1974 and became a founding member of the Pan Hellenic Socialist Party as well as a voice in the woman's movement. In 1981 when her party won the national election, Mercouri was appointed to the cabinet as Minister of Culture. Throughout her eight-year tenure in government, one of her most passionate causes was the return of the Parthenon Marbles (also known as the Elgin Marbles) from the British Museum. Taken by Lord Elgin in the early 19th century, these priceless sculptures, a series of friezes and metopes, were brutally cut away from the Parthenon and shipped to England. Elgin's men tried to remove the Caryatids as well, but the ship had only room for one, which was replaced by a brick pillar. At attempt to remove a second Caryatid resulted in its destruction. Mercouri had only one thing to say about the repatriation of her country's beloved treasures: "There are no such things as the Elgin marbles."

Mercouri's zeal was twofold: continuing to fight for the return of the marbles and to create a new space to house them once they returned. With the announcement of the Athens Olympics to be held in 2004, there was hope to have the new museum ready in time for the opening ceremonies. Yet protests by locals concerned about the archaeological remains in the construction area caused delays. Mercouri and her group held an international competition, won by Bernard Tschumi, who designed the highly modern structure atop pillars, raising the structure aboveground.

What is just as exciting about this new museum are the ongoing excavations that continue below the glass floors showcasing the acres of open trenches filled with potsherds, allowing you to admire the melding of past, present, and future in this one magnificent building. Children love to crawl across the reinforced glass surface and visitors of all ages have a chance to peer down into the earth far below and look into the past. (Ladies, just watch that you don't wear a skirt or dress that day!)

Finally opened to the public in 2009, the gleaming glass-and-steel structure sits adjacent to the Acropolis hill in the Makriyanni neighborhood and is oriented to line up with the Parthenon itself. Until the British Museum returns the long missing marbles, the top floor of this magnificent structure is filled with mostly white plaster reproductions of what should be the rightful heritage of the Greek people.

Politics aside, the ladies of the hour have their own platform—in fact, their whole entire level. Seen from both the first and second floors, the five remaining Caryatids are installed in a central corridor. Their luxuriant braids, snaking down their backs, are now fully visible beneath the Ionic capitals atop their heads, holding up the proverbial world. Behind the lovely marble ladies is a continually looping video showcasing the latest technology used to clean these priceless statues. A thin laser beam is trained on a layer of grit encrusted on the statue's braids, and the video shows it instantaneously being erased by the intense pulsing light.

The 14,000 square feet of gallery space holds more than four thousand objects, ten times more than the old museum. A lovely restaurant offers prime views of the Parthenon from both an indoor and outdoor veranda, and the gift shop is the place to buy. This classy venue is a welcome relief from the standard tourist shop, offering elegant notebooks featuring drawings of the Caryatids' well-coiffed heads and art books on the history of Greece's most treasured antiquities.

Mercouri, who died in 1994 at the age of seventy-three, summed up her Hellenic heritage, "You know, it is said that we Greeks are a fervent and warm-blooded breed. Well let me tell you something—it is true." Not only was she a goddess of cinema, she was a force of nature who founded a political party, changed Athens's cultural landscape and fought to preserve the rightful heritage  of the Greek people. I like to think of her alongside her Caryatid sisters as Greece's last goddess: regal, forthright, and standing proud...a woman holding up the world.

17 Men in Tights

THE ROYAL GUARDS AT THE NATIONAL PALACE AND QUEEN AMALIA OF BAVARIA

You've heard the saying, "Who can resist a man in a uniform?" But what about a man in tights? If you're intrigued, stop by the Parliament Building, located across from Syntagma Square, catty-corner to the Grand Bretagne and you will get an eyeful. Every day the changing of the guards occurs and a line of tall, gorgeous Greek men in uniform emerge from their sentry boxes to parade in front of tourists. But this is no ordinary Buckingham Palace changing of the guards—no Beefeaters hats or tomato-red and gold brocaded costumes for these guys. In Greece they do it their way: these hunks step out in silk garters and short kilts known as *fustanellas,* and do a high kick with a flourish of pompoms on their tailor-made clogs.

 I never tire of this extravagant and dramatic spectacle. Men may laugh at the somewhat ludicrousness of the guards' gear, but for women, it's time to get the camera ready. These guys are a seriously good-looking lot. Only men who are 6' 3" qualify, and must have impeccable personal credentials. The uniform—if you can seriously imagine anyone doing battle in such a cumbersome outfit—is derived from the attire

of the guerrilla fighters during the Ottoman occupation, which lasted from 1453 to 1821. These men, known as *Klephts* (thieves) or *Armatoles* (bandits), were outfitted in 400-pleat skirts and hand-embroidered waistcoats, which take more than a month to sew. But most notable are those shoes: more specifically, clogs, with gargantuan black pompoms attached to the top. Called *tsourachia*, these are also handmade on the premises and weigh several pounds each, thanks to sixty nails buried in the soles, ensuring the guards (known as *evzones*) don't slip and slide during their procession. These guys are as tough and hard to distract as their Buckingham cousins. One account states that, when a Molotov cocktail was thrown at a guard's booth, the stoic *evzone* didn't bat an eye as the wooden structure burst into flames. Now that is cool under fire.

Best time to show up is on Sundays at 1 P.M. This is when the granddaddy of all performances occurs, so arrive early, find a high perch nearby and have your camera at the ready. Keep an eye out for those sixty nails, clearly visible on the bottoms of the clogs as they goose-step in a parade of black and red ponytail silk-tasseled berets, which denote a difference in rank. The procession, done at an implausibly slo-mo pace, is specifically orchestrated to maintain the stamina necessary to stand still for hours at a time. So as you watch this quasi-theatrical production, don't let those puffy sleeves fool you. These guys are as ruggedly trained as their bayoneted rifles are real.

After the thirty-minute changing of the guard, be sure to take a walk around the Parliament Building. Visitors are not allowed inside, but you can admire this neoclassical structure designed by German architect Friedrich von Gartner, which once served as a residence for the Greek royal family. After the monarchy was abolished in 1929, the building became the seat of Parliament.

Directly behind the Parliament Building is Athens's National Gardens, a densely forested central park replete with park benches, ice cream vendors, and *kamakis* (literally "hooks"): innocuous young Greek men looking to pick up foreign tourists. When I was a college student living in Athens my friends and I would regularly be subjected to the kissing sounds and offers to "Seet down please, baby," as we strolled through the grounds.

This maze of walkways and exotic plantings covering thirty-eight acres was originally the personal garden of Queen Amalia. Born a Duchess in Bavaria in 1818, Amalia Maria Frederica married King Otto I of Greece in 1836. Only seventeen years old when she arrived in Greece, her fair hair and complexion made her a curiosity and wildly popular with the locals. Sensitive to the customs of her adopted country, she designed her royal court dress to emulate the clothing of the people, wearing the offset tasseled beret over her braided hair, wide-breasted trimmed waistcoats and flowing skirts.

To stock her private Eden, Amalia's personal gardener, a Prussian native named Friedrich Schmidt, was sent out to collect plants from around the world. Amalia even ordered the Greek Navy to bring back 15,000 seedlings from Italy, resulting in the wide array of subtropical species that populates the garden today.

Unfortunately, Amalia's popularity didn't last long. Unable to produce an heir, Otto had a scandalous fling with—gasp—his own father's paramour. After an assassination attempt on Amalia's life and a coup in 1862, the couple grabbed the family jewels and headed back to Bavaria. Amalia's primary gift to the city is the garden she so lovingly tended, and one of the city's main boulevards, Vassilias Amalias, which borders the Parliament Building and gardens, is named for her.

A huge semicircular building within the gardens, known as the Zappeion, was originally built for the 1896 Olympics held in Athens, the first of the modern era. Named after its benefactor, financier Evangelos Zappas, the neoclassical building, with its Corinthian style *propylaea*, or gate, is primarily used as an exhibition hall. The Zappeion, which housed the fencing competition in the 1896 games, is a favorite meeting spot for locals to discuss the politics of the day and is surrounded by some impressive gardens of its own.

Wandering through the lush canopy of the National Gardens is a treat on a hot Athenian afternoon and remains open all day. The park contains several ponds and is filled with statuary of celebrated statesmen and poets, a scattering of Corinthian column capitals, playgrounds and even a small zoo. Dazzlingly indigo and emerald peacocks strut across the serpentine pathways and other waterfowl can be spotted beneath the stately lines of palms, conifers, and cypresses.

Make a stop at O Kypos (the garden), the park's refreshment stand, and treat yourself to a cold frappe—or if it's after siesta—a glass of ouzo. If you do, the licorice-scented beverage will always be accompanied by a *meze*, often a snack of chips, nuts, or a plate of cucumbers and sausage bites stabbed with toothpicks. Greeks don't drink alcohol without an accompanying bit of food, so it's always a treat to see what little snack will be served with this traditional Greek refreshment.

My favorite respite after the gardens is a visit to the row of florist shops along Amalias Street bordering the park and Parliament Building. The buckets of yellow, candy pink, and ruby red roses exude an enticing fragrance, so even if you're not in the buying mood, satisfy your olfactory senses and make a mental note to thank Amalia for importing all her exotic plantings and bringing the adjacent jewel of a green space to grace Athens's central corridor.

❧

18 The Herodes Atticus Theater

MARIA CALLAS AND OTHER STARS
PERFORMING UNDER THE STARS

The first time I attended an event at this ancient theater, I was living in Athens as a college student. As I shuffled in with the large, cosmopolitan crowd, the air saturated with the scent of Chanel N°5 and Turkish tobacco, I recall looking up at the towering, ancient proscenium. Dramatically lit and soaring into a starry night sky, I stood there for a moment to take in the dramatic view of this magnificent structure and the dreamlike form of the Parthenon, seemingly floating above on the Acropolis plateau. My roommate's sister was a member of the Maurice Bejart dance troupe and I remember watching the performance, spellbound not only by the enormous talent of the dancers on the stage, but the sheer splendor and deep history of the theater surrounding me.

As you stroll down the pedestrian walkway beneath the Acropolis hill, you come upon the twin stone towers that mark the entrance to this commanding structure. With the columns of the Parthenon visible hovering just beyond, it's even more thrilling to realize that, not only can you admire the architecture, but you can also participate in this living monument by attending one of the many performances that are held here over the summer season.

The Herodes Atticus, also called the Herodeion, is known as an "Odeion" theater. Originally a closed structure, the ancient theater once had a roof fashioned of aromatic wood from the cedars of Lebanon. Erected in 161 A.D., the structure was built directly into the southern slope of the Acropolis hill. Named after a wealthy aristocrat who became a Roman senator, philosopher, and teacher, Herodus Atticus built it in memory of his wife Aspasia Regilla, who died in 160 A.D. Its vast auditorium with seating made of gleaming Pendelic marble was restored in the 1950s and has the capacity for more than 5,000 spectators. The original immense façade of the stage wall was three stories high and, in places, the remains of the tiered arched windows still reach to that height. Three doorways at the base of the stage wall provide egress for the thousands of spectators, above which are eight niches that once held statues; my guess is that Calliope (muse of epic poetry), Melpomene, and Thalia (muses of tragedy and comedy) as well as Euterpe (the muse of song) were among them, gazing down beatifically at the audience below.

Greek drama was born on this slope of this ancient hill, which lies adjacent to the theater of Dionysus. When the ancient writer Pausanias visited Athens, he described the Herodeion as the finest theater of its type. Less than a century after its completion, the building was destroyed in a fire during the invasion of the Herulian hoards in the 3rd century B.C. Afterwards, when the site lapsed into disuse, the locals used it as a stone quarry. Over time, the locale became covered in soil, and even crops were cultivated on this historic ruin.

After its independence from the Turks, the Greek government made a decision to promote its new identity by celebrating and restoring its ancient monuments. By putting its ancient theaters to use, it would serve to bolster the connection between the resplendence of ancient Greek culture and modern society. In

1955, under the celebrated statesman Konstantine Karamanlis, the building was brought back to its original glory, during a time when the Greek government was interested in reestablishing its identity to the world as a way to further the concept of Hellenism.

The ability to attend an arts performance outdoors is a singularly Greek idea. For more than fifty-two years the Herodeion has hosted the Athens-Epidaurus Festival that has highlighted the crème de la crème of Greek and international music, theater, and arts. From April through September, Athenians and tourists alike can be treated to a wide array of performances. Ancient plays by Aeschylus, Aristophanes, and Euripides are staged here, as well as work by modern Greek playwrights, dance, and philharmonic performances.

The Greek opera great Maria Callas gave numerous performances at the Herodes Atticus. During the German occupation of Greece,

Callas performed with the Greek National Opera, in the lead of Beethoven's *Fidelio*, and in 1957 she delivered a virtuoso performance of Wagner's *Tristan und Isolde*. Callas was a diva about as dramatic as they come. Born Cecilia Sophia Anna Maria Kalogeropoulos in 1923 to Greek immigrants in New York City, she became Callas as a child when her family shortened the name. After her parents separated, Maria moved back to Greece with her mother and sister. Although she was much younger than her peers, Maria showed so much promise as a singer that the Royal Academy of Music made an exception for her to begin studying voice. When she was just sixteen she made her debut at the Royal Opera in Athens and by her twenties she was singing a major role in Puccini's *Tosca*.

During World War II she entertained the enemy troops, and when Greece was liberated she moved to Italy. After singing roles in Wagner's *The Ride of the Valkyries* and Bellini's *I Puritani*, her career took off to international acclaim and she was offered multiple recording contracts. Her tempestuous affair with shipping magnate Aristotle Onassis kept her in the gossip pages for years to come, but after Onassis refused to marry her, instead wedding Jacqueline Kennedy, Callas suffered from a breakdown. Her voice was never the same and even though she made many attempts to resurrect her career, she ultimately succumbed to heart failure and died in Paris in 1977.

While Callas's memory leaves a tragic imprint on this monument, luckily this is not the case with many of her fellow countrymen who have graced this ancient stage. The celebrated Greek composer Mikis Theodorakis, with his heart-pounding rhythms and deeply patriotic music, has performed here, as well as many of his compatriots, including the Greek singer with the sexiest voice on record: Yiorgos Dalaras. Other famed performers at the Herodeion include Diana Krall, Patti Smith and her band, Sting, Pavarotti, and even back in the day, Old Blue Eyes, Frank Sinatra. The eminent Greek folk singer, Nana Mouskouri—famous for her distinctive thick black-rimmed glasses—is a popular artist who has performed at the Herodeion over several decades.

Originally the festival venues included only the Herodeion and the ancient theater at Epidaurus, located a three-hour drive from Athens. Today's Athens-Epidaurus Festival has expanded to include a wider array of concert locales, including a warehouse in Piraeus and other unusual recital venues. It is a unique and unforgettable experience to attend a performance in this magnificent ancient space. If you are fortunate enough to see a play by an ancient Greek playwright, keep one ear on the actors and with the other, listen for the rustle of ancient theater-goers, and imagine them sitting in these same seats, enjoying a performance by the same artist more than two thousand years ago. It's enough to send a shiver down your spine.

꙳

19 Dora Straton Theater

A LIVING MONUMENT TO DANCE

Imagine it is a full moon night, the silvery beams puddling and reflecting off the Parthenon marbles. You are walking up a cobblestone pathway, the lights and clamor of the Plaka district receding beneath you and the stars twinkling overhead. A slight breeze rustles the grasses growing along the walkway and a hush comes over the night. You feel as if you have traveled backwards in time two thousand years.

You enter an auditorium and hear the sound of feet brushing on the floor. Soon you sense the vibration of dancers on the stage, stepping louder, stomping to a strange and throbbing rhythm. A snakelike formation of women and men enter from the wings, their movements rising and falling like an infant's chest to the whining, ancient song.

These are the Dora Stratou Dancers. Every night in the summer, you can climb these ancient pathways and take a seat in this stadium and be treated to a display of dance that is as old as Greece. Greeks proudly refer to this dance troupe, a cultural institution since 1953, as a "living museum of Greek dance."

Situated on the Philopappou Hill, the theater is located directly across from the Acropolis monument. The program, which runs all summer long, boasts a dance company of some seventy-five members, including folk singers, musicians, as well as dancers. The theater, as are all ancient theaters in Greece, is situated outdoors and can accommodate 800 spectators.

As each performance winds its way across the stage, viewers are treated to a parade of the various costumes and headgear of different regions of Greece. Male costumes range from rich blue *kaltses*, or leg coverings, tassled headscarves called *sariki* and stomping-worthy leather boots of the Cretan islanders. Women often are adorned in the snug-fitting *bodia* or aprons, flowing chemises called *poukamisa* and elaborate scarves called *mandilia*, which can often be festooned in tiny golden coins. It's hard to imagine how one can dance in these thick woolen brocaded skirts, heavy scarves, and layers of gleaming pectorals and necklaces wound around their necks. Dizzyingly patterned stockings, richly embroidered vests, and ballooning sleeves add a visual opulence to the troupe as they wend their way across the stage while the poignant and sometimes haunting strains of traditional Greek music perforates the sultry evening air.

Often men, holding a white handkerchief, lead the dances with movements such as leaps, spins, and high kicking, heel-slapping flourishes, while the rest of the company keeps the beat, repeating the intricate steps. With more than two hundred dances in the theater's repertoire, that's a lot of high kicks, and we have one woman to thank for bringing this fantastic display of dance, music, and rich costuming to the public.

Dora Stratou was born in 1903 to an upper-class Athenian family. As a privileged child, the daughter of Maria Koromila and Nikolaos Stratos, a politician, she took piano lessons from Dimitri Mitropoulos, who later went on to become the conductor of the New York Philharmonic. Exposed to fancy balls and palace events, she mixed with influential families as she engaged in her studies of voice and foreign languages while attending theatrical performances. After her father was charged with high treason and sentenced to death in 1922, her family lost its fortune and she moved in and out of the country for the next ten years until she settled back in Greece in 1932.

After seeing a Yugoslavian folk ensemble perform in 1952, Dora decided to found her own company and bring the rich cultural heritage of her country's tradition of dance to the public. Not only was she a curator of dance, she spent tremendous effort over the years to collect more than two thousand traditional regional costumes from around the country, including shoes, scarves, bells, and swords, to keep this tradition alive. Her love of Greek dance led her in 1979 to write the book, *Greek Traditional Dance*. Over the years, she did ethnomusicology research with the famed Simon Karras, filming regional dances, interviewing villagers, and recording music throughout Greece.

❊ www.grdance.org/en

Even though many tourists attend these performances, there is good reason not to skip this treat. Seated in the massive outdoor auditorium, you can savor the dancing, set against a backdrop of pine forest, nestled at the back of Philopappou Hill. The ninety-minute show continues without intermission and beverages are available from a nearby kiosk so you can enjoy a cool drink while taking in the show. Every two weeks the performance program will shift, so an entire new set of dances will be presented throughout the summer season, accompanied by seventy-five musicians performing on traditional instruments such as the bouzouki, lyra and bagpipe-sounding *tsabouna*.

Variously described as a national treasure, this living history of Greek music, dance, costuming, and culture is a must see for any visitor to Athens during the summer. The feeling of the performance momentarily takes you away from the hubbub of downtown Athens and you are magically transported to a small village square where these kinds of performances go on all over rural Greece in honor of saints days throughout the year. For hard-core lovers of Greek dance, the Dora Stratou Theater also offers lecture programs and research opportunities. And if you are inspired to learn a few of these intricate steps themselves, such as the *Hasapiko* (Dance of the Butcher) *Syrtos* or *Zeibekiko*, you can take lessons at this famous theater. With a little practice, who knows? You might end up like Zorba dancing on the beach! *Opa!*

᪥

20 Cycladic Museum

DOLLY GOULANDRIS AND CYCLADIC FIGURINES

Known for her passionate collecting and preservation of Greek antiquities, Dolly Goulandris worked her whole life to bring the treasures of Greek art into the public domain. However, the Cycladic period, which dates from 3300 to 2000 B.C. and is known for its modern-looking marble figurines, was not always the well-known and documented era of Greek art that it is today. In large part due to Goulandris and her husband, shipping magnate Nikos Goulandris, the world can see and appreciate these elegant, almost Picasso-like sculptures in the Goulandris Museum for Cycladic Art in Athens. In fact, these objects are thought to have inspired both Picasso and Brancusi, known for their bold abstract sculptures.

These highly stylized, creamy marble figures are named after the island group in which they were found, which forms a rough circle around the sacred island of Delos. A gorgeous translucent variety of marble is found in the Cycladic chain, including Paros, and Delos itself, which the ancient artists used to sculpt these figures for over a thousand years.

The majority of these figurines were found in burial sites, leading experts to believe they were used in funerary rituals. The fact that most of the figures depict females opens up a variety of reasons for their use: were they meant to depict the deceased, or as companions to comfort them in the afterlife? Different groups scattered throughout the islands made these figures, resulting in a variety of unique designs. Civilization in the early Aegean period was associated with the mother, reproduction and fertility, so it is very likely that the figures are representations of the ancient goddess, whose worship was still active at this time.

The museum opened to the public in 1986, and is housed in two buildings. One is a neoclassical structure designed by the famed Bavarian architect Ernst Schiller, a former residence replete with the towering white cupcake fussiness endemic to this period of architecture. Known as the Stathatos Mansion, this building houses the temporary exhibitions and is a visual treat. A circular central staircase winds up to the original main drawing room, dining room, and bedrooms, all in their original state. Wooden revetments are installed to cover chandeliers, fireplaces, and other decorative features during exhibitions.

Follow a glass walkway to the ultra modern main gallery of the museum across the street. Built in 1985 by architect Ioannis Vikelas, the building is constructed with white marble and granite, and the massive glass windows reflect the blue sky, creating the ethereal feel of the stark Cycladic landscape. This sleek and compact four-story structure includes a collection of Mycenaean and Hellenistic pottery, but the primary exhibition space is devoted to the lyrical and somewhat mysterious marble female sculptures. Made of the luminous, almost transparent marble from the Cycladic island group, these figurines represent the female figure in its most schematic form. With arms crossed across the chest, the head is often triangular in shape with the only distinguishing feature being its nose. Legs are often separated by a narrow cleft and a stylized pubic triangle denotes the gender. A few figurines are fashioned in a violin-type shape, and several are depicted playing instruments, including a harp player. Two figures depict a pregnant woman and one who has just given birth, still showing stretch marks on her belly. A series of frying pan-like objects, whose function remains unknown, is also on display. Made of either clay or a hard stone known as schist, these pans are elaborately decorated in a typical Cycladic geometric pattern of interconnected spirals, zigzags, and hatch marks.

✳ www.cycladic.gr/frontoffice/portal.asp?cpage=NODE&cnode =1&clang=1

Be sure to make a stop at the museum's hip little gift shop, located on the main floor, which offers distinctive designer jewelry and elegant reproductions of the artifacts. I made a point of purchasing a number of gifts for loved ones back home, including little dishes of recycled aluminum and bronze in the shape of a pomegranate, inspired by my favorite goddess, Persephone. The shop also sells a wonderful selection of children's educational books and toys, and there is a small café and courtyard for those with museum fatigue.

Until Goulandris donated her considerable resources to protecting and preserving these figures, as well as educating the public about Greek antiquities, these elegant and unusual works of art remained largely unstudied and unknown. She instinctively appreciated the aesthetic beauty of these minimalist forms and wanted others to have the opportunity to admire their timeless charm. Thanks to her efforts, this distinctive civilization has joined the canon of ancient Greek culture, and the name of Dolly Goulandris will forever be synonymous with Cycladic art.

21 *Benaki Museum*

PENELOPE BENAKIS DELTA

If you want to see classical statues, go to the National or Acropolis museums. If you are interested in a peek into the life and culture of Greece's more recent past, particularly the life of women, then consider the Benaki Museum your personal portal. Touted as Greece's oldest museum (and that's saying something in a country filled with antiquities), the Benaki today is actually a collection of

several satellite campuses around Athens. The museum's massive collections include artifacts spanning multiple periods, including ancient, Coptic, Byzantine, Chinese, and Islamic arts. After a significant renovation project in 2000, the main building in central Athens remains the headquarters of the Benaki's most notable collection, with its focus on the culture and history of Greece.

Situated on a tree-lined street near downtown Athens's Syntagma Square, the museum is the former mansion of the esteemed Benakis family. Founded by Antonio Benakis in memory of his father and donated to the Greek state in 1931, the Benakis' mission is to present the story of Greece's glorious history, and unique and important pieces are showcased from all periods, including Geometric,

Archaic, Classical, Hellenistic, Roman, and Byzantine eras. But the post-Byzantine era shows us a more recent and approachable Greece. By far the most remarkable exhibits are those that showcase art forms that are closer to the people. Throughout the country's modern history, wars were fought, most notably the Greek War of Independence in 1821, but the individual life of the family went on. Objects from everyday existence are what make the heart of this museum, and this opulent, wedding-cake tiered neoclassical building is chock full of costumes and traditional clothing, embroidery, ceramics, and those arts most closely associated with women: jewelry and weaving.

✳ www.benaki.gr/index.asp?lang=en

Thick, heavy embroidered coats! Elaborate headdresses and neckpieces formed of dozens of golden coins! Visitors literally can marinate in Greek home life throughout the ages; intricate embroidery dazzles the eye, and each article of thick woolen clothing shows a masterpiece of needlework. Tanagran bridal costumes from Boeotia with their hammered brass pectorals make you wonder if women from this pre-modern era enjoyed the heavy Valkyrie gear that appears to come straight out of a Wagnerian opera. Each gown is like a multi-tiered layer cake: a base of cream-colored wool overlaid with intricate needlework, usually in red, black, and golden tones. The whole outfit is then topped with scarves that are festooned with hundreds of tiny, thin coins. I like to imagine the sound these costumes must have made as the women moved about their houses, the thick swish of the woolen skirts brushing together, the light step of the slippered feet and the jangling of metal coins that practically dripped from the forehead and neck. It almost makes you wonder if they could move at all!

Many of the dresses are actually bridal gowns, and from the looks of many of them you'd believe women didn't just inherit their dowries, but also wore them! While the suffocating weight of some of the gear can make you wilt in a typical Athenian summer day, the installations recreating family homes from the late 18th and early 19th centuries put the clothing into perspective. A formal reception hall, carved in Constantinople, was shipped in its entirety to the island of Hydra, and the display shows a scene of women gathered, wearing bridal gear and town costumes that were fashionable in the Greek islands around the turn of the 19th century. The Ottoman effect on Greek culture is evident in these costumes, some of which come from Constantinople, or modern-day Istanbul.

Many members of the Benakis family, who immigrated to Athens from Alexandria, made their mark on the country's history. Antonio's sister, Penelope, became a famous writer, responsible for many children's books focused on patriotic themes. Penelope Benakis was born into wealth, one of five children of Emmanuel Benakis and his wife Virginia Choremi. She grew up in Alexandria, Egypt, a Greek colony known for its intellectual society, and Penelope's literary aspirations were notable from the start. Her books were all influenced by Greece's history and often focused on patriotic and religious themes, but she was also known for the amusing tales, including *Crazy Antonis,* which was modeled on her brother. Her marriage to businessman Stephanos Delta resulted in three daughters, who were raised in the same literary and entitled environment that she had been. Penelope's literary interests expanded to preserving oral tradition, and over time she collected narratives about critical historic events from her time and interviewed veterans about the struggle for Macedonian freedom.

Penelope engaged in a love affair with Ion Dragoumi, a Greek diplomat, writer and sometime revolutionary. The affair eventually ended, but the two carried on a passionate exchange of letters during which Penelope tried to commit suicide. In the following years she wrote a series of novels, some set in the Byzantine era. During her final move back to Athens, she contracted polio. Her subsequent novels mirrored the political events of the time and were, according to some, conspicuously autobiographical. After her former lover, Dragoumis, was assassinated, she wore the black of the mourning widow.

As her paralysis advanced, she received Dragoumis's letters and diaries, and spent her time dictating commentary on his work. Her dedication to Greece's cultural history was so powerful that, when the Germans invaded Athens in 1941, she made a zealous and irrevocable decision. Unable to withstand the desecration of her beloved country's honor, on April 27, 1941, she committed suicide by ingesting poison. She died two days later and was buried at her estate in Kifissia, a suburb of Athens.

❧

22 Heinrich Schliemann's House

SOPHIA SCHLIEMANN, RICH IN GOLD

Long closed to the public, this massive, formerly private estate on Panepistimiou Street in downtown Athens—located a few blocks from the city's central Syntagma Square—opened in 1999 as the city's premier numismatic museum. Originally known as the *Iliou Melathron*—house of Ilion—it was built between 1878-1879 by Ernest Ziller. This famed architect was responsible for many of Athens's most notable neoclassical structures, such as the Presidential Mansion and the National Theater; yet more intriguing is that this was the former residence of the infamous businessman turned archaeologist, Heinrich Schliemann.

German born, Schliemann was a passionate Hellenophile from a youthful age. After having read Homer's classic poem, *The Iliad*, the eight-year-old Schliemann declared he would one day locate the fabled city of Troy. An avid linguist, he eventually mastered more than a dozen languages, and by some accounts memorized both *The Iliad* and *The Odyssey*. After amassing a fortune in Russia, he dedicated his life to locating the sites he had read about in Homer's epics.

Schliemann's discovery of Troy and Mycenae—two of the most famous sights of antiquity, previously believed to have been only the subject of myth—made him famous worldwide. Yet his archaeological practices drew the ire of many. Schliemann was roundly criticized by the academics of his era for his lack of professional training in the field of archaeology, and was accused of "peppering the tombs" with gold treasure after shutting down excavations and sending the workers away. Whatever the truth is about his practices, he was bigger than life, both in his professional and personal life, and his approach to finding a suitable wife was followed with the same single-mindedness he devoted to his work.

Writing to a Greek friend, he posted an ad in an Athenian newspaper, stipulating his made-to-order bride should include the following characteristics: the angelic temperament of his mother and sister, young enough to have children, enthusiastic of Greek art and willing to travel with him. Schliemann commented that Greece offered up girls "as beautiful as the pyramids" and "as poor as rats." After being shown photographs of two potential brides, he pronounced one of them, Polyxena Giusti, "bossy, authoritarian, despotic, irritable and vengeful. I think she has developed these faults due to her métier of school teacher." On the other hand, he found the image of Sophia Engastromenos most pleasing, stating she "is a splendid woman, open, indulgent, gentle and good house-wife, full of life and well educated."

Heinrich decided Sophia was a suitable match, and they were married on September 23, 1869. The union produced two children with the larger-than-life names of Andromache and

Agamemnon. Sophia dutifully followed him on his pursuit of ancient civilizations, yet her sometimes-delicate emotional state caused struggles in their marriage. Heinrich's persistent concerns that a young woman wouldn't be attracted to an older man for his looks made him eternally suspicious that he would not be truly loved. He wrote to her: "But I've thought that a woman endowed with a character that perfectly harmonises with mine and enlightened by the same enthusiasm and desire for knowledge could respect me...then I dare hoping that with time she would learn to love me..."

Because they were searching for one of the world's greatest treasures, Sophia eventually adapted to the harsh life of excavating on foreign soil, and the couple learned to work together side by side in the field, as Heinrich recalls from his letters:

As my darling Sophithion placed her hand in mine, we looked toward the mound rising from the flat land, and allowed our eyes to sweep the Trojan plain we knew so intimately. Is this spot friend or foe, adversary or challenge? With our hands joined like two ends of electricity, we knew with certainty that our excavations would be memorable. My beautiful Sophithion would never have come here were it not for me; I would never have progressed so far were it not for her assistance both physical and emotional. Together our love and faith has brought us to the brink. Never before has this love been so fully consummated as at the moment we paused, before attacking.

Schliemann was chided by scholars of his time as a "romantic financier with the destructive manner of a grave robber." The book *One Passion Two Loves* by Lynn and Gray Poole recalls that fateful day Schliemann found the Treasure of Priam at Troy:

Sophia and Heinrich, sweaty of body and dry of mouth, were digging together, but without a crew, on a level flagstone floor between two walls. One was the wall of the house that Heinrich thought was the Palace of Priam; the other, a high fortification wall, Heinrich, standing apart from Sophia, struck metal, a strike that triggered the most sensational archaeological news of the 19th century and sparked archaeological interest not matched until 1922, the year Lord Carnarvon and Howard Carter discovered the tomb of the Egyptian boy king Tutankhamen.

One of the most famous photographs from this period of archaeology was that of Sophia, whom Schliemann adorned in the elaborate golden fringed headdress, earrings, and enormous loops of necklaces from his excavations at Hissarlik (the site of ancient Troy), which became known as "Priam's Treasure." But Sophia was more than just a model for the golden treasures from their excavations; she dug alongside her husband in the field, at one point rescuing some workmen who had become trapped under a collapsed wall, as the Pooles describe:

> *Astonishment gave way to respect for the compassionate lady, who, after risking personal injury in the successful attempt to rescue the men, had nonchalantly returned to work. When news of the mishap reached Heinrich, he hurried to Sophia, finding her with clothes ripped, fingernails broken, and hands nicked by stone. In a letter bubbling with pride, he described the accident to Madame Victoria, assuring her that her daughter was a heroine at the excavation.*

Schliemann may not have been the best-trained or most skilled archaeologist, but he was certainly one of the luckiest. When they weren't in the field, Heinrich and Sophia enjoyed the pleasures of their elegant home in downtown Athens. The Schliemann mansion was at its time the most magnificent estate in Athens, with its massive three-story façade, replete with arched, colonnaded porticos, and larger-than-life statues of gods and heroes towering above the roofline. Ziller's signature renaissance revival style is evident on the exterior; for the interior, Schliemann favored décor inspired from his favorite sites and themes: Pompeii, the Trojan War, and other famed Greek epics.

Visitors will find themselves surrounded by fluted columns topped with delicate Ionic capitals, and walking along floors of marble and mosaics in both geometric Greek key patterns and natural seascape designs. Arched ceilings and walls are festooned with a riot of floral garlands, cherubic putti, and contrasting oval and rectangular geometric shapes.

The magnificence of the house extends to the manicured grounds outside, which Schliemann named the Garden of the Muses, for the mythological figures that stand beneath the fern-like trees. In the summer, concerts are held in the courtyard and you can enjoy a frosty frappe in the evening while listening to jazz, classical, or traditional Greek music. With the building's modern incarnation as a numismatic museum, you may be here to admire the cases of shimmering coins, such as magnificent gold staters of Alexander the Great, and hoards of silver spilling from tipped pots. Yet you might want to take a moment and imagine Heinrich, resplendent in his top hat, and Sophia in her ruffled collar and bustled dress, surrounded by all the elite of Athenian society, while in the background—tended to by a flotilla of servants—their children with the epic names race up and down the marbled hallways.

∗⁓

23 Rebetika

ROZA ESKENAZI: FROM THE CANARY TO QUENTIN TARANTINO

Haunting, mysterious, faintly baleful. The first time you hear Rebetika music, it will hit you somewhere in your gut, and it will likely stay with you. That's because, as with all music that finds its genesis in suffering and sorrow, it comes from a place that is astonishingly and undeniably authentic.

Originating from within the socioeconomically oppressed classes, Rebetika may be Greek in its adolescent and adult stages, but it was Turkish in its infancy. As Dean Kalimniou, in his weekly column on the blog Diatribe, states, "For the homeland of Rebetika is also the traditional land of the Great Mother Goddess, Cybele, the Love Goddess, Anahit and the nurturing but ultimately dark and chthonic Hecate. It is in the early hymns of their praise, sung by their female devotees that we could probably try at least, to tentatively trace the origins of Rebetika." Kalimniou goes on to say, "Sometimes called the 'Greek blues,' Rebetika is as much the music of defiance, as it is of survival."

Most who listen to this deeply sonorous, sad, and even bitter music associate the genre with its most famous male primogenitors, Markos Vamvarakis and Loukas Daralas, to name two. Vamvarakis and many others were displaced from their homeland in Asia

Minor, ending up in the shanties of Athens's main port, Piraeus. There they spent their days smoking hashish and teaching themselves the music that would resonate with the pain of oppression, war, and dislocation from one's homeland. All cultures have their own expression of this form of music: in Portugal it is the Fado, in Spain, the Flamenco, in Argentina, the tango, and in the United States, the blues. All can be roughly grouped in the same category. Music that comes directly from the soul, telling it like it is, even if it's about excruciatingly painful times.

In 1921 and 1922, a mass extermination of Greeks occurred in the city of Smyrna, now known as Izmir, Turkey. This colony was formerly the home of many of Greece's intelligentsia and artists, and those who were able to escape fled mostly to Athens, where they had to adjust to life in a different country. My former Greek teacher, Mary Critzas, one of those who escaped the massacre of Smyrna, was subjected to teasing by schoolmates. Being told she wasn't really Greek and called a "little Turk" because of where she was born, she reported to me that she always responded curtly and self-assuredly by telling her bullies, "If a cat gives birth in an oven, does that means its kittens are biscuits?"

If you go into any Rebetika club in Athens, often the singer will be male, but many women have led long and successful careers singing the blues. The most famous of all was Roza Eskenazi. A Sephardic Jew born in Constantinople (now Istanbul) in the late 1800s, Roza's given name was Sarah Skinazi. Her working-class family moved to Thessaloniki, still under Ottoman control, where a youthful Sarah became enamored of the world of singing after seeing performances at a local theater. Determined to become a singer and dancer in spite of her family's objections to the life of an *artiste*, Sarah moved away to the port town of Piraeus, ground zero for the Rebetika movement at the time, and changed her named to Roza Eskenazi. Initially she began dancing and eventually singing

with an Armenian troupe, and by the 1920s her talents were recognized by a famous Greek composer who noted the rapt audiences
who attended Eskenazi's performances. He offered her a recording contract and a star was born. Eskenazi sang not only in Greek
and Turkish, but Yiddish, Arabic, Italian and Armenian and she
became known as "The Canary" for one of her most famous songs,
which became the title of a documentary made on her life in 2011.

My sweet canary
you took my mind,
the morning you wake me up
when you chirp sweetly.

Ah you jealous bird
you will drive me crazy,
with your sweet speech
you will make me your slave.

Come to me, in my arms
ah one night in my bedroom.
Come to me, in my arms
to glut you with my kisses.

During the German occupation of World War II, Eskenazi
operated a restaurant in Athens. In spite of being Jewish, she managed to avoid detection by having an affair with a German officer.
According to Laura Barton, who wrote an article on the singer for
The Guardian, Eskenazi "hid resistance fighters and British agents in
her home and saved the lives of many Jews—including her own family—until she was finally exposed in 1943. She spent three months
in prison before being released, thanks to campaigning by her
German lover and her son."

Eskenazi, whose voice has the soulful breadth and passionate depth as such famous cabaret singers as Edith Piaf, also recorded a song that has been recycled in a surprising way. If you've ever seen Quentin Tarantino's 2004 cult classic, *Pulp Fiction*, then you watched Uma Thurman undulate and vamp with John Travolta to the hypnotic, thrumming beat and faintly Middle Eastern flavor of the updated version of Eskenazi's famous recording *Misirlou*.

In all, Roza recorded over five hundred songs and had a career that spanned decades. She gave birth to one son who gave her three grandchildren, but her long and prolific life ended much the way it began. She died in relative obscurity and was buried in an unmarked grave near Corinth. In 2008, local residents raised money to inscribe her grave with a simple dedication, "Roza Eskenazi, Artist."

If you'd like to sample this fundamental art form of modern Greek culture, there are several clubs in Athens. Possibly the most famous is Stoa Athanaton, located in the Central Market at 19 Sofokleous. Another favorite listed on Matt Barrett's Greek Travel pages is a small café called Kapnikarea near the eponymous church at 57 Ermou.

და

24 *Mani-Sonnenlink*

A MEDITATION AND ARTS ECO-RETREAT
WITH A VIEW OF THE SEA

When you first meet Burgi Blauel, you'll feel as though you were hit by an eighteen-wheeler. Artist, business entrepreneur, and political activist, Burgi is a fireball of energy, and, along with her husband Fritz, she runs one of the most unusual resorts in Greece.

When my sister, Deb, and I were driving around the Peloponnese one November, we decided to hit the middle finger of land known as the Mani on this hand-like peninsula which points down into the Aegean. Deb was making a film of the olive harvest in Greece and wanted to know where some of the more organic operations were. Thanks to friend and Greek food blogger and writer, Alexis Adams, we were directed to this unique bio-hotel and self-described "multifunctional vital energy Feng Shui resort."

Back in the 1970s, Burgi's husband, Fritz Blauel, moved to Greece in search of paradise. He spent the first decade in his newly adopted country pursuing a hippie lifestyle, meditating in caves and following his passion for Zen Buddhism. Then a friend mentioned how much they enjoyed the local olive oil. With access to an abundance of the best olive groves in the country—if not in the whole of Europe—Fritz realized he was sitting on a veritable gold mine. After becoming aware that a lot of local olive oil left the country bound for Italy, Fritz did something unusual; he sat down and began bottling the Greek liquid gold by hand.

In the early 1980s, Austrian-born Burgi arrived on the scene, and their small manufacturing business flourished. Combining their love of the olive with a keen sense of environmental stewardship, the Blauels started out modestly with a small operation, bringing to Greece an entirely new concept for the time: organized organic farming. Instead of growing their own orchards, they built a small press and began to process the fruit of the land. Local farmers came to know and trust the Blauels and the operation grew over the following decades to what it is today: a leading industry of olive oil processing and exporting.

But the gleaming 1,000-square meter olive processing plant is not the only draw the Blauels had in mind. With their love of meditation, music, and the environment, they set up a small resort on the hillside overlooking the cobalt Messenian Gulf. Over the years they have added more apartments, and recently received a permit to build a series of tent-like yurts that offer a more rustic way of experiencing this magical region of Greece.

"I wanted to create a venue for relaxation, rejuvenation, therapy and meditation," Burgi says. "What came out is a bio hotel with seminars, a music festival, and lots and lots of love."

Now Greece's first certified organic resort, Sonnenlink uses only 100 percent organic detergent and materials, as well as offering organic meals from the resort's own gardens. Guests can hike along old donkey trails in the lavender-infused hills, or swim at Zorba's Beach in Stoupa, a small town located at the bottom of the hill, where Nikos Kazantzakis lived and was inspired to write *Zorba the Greek*. After a yoga session overlooking the sea you can unwind on natural coco-mat beds, a line of natural sleep products such as mattresses, duvets and pillows lovingly handcrafted in Greece.

✳ www.mani-sonnenlink.com/mani-sonnenlink/Intro.html

In addition, the Blauels have constructed a small amphitheater where they host a series of performers and musicians during a summer-long season of artistic events. Running from July through September, the series treats visitors to outdoor concerts featuring classical music, Greek favorites, and Gypsy Jazz. Meditation retreats are offered regularly and visitors can enjoy doing their downward dog position or chilling in front of a serene Zen rock garden in a room specially built with a glass wall front and wooden floors that takes advantage of the gorgeous view to the sea below. A small hearth keeps the room warm in off-season months.

Guests can also enjoy the main parlor that houses a concert-sized piano, complete with a kitchen for group dining and entertaining. In addition, each suite is equipped with a full kitchen so guests can cook using the Blauel's special olive products, or take a soak in the oversized bathtubs in the beautifully appointed bathrooms. Each apartment has views of the garden and sea below, and is stocked with candles, olive oil soaps and soothing spiritual CDs and players for your listening pleasure. With the series of interconnected rooms surrounding the soothing public spaces, one guest commented, "It's like living in a beautiful mansion!" During our visit, we attended a special meditation session with a recording by the spiritual writer Eckhart Tolle. With a fire crackling in the kiva-like fireplace, we sat on our Zen cushions and basked in the warmth of the November sun while taking in the view of the Aegean glimmering far below.

❈ www.blauel.gr/en/welcome.html

On our final evening, the Blauels invited over some friends for an impromptu gathering. We put together some appetizers using the Blauel's line of olive products, and with Deb accompanying on the piano, Burgi played a concerto on her violin while we sang to the guests. With moonlight streaming into the enchanted living space and the silver Aegean gleaming just beyond, it was a magical evening I won't soon forget. So if you are traveling in the southern Peloponnese, track down Mani-Sonnenlink, secreted in the hills above Stoupa, and I can promise you won't be disappointed. With access to both the arts and the serenity of nature that this unique bio-hotel provides, I've no doubt you will find some of that magic for yourself.

※

25 *Spetses*

THE LEGEND OF LASKARINA BOUBOULINA

I can't think of the island of Spetses without thinking of my favorite novel of all time: *The Magus*, by John Fowles. Spetses is the setting for the fictional Greek island of Phraxos, where an itinerant Englishman decides to take a job teaching English at a boy's school in the 1950s. While living on the island he crosses paths with a mysterious local, who leads him on a terrifying journey that changes his life. The book was made into a disappointing movie, the only redeeming quality being Candace Bergen in the twin roles of June and Julie, whose goddess-like stature is captured on film as she stands at the prow of a boat, gliding across the silken waters of the Argolic Gulf.

One of my favorite videos is of Fowles returning to his fictional Phraxos after some forty years. There he recalls the island of his youth and visits the boys school where he taught, as well as the remote beach house of the infamous islander and reality-shifter Conchis, who inspired his psychological tale of love and betrayal. Fowles's character, Nicholas Urfe, describes the first time he sets eyes on the island, which remains furred in emerald pine and as fragrant in sage as it was during Fowles's residency:

> *Phraxos was beautiful. There was no other adjective; it was not just pretty, picturesque, charming—it was simply and effortlessly beautiful. It took my*

breath away when I first saw it, floating under Venus like a majestic black whale in an amethyst evening sea, and it still takes my breath away when I shut my eyes now and remember it. Its beauty was rare even in the Aegean, because its hills were covered with pine trees, Mediterranean pines as light as greenfinch feathers. Nine-tenths of the island was uninhabited and uncultivated; nothing but pines, coves, silence, sea. Herded into one corner, the north-west, lay a spectacular agglomeration of snow-white houses round a couple of small harbours.

"The whole island abounds with magic," says a friend who has lived on Spetses for many years. "On the west side near the beach of Agia Anagiri there is a cave that you can swim into...it is said to have been used by Bouboulina to hide women and children from the Turks." Who is Bouboulina, you might ask? Aside from being famous for the inspiration for *The Magus*, Spetses is the home of perhaps one of the most famous women in Greece. We've all heard of famous dames like Athena and Aphrodite, Irini Papas and Melina Mercouri...but Spetses has Laskarina Bouboulina.

Laskarina Eleni Boubouli is one of Greece's most revolutionary and revered women, known for her lifelong battle against the Ottoman Empire. Bouboulina, as she became known, was born in a prison cell in Istanbul, where her mother had gone to visit her father, who had been arrested by the Turks. After her father's death, mother and child returned to Greece and moved to Spetses.

As a child, Bouloulina loved to play by the sea, listening to stories of sailors who fought for the freedom of Greece, which had been under Ottoman occupation for one hundred years. By 1811, Bouboulina was the mother of seven children and had been twice widowed. Married at seventeen to a ship's captain, she remarried at thirty when her husband died. When her second husband died at forty—both killed in naval battles against pirates—she inherited her husbands' fortunes. Managing her wealth well, she grew it with

various commercial activities and used it to build four ships. Yet in 1816, her property was confiscated by the Ottomans, who declared her husband's ships had been used in the Russian-Turkish conflict on the side of the Russians. Her activist passions ignited, she joined a resistance movement as the only woman and fought alongside revolutionaries.

✳ www.visitgreece.gr/en/greek_islands/spetses

In an attempt to recoup her fortune, Bouboulina sailed to Constantinople to meet with the Russian ambassador and seek his protection, citing her husband's brave actions on the Russian side during the Russian-Turkish war. She was sent to Crimea to live in a Tsar's estate where she met the Sultan's mother, who was impressed by Bouboulina's character. The Sultana asked her son, the Sultan Mahmud II, to issue a decree to release her fortune and Bouboulina was free to return to her beloved Spetses.

Once back home, Bouboulina became an illegal arms dealer, hiding munitions in her own home, and fortifying her nation against imminent attack. She joined an underground organization known as the *Filiki Etaireia* (the friendly society), where she helped organize the revolution against the Turks. Using her fortune, she supplied the locals with food, weapons and ammunition as they readied for battle.

Shortly before the official revolution began on March 13, 1821, Bouboulina set off her country's revolt by raising the pennant on her flagship Agamemnon in Spetses's harbor. Days later, other islands followed. Commanding a fleet of eight ships, Bouboulina sailed to Nafplion and participated in fiery battles there as well as

Momenvasia and Pylos. The captains of the other vessels included her sons and half brothers.

Her bravery in warfare made her famous, and other generals considered her an equal. After the war she lived in the newly independent country's capital of Nafplion. Unfortunately, opposing post-war factions soon developed and began to fight one another. Bouboulina was arrested twice and ultimately expelled back to Spetses. A tempestuous woman in every sense of the word, Bouboulina's exploits were not limited to the battlefield—she was purportedly known to seduce men at gunpoint!

Sadly, Bouboulina's life came to an end in as turbulent a way as it began. Her fortune depleted and surrounded by local politicians' infighting, Bouboulina was caught in a family scandal. When her son eloped with the daughter of a neighboring family, Bouboulina was involved in a dispute in which she was shot and killed. She died on May 22, 1895, penniless and alone, but since has been celebrated as one of Greece's most beloved naval heroes.

❧

26 *Mykonos*

SHIRLEY VALENTINE AND MANTO MAVROGENOUS

The droopy hound dog eyes, that sexy Greek accent—Tom Conti's character, Costas, is unforgettable in the film *Shirley Valentine*. But it was Pauline Collins in the movie's title role who captured my heart. Leaving her husband behind in rain-splattered London, she heads out with a friend who has won a holiday for two in sunny Greece. As a middle-aged housewife, she is accused by her incredulous daughter of being on a "granny grabber fortnight," and while Shirley does have a fling with Costas, she ultimately falls in love with someone even more enchanting, a person she comes to know intimately while living on the island of Mykonos: herself.

One of my favorite scenes in the film is after Shirley ditches her friend in the Mykonos airport and leaves her luggage behind at the airline check-in counter. She returns to Costas's place only to find him romancing another woman. Undeterred, Shirley asks him for a job and settles in to her new life. Her first morning on the island alone, she awakens, a stunning view of the Mykonos coastline seen through her window. Over the weeks, as she wanders through the bustling marketplace and along the harbor front, Shirley discovers her own independent spirit and learns how beautiful life can really be. Not surprising, for Mykonos is a good place to do this.

With its whirling iconic windmills and chalk-white houses stacked along the implausibly turquoise shores, Mykonos is one of those islands you probably have heard about. Devotedly popular with tourists, the main town of Chora with its picturesque, half moon-shaped harbor, is emblazoned on many a postcard, as is the ersatz mayor of Mykonos, Pete the pelican, who has a paparazzi-like following among vacationers eager to take his photo.

✳ www.mykonos.gr

Mykonos is well known for its string of pristine beaches, some of them dedicated to the topless and nudist crowds, and the island was one of the early meccas for gay tourism. Paradise and Super Paradise beaches are the most famous for *au naturel* sun worshippers, while Paranga and St. John's have become more popular in recent years, and Ella has become a mainstay for gay vacationers.

If topless beaches aren't your thing, Mykonos has its share of more secluded shores, such as Frangias with its remote natural scenery and Kapari, which overlooks the island of Delos—but there are many other things to love about the island. You can spend the whole day wandering through Chora town with its idyllic whitewashed Cycladic architecture, or take a detour over to Little Venice, a collection of old fishing dwellings perched precariously over the azure Aegean coastline. Some buildings date back to the 18th century, and over the past decades the area has become an artists' quarter. Visitors can explore a variety of galleries and exhibitions and enjoy a drink at one of many snug abodes that has been converted into a chic bar. Order up an ouzo at Semeli or a fresh fruit cocktail at Scarpa, sink back into the plush pillowed banquette and watch the sun slip like a ripe mandarin behind the olive-colored sea.

Archaeological evidence indicates that these breathtaking shores have been inhabited for millennia. Excavations at the site of Ftelia show that the island was inhabited in the Final Neolithic period, around 3000 B.C. Later, the Phoenicians came to settle, followed by the Egyptians, Minoans, and Ionians. The island's proximity

to Delos made Mykonos an important supply station and its fortunes were tied for many centuries in antiquity to this sacred and
archaeologically rich island. During the Hellenistic period, under
the leader Alexander the Great, Mykonos came into its own as a
commercial center for maritime and agricultural trade, and the
island gained enormous wealth during the Roman period during
the reign of Augustus Caesar. Under Venetian and later, Ottoman
rule, slave trade was common and thousands of islanders were
abducted. This sparked a revolutionary movement in 1821-1828
during which islanders, known as great sailors, helped in the Greek
war of independence against Turkish rule.

As is often found in Greece, the Dionysian and Apollonian elements can exist side by side. After a sybaritic day of sunning topless
at Paradise Beach, take a drive up the mountain to the church of
Panagia Tourlian that contains a mysterious and powerful icon.
Every August 15, the Orthodox Holiday dedicated to the Virgin,
pilgrims flock here in search of healing, as they believe the relic
possesses curative powers. Even though the monastery attached
to the church is dedicated to the BVM, it's still a male-only club;
however, one woman figures largely in Mykonos' history. The most
famous—Manto Mavrogenous—professes a real riches to rags story
filled with war, love, and all that is in between.

Born in Trieste in 1796, Manto Mavrogenous was the daughter
of a wealthy merchant and member of a secret society, *Filiki Eteria*,
formed to overthrow the Ottoman rule that dominated most of
what is now called Greece. One of her ancestors was a *dragoman,* or
interpreter for the Ottoman fleet. Raised by an educated family
during the Age of Enlightenment, Manto studied history and phi-
losophy in Trieste and spoke several languages fluently, including
Turkish, Italian, and French.

After her father' death, she took up his struggle. Moving to
Mykonos, she chased off pirates by purchasing and stocking two ships

which she herself commanded, then proceeded to organize a series of revolts against the Ottomans. After inheriting her family's fortune, she gave it away to support the War of Independence and encouraged her friends to donate weapons and money to the Hellenic cause.

In spite of a hot temper, she was a gifted leader who led many military expeditions into battle. Over time, she put together many different campaigns to other parts of Greece, including a fleet of ships and infantry and participated in the battle of Karystos in 1822. She even sold her jewelry to support the different campaigns around the country. In her zeal, she embarked on expeditions in Europe to drum up support for her cause, even speaking to groups of women in as far-flung places as Paris, before returning to Greece. Apparently her own mother was not a fan of Manto's activities, and supposedly hated her for leaving her family behind and choosing her cause instead.

Manto did take time out for other things. During the war she had a love affair with a man named Dimitrios Ypsilantis, but Ypsilantis later dumped her and left her alone. When her house burned and she was left with nothing, she was forced to rely on a priest for food. She died in 1840, penniless and alone. Today her name has been emblazoned on commemorative coins, several streets around the country are named after her, and a statue of Manto has been erected and prominently displayed in the main square of Mykonos's Chora town in her honor.

As you sit by the harbor and watch the sunset, order an ouzo and watch the light turn the water shades of orange, pink, and mauve while the island's iconic windmills spin lazily in the background. And be sure to raise your glass in a toast to Manto, for one thing is for sure: her love of Mykonos is legendary. If she were able to see the beauty of Mykonos today, there's little doubt she would still feel it is a place worth fighting for.

❧

27
Skopelos

MAMMA MIA, IRON CHEF CAT CORA,
AND A MATRILINEAL SOCIETY

Do you recall that movie where Meryl Streep belts out Abba tunes with her girl group? The glittering sea beneath her B&B where a chain of men danced in scuba fins along the rocky shores, and the tiny church on top of that impossibly high cliff where her daughter's wedding is supposed to take place?

It's not surprising that the popular chick flick *Mamma Mia* was filmed on lovely, ethereal Skopelos. The island, as are many in this chain, is matrilineal, a custom in which the parents of the bride provide the couple with a house and property that must stay in the woman's name. The land is passed down from generation to generation through the female chain, unlike most of the rest of Greece where property is passed down via the male line.

Meryl Streep is not the only famous woman to have graced the island's shores—famed Iron Chef Cat Cora has links to Skopelos as well, where she is known as Katerina Karagiozi. Cat was raised in Mississippi, but according to her website, "meals at the Cora house often combined spices from the South with fresh cheeses and home-cured olives sent by relatives from the island of Skopelos."

So what is so special about this lush island forested in fir pines and graced with turquoise shores? There's something greener about the greens, bluer about the blues, and whiter about the whites. Everything on Skopelos stands out in high relief, with the stark vibrancy of an Ansel Adams print or the explosive color palette of one of Gauguin's Tahiti landscapes. Some say that this island, studded with Aleppo pines, is the greenest in Greece.

✳ www.visitgreece.gr/en/greek_islands/sporades/skopelos

Called Peparethos in antiquity, the island was a Minoan colony, that great civilization that worshipped the goddess. Apparently the island has a half divine founder in Prince Stafilos, son of the god Dionysus and Ariadne, daughter of King Minos and the girl with the golden thread who led Theseus out of the Minotaur's labyrinth.

Skopelos is part of the Sporades, a chain of islands off the northeast coast of the Greek mainland and one of the largest areas of marine conservation in Greece. Along with Alonissos and Skiathos, where part of *Mamma Mia* was filmed as well, a multitude of tiny islets dot this area of Greece known as the "The Gates of the Wind." Kayakers will find themselves in heaven if they wish to explore these emerald specks in the surrounding cerulean seas.

The remains of an *askeplieon,* or ancient sanatorium, are located near the port of Chora, and the Romans built baths near Loutraki, so it appears that ancient Skopelos was considered to be a site of healing in antiquity. The ancient Greeks are known for their penchant to worship gods of contrasting sensibilities, so there is a cave dedicated to Pan, god of the wild, for good measure.

If castles are your thing, the Venetians left one just for your viewing pleasure. Locals say that if you decide to climb to the top, you can be treated to the melodies of Giorgios Xintaris. A renowned Rembetika musician, he plays the music of the Greek underground that was first composed at the turn of the 20th century and experienced resurgence during the junta period of Greece in the late 1960s and 1970s, when the military ran the country.

Foods not to miss are the island's Pelion olives (larger and more round than the traditional Kalamata variety), honey scented with pine from the island's forests, *damaskino avgato* (a plum-flavored spoon sweet), and a special cheese pie made of twisted phyllo dough and deep-fried.

No visit to Skopelos would be complete without a swing by that amazing church in *Mamma Mia*, perched on the edge of a cliff. Remember when Meryl sings to Pierce Brosnan (thank goodness he only listened!) while waving her red scarf against the stunning backdrop of the church? Agios Ioannis Kastri sits atop a precipitous rock face high above the sea, and can be accessed via a narrow winding path cut directly into the rock. If you feel like climbing all 110 steps you can peek into the tiny church. The only rub is that you must be Greek Orthodox to enter!

Skopelos's matrilineal culture celebrates the female as well in a festival known as Valch's Wedding. For ladies only, this annual celebration is when women outfit themselves in their finest bridal gear and take to the streets, dancing and parading through the main town of Skopelos. This brightly costumed event celebrates the island's matrilineal customs, and onlookers and participants alike partake of wine and desserts as the procession makes its way through the streets to the strains of local bands. If you want a real wedding on Skopelos, look no further than Daphne Weddings. This Dutch born entrepreneur, married to a local Greek, can create the wedding of a lifetime. Bride and groom can exchange vows against the shimmering Aegean and follow it up by parading through the village's picturesque streets with strolling musicians playing guitar and violin.

✳ www.daphneweddings.com

The island's name means "rocky," so if you want to get to Skopelos, you have to take the ferry, as there is no airport. Yet it's well worth your effort, as there's a little something for everyone on this distinctive, out-of-the-way island. If you want to see first hand the lush location where Meryl and friends danced and sang in *Mamma Mia*, or you just love the color green, add Skopelos to your list of must-see islands in Greece.

28 *Santorini*

ISLAND OF *SUMMER LOVERS, SISTERHOOD OF THE TRAVELING PANTS,* AND SAINT IRENE

Maybe you've seen the movie *Summer Lovers*? The late film critic Gene Siskel referred to it as a guilty pleasure: a white-blond, tanned, and youthful Daryl Hannah and her boyfriend engage in a three-way affair with a chic French archaeologist while frolicking on this blindingly white and blue island. In one memorable scene they stage an olive oil fight on the terrace of their cliffside dwelling.

Then there is the hit chick-flick *Sisterhood of the Traveling Pants.* Four teenage girlfriends spend the summer apart but mail back and forth a pair of magical blue jeans that brings each of them luck. One of them, a Greek American named Lena, played by Alexis Bledel, returns to Greece to stay with her grandparents and falls for the son of her family's sworn enemy.

Not surprisingly, both movies are about love—the forbidden kind. And Santorini is a forbidding kind of island. Formed in a cataclysmic volcanic eruption, today's Santorini is what's left of the ancient crater. Sailing into its harbor is one the world's most unforgettable experiences, and sitting on the edge of the crater and looking down is one of the world's most extraordinary views.

"Unbelievable. Amazing. Never seen anything like it." Or just plain, "Wow." Whether you arrive via ferry, cruise ship, or puddle jumper from Athens, the reaction is always the same. Santorini is one of those places where the superlatives are absolutely warranted. The views, from the water up, or from the edge looking over the caldera, are of the once in a lifetime category. Even arriving at night, as my husband and I did a few years back, the island stuns. Landing at the airport in the middle of a thunderstorm, we could see the outline of the island and the small cliff dwelling town of Oia in the distance, lit up by the lightning with jagged sections of cliffs, billowing cumulus, and a metallic sea flashing on and off like a paparazzo's light bulbs.

Santorini (also known as Thera) is named for Saint Irene, from the contraction of Santa Irini. Born in the northern Greek city of Thessalonika, her sisters, Agape and Chionia, were persecuted and brought before the Governor of Macedonia for the crime of not eating meat offered in sacrifice to the gods. Agape and Chionia were burned at the stake for their offense, but Irene was targeted for the crime of keeping Christian books in her possession. Some accounts say she was ultimately burned alive like her sisters, but others say she escaped to Thera, where she died in exile in 304 A.D.

Irene means peace in Greek, and the island certainly appears that way. As you approach, seeing the sheer, diorite-colored rock rise from the sea like a massive chocolate sundae, with white cubist dwellings clinging to the top like copious amounts of whipped cream, it is deceptively serene. But boiling deep underneath is a dormant volcano, reminding visitors that where they are standing used to be an entire crater, half of which collapsed into the sea some 3,500 years ago, leaving the crescent moon shaped island we are so familiar with today.

The eruption of ca. 1450 B.C. is believed by some to be the pillar of fire mentioned in the Bible, and responsible for a tidal wave that destroyed the Minoan civilization of Crete. Salt deposits have been found far inland in the Nile Delta of Egypt, lending credence to the tsunami's power and reach.

Each time I have visited the island, I have felt the spirit of the Hawaiian goddess of the volcano, Pele, to be very much present. Visitors can take a small boat to Nea Kameni (literally new burnt), one of the black islets in the caldera that once formed the missing half rim of the island's crater. Plumes of smoke emanate from fissures in the sharp, rocky earth and views aplenty exist for the ideal selfie with the island in the background. On the way back to the boat, make sure you've packed your bikini as you can take a dip and feel the hot, sulfurous waters bubbling up from the depths.

Lovers of archaeology should not miss Akrotiri. This fantastic site, dating to the second millennium B.C., was perfectly preserved by the pumice and volcanic ash that rained down from the ancient eruption. Like at Pompeii, here you can easily imagine the layout of the city from the staircases and walls of houses. Yet unlike Pompeii, no bodies were found; initial earthquakes gave the inhabitants time to flee with their jewelry, animals, and personal effects, leaving behind large storage jars and gorgeous frescoes that illustrate the daily life of the ancient inhabitants. The frescoes today are displayed in the National Museum in Athens; be sure to make a stop to see these lyrical and stunning images of beautifully attired Minoan women in elaborate costume and hoop earrings, their black hair snaking down their backs, as well as a famous painting of two girls playfully engaged in a boxing match.

The dense, rocky soil might seem inhospitable for agriculture, but some of Greece's finest wines are grown on the island. My favorite white, Boutari, hails from Santorini, and wine tours are offered every day except Sunday. This sparse but fertile soil also produces succulent, tiny tomatoes and plump capers that grace the island's salads. While you can dine at tavernas literally hanging over the edge of the caldera and enjoy treats such as *chloro*, an island cheese made from goats' milk, and tiny homemade sausages, my favorite dining spot is at the bottom of the steps in Oia. Ammoudi Bay is where some of the love scenes in *Sisterhood of the Traveling Pants* were filmed, and two rival tavernas both offer up fresh seafood and views of colorful bobbing fishing boats. As the waves slap at your feet, gobble up platters of *atherina* (tiny matchstick-sized fried fish), *skordalia* (a garlicky seafood dip made with mashed potatoes), and wash it down with local Boutari wine, white and cold.

Whether you stay in the main town of Fira or the smaller village of Oia in the north, shopping opportunities abound. Those wishing to walk the hundreds of steps from the port are welcome to, but the cliché donkey ride is a fun way to avoid the grind—or better yet, take the ski lift-style gondola that zips visitors up and down the cliffs to Fira town. Wend your way around the endless, narrow lanes and steep steps where lacy bell towers, dovecotes, and robin's egg-blue church domes appear between the chalk-white houses.

Fira is the more happening place in the summer, with nightclubs and bars, while Oia is a little more sedate, with more traditional shops and *skafta*—barrel-vaulted dwellings that are built directly into the cliff (I have had many a fantastic dream in these *skafta*, as the curved ceiling over your head is thought to bring on purple reveries). Oia is also the place to watch the sunset. Join the others gathered along the cliff walls where you can watch the sun plunge, like a blazing tangerine, into the Metaxa-colored sea, and applaud with the group before heading to a nearby bar for an ouzo aperitif.

While the caldera side isn't for beachgoers, the outer ring of the island is rimmed with black sandy shores, thanks to the dark volcanic soil. One of my favorite ways to get around is via moped, but with a major caveat—many a rider has succumbed to a sharp curve, skidded, and broken an arm or leg, so beware.

While there is so much to do on this fantasy island, you may choose, as I have, to do nothing. Just sitting on your balcony and watching the cruise ships glide by a thousand feet below, listening to the swallows dip and slice through the honeyed air, and letting yourself be mesmerized by the aerial views of the glittering sea and faint, molten outlines of islands in the distance, is a vacation unto itself. But if you do venture out and happen to see a gaggle of young women sunning topless, or a teenaged girl secretly meeting her Greek lover at the bottom of the steps leading to Ammoudi Bay, pay a silent homage to Daryl and Alexis for enticing you to visit this unforgettable place—but keep in mind that the commanding allure of Santorini extends far beyond the decadent delights of olive oil parties and the mysterious magic of the Sisterhood's Traveling Pants.

᳓

29 *Kefalonia*

PENELOPE CRUZ AND THE ISLAND OF
CAPTAIN CORELLI'S MANDOLIN

After spending the last thirty years returning to the Ionian island of
Ithaka, famed from Homer's *Odyssey*, I have long regarded Ithaka's
larger sister island to the west, Kefalonia, as a necessary hiatus on
the way. Most ferries from the mainland stop here first before
chugging on to Ithaka, and I have spent many a year watching endless streams of trucks, buses, cars, and motorcycles disgorge from
the ferry at Kefalonia's main port of Same before reaching my
beloved final destination. Yet in recent years, I decided to delay
my arrival in Ithaka and get off the boat in Same; and I'm glad I
did, for I've had the chance to explore this immense and infinitely
fascinating island.

Many people might remember Louis de Bernieres' clas-
sic novel, *Captain Corelli's Mandolin*. The book is set on Kefalonia,
and the movie, starring the lovely Penelope Cruz along with
Nicolas Cage, was also filmed on the island. In the lead role of
local girl and freethinking physician's daughter, Pelagia, Cruz's
character, meets Corelli, an Italian army captain who is posted
to Kefalonia and assigned to live in her home after the Italian
invasion of Greece. Pelagia is determined to hate the invading
soldiers, but Corelli's humor, sense of honor and consummate

mandolin-playing skills win her over in this sweeping World War II epic. Pelagia and Corelli eventually fall in love against the stunning backdrop of the island's pine-encrusted mountain villages and glittering shores, and their powerful bond manages to survive a massive earthquake that levels almost the entire island. While the lead characters certainly headline this ambitious film, Kefalonia is the true star, and the movie does justice in portraying this stunning and sprawling island, the largest in the Ionian chain, located off the western coast of Greece.

I have touched on some of Kefalonia's attractions in other chapters, but in addition to the festival of the snakes (Chapter 42) and the magical Melissani Lake and Drogarati Cave (Chapter 15), there is much more to see. As an archaeologist and perhaps, more important, as a romantic, I believe that modern Ithaka is the self-same island Homer was referring to in *The Odyssey*. All the pertinent geological features mentioned in Homer's text have corresponding locales on Ithaka, such as Raven's Crag, the Cave of the Nymphs and the Fountain of Arethusa. However, archaeologists and philologists have disagreed on this point for centuries, and many believe that nearby islands, including Kefalonia, are in fact the true site of Homer's *Odyssey*. Most recently a British engineer named Robert Bittlestone put forth a theory that, due to shifting sea levels, the Paliki peninsula of Kefalonia was actually an island in antiquity, which he believes was the true Ithaka.

Whether it is the original Ithaka or not, Kefalonia did flourish during Odysseus's time and is the site of several Mycenaean settlements. In 1991, near the village of Poros, a beehive-shaped *tholos* tomb was discovered at Tzannata. The tomb is considered to be a royal burial, as golden jewelry, royal seals, and precious stones were found inside. It is the largest known *tholos* tomb in the Ionian Islands, and the glittering finds can be viewed at the Archaeological Museum in the main city of Argostoli.

A large, bustling city surrounded by lush countryside, Argostoli is a primary destination for those seeking a classic Greek beach vacation. With its own airport, flights arrive directly from Europe without having to route through Athens, and vacationers can be on the beach within a matter of hours at one of the area's many resort hotels. As depicted in *Captain Corelli's Mandolin*, much of the island, including Argostoli, was destroyed in a massive earthquake in 1953, and the city, with its narrow streets, palm-lined harbor and generous bay was rebuilt with donations from emigrants. Keep an eye out for the giant loggerhead turtles that swim in the bay as you stroll along the harbor's mosaic-pebbled promenade.

For horse lovers, take a side trip to Mount Ainos, a 5,000-foot peak where wild horses live in Mount Ainos National Park. Abandoned in the wild, the herds have existed for more than a century and run free throughout the rough terrain, pocked with deep ravines and valleys among the island's lush native fir trees, *Abies cephalonica*. The horses are said to be offspring of a breed inhabiting the Pindos mountains in northern Greece, and the many decades of isolation has resulted in a separate breed. Local lore states the horses are directly descended from the horses of Alexander the Great; be quick with your camera, because these shy creatures tend to disappear like unicorns into the dense woodlands when they sense the presence of humans.

My favorite village on the island is on the northeast coast, facing Ithaka. Fiskardo was spared in the 1953 earthquake; as a result the village's Italianate feel remains intact. Pastel, 18th-century Venetian houses grip the village's picturesque harbor, which is regularly filled with pleasure yachts and fishing boats; be sure to stop by in early morning to see the fishermen unload their daily catch. In the evening, Fiskardo takes on a completely different atmosphere. Twinkling lights reflect off the water and blend with the sounds wafting from the shorefront cafés and tavernas, making a stroll along the harbor the perfect summer evening Greek village experience. Make a point to visit the Roman cemetery, located by the sea. Dating from the 2nd century B.C. to the 4th century A.D., the site contains twenty-seven tombs, some of them engraved, which yielded a large number of finds, including pottery, jewelry, glass, and coins. Remarkably, the front of one tomb has a door that still pivots perfectly on two stone points after all these centuries, opening and closing today just as it did in antiquity.

Before leaving Fiskardo, be sure to taste some of the island's wines. With its vast tracts of vineyards, Kefalonia produces some terrific vintages, including the bright Robola, wrapped in its distinctive burlap sleeve. With its pale green color and citrus bouquet, Robola is known throughout the world as a fresh wine, best consumed within two years of harvest. As you sit astride the harbor, with the lights of Ithaka sparkling in the distance, make a toast to an island that, like Pelagia and Corelli's fated love affair, has survived invasions, wars, and earthquakes, only to emerge more resilient and beautiful than ever.

30 Corfu and Sissi's Palace

AN AUSTRIAN PRINCESS'S
MEDITERRANEAN RETREAT

This story has all the ingredients of a Greek tragedy—or a soap opera. A beautiful Austrian princess, enamored of all the finer things, is living a life of luxury in her native Bavaria when she loses her precious only son, the Crown Prince Rudolf. Her name is Elisabeth von Wiltesbach, Empress of Austria, but she became known by those who loved her as Sissi.

Taking a cruise through the Mediterranean to forget her problems the following year in 1890, she fell in love with the idyllic, Italianate island of Corfu that lies in the Ionian Sea between Greece and Italy. There she built a summer palace in memory of her son called the Achilleon after Achilles, the seemingly impervious hero whose weakness—his heel—was exploited by his enemies in Homer's epic poem, *The Iliad*.

It's not hard to see why Sissi fell in love with Corfu. Unlike the dry, rocky islands of the Cyclades, or the awe-inspiring sheer cliffs of Santorini, this is a green island—replete with fir-covered mountains and surrounded by parfaits of emerald and turquoise slices of coastline. With its more seasonable climate, Corfu has understandably been a favorite of Europeans and other expats over the centuries. The author Lawrence Durrell first came to Corfu in

1935 with his wife Nancy, and soon afterwards his famous literary family followed, including his brother, the naturalist Gerald, who narrates the family's exploits in the memorable *My Family and Other Animals*. Lawrence Durrell went on to write *Bitter Lemons* and most famously, *Prospero's Cell*, about his years living on the island with his wife and curious neighbors.

Built in 1892 by the Italian architect Raffaele Carito, Sissi's immense white, wedding cake-like palace is distinctly out of place with the rest of Greece's modern island architectural style, but it finds its roots in classicism. Soaring columns, impressive colonnades, and a grand sweeping entryway are all testament to the neoclassical style that celebrates the best of ancient Greek architecture. Staring at the massive structure and grounds, one can't help but imagine that the formidable building was in fact a tribute to her only son, a monument she could inhabit and where she could sense his presence within the palace's ornately decorated walls. Situated on a hillside, the palace offers commanding views of the verdant valleys and gleaming Ionian in the distance.

The imagery of Achilles is everywhere, including the entryway, with its coffered ceiling painted in the primary colors of red and blue that would have decorated an ancient temple. Guests are greeted by twin bronze statues of Achilles straddling the grand staircase that rises from the black-and-white terrazzo marble floors. The palace interior and grounds are filled with statues depicting dramatic scenes from the Trojan War created by German artist Ernest Herter, who was commissioned to sculpt figures inspired by Greek mythology.

A local Corfiot named Petros Vrailas Armenis must have been enamored of the beautiful Austrian princess. He originally gave Elizabeth the property as a gift, and in turn was presented with a piece of heirloom jewelry: an enormous diamond-encrusted brooch that he passed down to a lucky daughter-in-law.

Elizabeth's royal line boasted Byzantine emperors, and she set about learning fluent Greek so she could communicate in her adopted home. The palace is located in the little village of Gastouri, not far from the main village of Corfu town. The area was known for its culture, as the first philharmonic orchestra was established here in 1898.

Corfu's history, while culturally abundant, also tells of a more mysterious and foreboding side of the islands in this Ionian chain, as if a certain sadness or melancholy impregnates the very air, which Lawrence Durrell describes in *The Greek Islands*:

> ...there is something faintly sinister, faintly menacing. Little pockets of wind moving about on bare hillsides, the swish of the sea; then an enormous still- ness with an echo. In the midst of a siesta or in the middle of the night, one is suddenly completely awake and on the qui vive, one does not know why. A thrilling moment of anxiety intervenes; as if on the veldt one awoke in one's tent to hear a lion breathing at the entrance. A sudden loneliness assails one. And then, abruptly, the influence, the ghost, the cloud—whatever it is— passes; the wind revives, and the whole island echoes once more like a seashell to the deep reverberations of history. Yes, other islands off Dubrovnik are just as beautiful, but they seem to hold nothing.

Near Gastouri, nestled into the valley of Pachalatika, there is a spring that flows through a deep ravine filled with pine trees and a smattering of kumquat. Local lore says that Sissi used to visit the val- ley and drink from the spring and today it is known as Sissi's Spring.

Sissi returned to Corfu and her beloved Achilleion over many years, but her life came to a tragic and abrupt end. In 1898 she was visiting Geneva when she came into the crosshairs of an Italian anarchist named Luigi Lucheni. He despised her for her lavish lifestyle, and hoping to incite fear in the hearts of royals, Lucheni assassinated the princess. Sissi died as tragically as her son. After her death, the Achilleion was purchased by Kaiser Wilhelm II in 1907. Wilhelm used the property as a summer palace, as did Sissi, but over time the palace became more of a diplomatic center with many visitors.

During World War I, the palace was used as a military hospital, and in World War II, it became a military headquarters. In 1994 and 2003, it hosted summit meetings of European leaders, but Sissi's spirit might be pleased with the building's use in more recent years. Under the Hellenic Tourist Organization, her beloved Achilleion has now become a permanent museum, a testament to her vision of a peaceful, elegant, and cherished retreat from an uncertain world.

❧

31 Crete and the Palace of Knossos

MINOAN SNAKE GODDESSES, BULL LEAPERS, AND HAYLEY MILLS

When I think of Crete, I think of these women: Ariadne, the daughter of the Cretan King Minos, the Minoan Snake Goddesses, those little figurines of women holding up snakes in their hands, bull leapers—divine "catchers" resembling young girls who competed with boys in leaping over bulls in a toreador-like contest—and...Hayley Mills.

You got that: Hayley Mills. If you've never seen the vintage Disney flick *The Moon Spinners*, queue it up right now on Netflix. Filmed on the island of Crete, it follows the escapades of a young English girl chasing down a jewel thief with the help of a handsome fellow Brit. But more importantly, it showcases this beautiful island in the Mediterranean whose mountains, ravines and vast plains make it seem more like a country unto itself than another Greek island. I'll never forget the first time I watched Mills's character trying to escape a windmill. Hanging onto the sails for dear life, she rotates around and around, the whitewashed houses, verdant olive groves and mysterious landscape mesmerizing in the background.

But I digress. Crete is a place fit for movies—and palaces. When I first visited the Palace of Knossos, I was a student living in Greece. I made the mistake, as many tourists do, of assuming the beautiful displayed frescoes were all original, not realizing they are actually reconstructions—some of them inaccurate—by an over-zealous archaeologist named Sir Arthur Evans in the early 20th century. But what caught my attention more than Evans's passionate desire to rebuild the monument in the image he wished, was the fact that one of them depicted a ceremony dedicated to bull-leaping.

Scholars have studied this ceremony for years and disagree as to its meaning. Some believe the ancient inhabitants' activity of vaulting their bodies over charging bulls was religious in nature and not athletic, while others maintain it was an actual sport. A fresco, entitled *The Bull-Leapers,* depicts the sinewy figures of young men, and equally importantly, women, making a case for the relative equality of the sexes during this Bronze Age period of 3000 B.C. The original image, now in the Archaeological Museum just a few kilometers away in the main town of Heraklion, once decorated the east wall of the palace's upper story, and visitors can see these nimble and energetic young men and women getting ready to do their best toreador-worthy stunts.

You could spend an entire afternoon wandering through the structure. In spite of Evan's scandalous reconstructions, such as substituting a monkey's head for a boy's in the *Saffron Gatherers* fresco, these brightly colored images do give a sense of what life must have been like for palace inhabitants. Indoor plumbing, brightly painted walls with designs from nature, and even a throne room make the most fatigued traveler feel royal.

Some of the most intriguing artifacts from this ancient civilization are the snake goddess figurines. Known as the goddess of the household, these statuettes, often made of faience or glazed earthenware, depict a woman holding a snake in each upraised arm and an owl perched on her head. According to Dr. Alena Trckova-Flamee, "She is called also Household Goddess due to her attribute of the snake, which is connected with welfare of the Minoan house.

But the snake is also symbol of the underworld deity, so the Snake Goddess is related to chthonic aspects too. It is possible, that the worshipping of the Minoan Snake Goddess was in some context to the rebirth, resurrection or renewal of the life."

The Minoan culture is known for its sophisticated ethos, love of nature, and peaceful rule. According to Christopher L.C.E. Witcomb, "Conspicuous in their absence are the usual signs of a male-dominated society common to the Eastern Mediterranean in the second millennium bce: no walled citadels, no fortifications, no temples to the gods, no large public sculpture, no clear evidence of a hierarchically structured society ruled by kings and priests, no boastful inscriptions."

The palace's peaceful setting, free of ramparts and buttresses, offers a vast panorama of the surrounding plain. Just close enough to the sea, the palace was destroyed by a tsunami caused by the massive 1600 B.C. eruption of Santorini, just eighty-eight miles to the north. Minoan civilization continued after the disaster in one form or another, but never reached the same height of glory.

Wandering around these ruins, the story of Ariadne and her ill-fated affair with the man-god Theseus fires up the imagination.
The subject has inspired countless painters, sculptors, and composers, including Richard Strauss, whose epic, *Ariadne auf Naxos*, has rocked opera houses for centuries. In an attempt to help her beloved, Theseus, escape the labyrinth of the fabled half-man half-
beast, the Minotaur, Ariadne left him a string of thread. Following the golden strand, he made his way out and promptly professed his love to Ariadne. Together they sailed towards Athens, but were waylaid on the island of Naxos. In a tragic twist, Theseus left her

there to return to Athens and Ariadne ended up in the arms of the wine god Dionysus.

Wandering through the rooms of the Palace of Knossos, one is reminded of a series of remarkable women whose echoes can still be heard today: Ariadne in the labyrinth helping her lover escape, the lithe and athletic girls leaping over bulls and competing as equals with boys. Bare-breasted snake goddesses, their upraised arms holding a snake in each grasped hand remind us of their connection with the earth, and with a matriarchal religion that once suffused this part of the world.

And then there's Hayley, blond hair blowing in her face, racing across the windswept plains and spending a night in a haunted ruins. Thank you, Hayley, for introducing me to the wonders of Crete. And to Ariadne and the snake-wielding ladies, as well, for luring me to the wonders of Knossos. The palace may be named after a king, but it is the spirit of women that lives on within these walls.

32 The Caves of Matala

JONI MITCHELL AND THE CAVE-DWELLING FLOWER CHILDREN

Maybe I'll go to Amsterdam
Maybe I'll go to Rome
And rent me a grand piano
And put some flowers 'round my room
But let's not talk about fare-thee-wells now
The night is a starry dome
And they're playin' that scratchy rock and roll
Beneath the Matala Moon

Come on Carey get out your cane
I'll put on some silver
We'll go to the Mermaid Café
Have fun tonight

The wind is in from Africa
Last night I couldn't sleep
Oh you know it sure is hard to leave here
But it's really not my home

These are the words of music legend Joni Mitchell's famous song
Carey. Written after a trip through Europe in early 1970, Mitchell
ended up spending some time on the island of Crete and more
specifically, living in the caves of Matala. This network of caves is
situated on the southern coast of Greece's largest island, Crete, and
with its own dialect and customs, some might consider it a country
unto itself. Even the pronunciation of words is different, as I first
learned Greek when I lived with a family in a small mountain village
in Crete. Locals articulate words like "ohi" or *no*, as "oshi" using
the distinctive Cretan "sh" sound that replaces the "ch" words in
the rest of Greece. While I lived on Crete years after Joni graced
the island with her presence, I've been fascinated by her adventures
in Matala ever since.

Located about a one-and-a-half-hour drive from the main city
of Iraklion, Matala's caves were likely first occupied in prehistoric
times. Carved out of the sheer sandstone cliff, this porous rock
face, pocked with grottos and sloping towards the sea at an odd
angle, is a remarkable site. It is believed the caves were originally
used as burial chambers in the Roman or early Christian periods,
and were painted, both in antiquity and again when the love children of the 1960s redecorated their temporary housing with glow-
in-the-dark paint. Mythology tells us that the beach at Matala was
where Zeus first brought Europa, one of his many conquests, after
transforming himself into a white bull and carrying her away from
the island of Kos.

With the advent of the 1960s, sex, drugs, and rock and roll
ruled the world, and the remote outposts of Greece were no
exception. Hippies from all over the world descended upon this
tiny remote hamlet in southern Crete, and for a few years, a sort
of utopian era reigned supreme. Over the years the expat hippie
culture both amused and confounded locals who didn't know what
to do with these hairy, grubby young people who appeared in their

small corner of the world. Eventually, the cave residents, who set up houses and raised children in the ancient rock-cut tombs, tried the last patience of the exasperated locals. Villagers called upon the local bishop to drive the hippies out, but they scattered to nearby locales only to set up shop once again.

Mitchell describes the village in a 1971 *Rolling Stone* interview:

Matala was a very small bay with cliffs on two sides. And between the two cliffs, on the beach, there were about four or five small buildings. There were also a few fishermen huts. The caves were on high sedimentary cliffs, sand-stone, a lot of seashells in it. The caves were carved out by the Minoans hundreds of years ago. Then they were used later on for leper caves. Then after that the Romans came, and they used them for burial crypts. Then some of them were filled in and sealed up for a long time. People began living there, beatniks, in the fifties. Kids gradually dug out more rooms. There were some people there who were wearing human teeth necklaces around their necks.

The village pretty well survived from the tourist trade, which was the kids that lived in the caves. I don't know what their business was before people came. There were a couple of fishing boats that went out, that got enough fish to supply the two restaurants there. Then the cops came and kicked everyone out of the caves, but it was getting a little crazy there. Everybody was getting a little crazy there. Everybody was getting more and more into open nudity. They were really going back to the caveman. They were wearing little loin-cloths. The Greeks couldn't understand what was happening.

Both Carey and the Mermaid Café are real, according to the article. Cary Raditz was a redheaded, turban-wearing hippie who worked as a cook at a restaurant owned by Stelios Xagorarakis. Their meeting was explosive, to say the least, as Mitchell recalls. Carey "blew out of a restaurant in Greece, literally. Kaboom! I heard, facing the sunset. I turned around and this guy is blowing out the door of this restaurant. He was a cook; he lit a gas stove and it exploded. Burned all the red hair off himself right through his white Indian turban. I went, 'That was an interesting entrance—I'll take note of that.'"

In a more recent *Wall Street Journal* interview, Mitchell recalls that living and sleeping in the famous caves wasn't all it was cracked up to be. "...sleeping up there was tough. To soften the surface, beach pebbles were placed on the stone slab and covered with beach grass. I borrowed a scratchy afghan blanket and placed it on top. But there was no real comfort. When the waves were high and crashed on the beach, they shook the stone in the caves."

In spite of the occasional dynamic surf, Matala is one of 400 beaches in Greece that has been awarded the Blue Flag, which denotes beaches with environmentally correct practices monitoring clean water, safe swimming, and the availability of restrooms and showers. The Sea Turtle Protection Society is also in operation, safeguarding the protection of *Caretta Caretta*, the giant loggerhead turtle that reproduces off and on these shores. Snorkeling is a favorite pastime, and visitors can view antiquities beneath the clear waters of Messara Bay. Located near the Messara plain, this area was the site of numerous ancient Minoan settlements dating to the second millennium B.C., such as Phaistos, Aghia Triada, and Gortyna, all within close driving distance.

Today the caves are protected by the Archaeological Service of Greece. Entrance is free, but if you were hoping to sleep in the caves and channel your inner Joni, you will be disappointed, as visitors are no longer allowed to spend the night. However, that hasn't stopped generations of visitors from trying; along with fisherman, lepers and hippies, the famous Roma, or Gypsy people have also made their homes in these caves over the past decades.

Just in case you were wondering, Joni Mitchell isn't the only celebrity to have graced these cliff dwellings. Some accounts claim that Joan Baez, Bob Dylan, Janis Joplin, and Cat Stevens dropped in on Matala at some point during the '60s and '70s love fest. But the draw of the caves goes back even further into history. It is speculated by some that the world's most famous traveler, Odysseus, also made a stop at the caves during his epic odyssey home from the Trojan War!

33 *Lesbos*

SAPPHO AND THE THESMOPHORIA

It's well known that our modern word lesbian comes from the name for a Greek island—Lesbos. The third largest in Greece, this lush green, puzzle piece of an island with deeply recessed, womblike bays lies tucked into the corner of the Aegean Sea where Greece meets Turkey. Less developed than other Greek islands, Lesbos is just far enough away from the more touristy islands, but well worth the twelve-hour ferry or six-hour hydrofoil ride from Athens, because it is large enough to get lost on.

Lesbos's most famous citizen may be Sappho, a poet who wrote some of the most beautiful and sometimes homoerotic love poems in antiquity; but she isn't the only woman the island is famous for. Once a year, women in ancient Greece were allowed time away from their husbands to gather with other women. Today it would be called a girl's road trip—in the 5th century B.C. it was called the Thesmophoria.

While modern women have spa treatments and mani-pedis, drink and gamble, women back then enjoyed time away from their families and routines by drinking, swearing, and throwing baby piglets into a cave. Thousands of years before Las Vegas appeared on the map, the saying could just have easily have been "What Happens in Lesbos Stays in Lesbos," but this was no ordinary girls' night out—this was considered a sacred practice.

The Thesmophoria was an ancient festival held in honor of the goddess of agriculture, Demeter. These secret rites were celebrated on Lesbos, as they were in many parts of Greece, and participants were limited to married women who spent three days every autumn worshipping in this annual ritual. The first day was called *kathodos* (going down) and *anodos* (rising up). Earlier in the season, piglets—animals that were sacred to Demeter—were thrown into subterranean caves to rot, along with seed cakes in the shape of phalluses and pinecones, all symbols of fertility. On the first day of the festival the women, after having purified themselves and abstained from sex, went down into the caves to retrieve the pigs. Along the way they clapped loudly to scare away any snakes that might be in the caves and shouted obscenities. The ritual of swearing is thought to be connected to Baubo, an old woman who told obscene jokes to cheer up Demeter over the loss of her daughter Persephone, who was abducted by the god of  the Underworld, Hades. The women would gather the remains of the pigs and mix them with grains and seed cakes to be placed on an altar.

The second day, *nesteia,* was a day of fasting, in which participants sat on the ground in commemoration of Demeter's grief over her missing daughter. Only pomegranate seeds—which Persephone ate when she was in the Underworld—were ingested, and the insults and swearing continued. On the third day, *kalligeneia,* or fair birth, the women indulged in a meat feast and scattered the seeds and remains of the piglets into the field to ensure a good harvest.

Drinking was a part of the proceeding, as the ancient playwright Aristophanes indicates in his comedy, *The Women at the Thesmophoria.*

First Woman to Mnesilochus, a man spying on the ritual.

Now stranger, tell me

What first we practiced on that holy day.

Mnesilochus.

Bless me, what was it? Why, first we—drank.

First Woman.

Right; what was second?

Mnesilochus.

Second? Drank again.

First Woman.

Somebody's told you this. But what was third?

Mnesilochus.

Well, third, Zenylla had a drop too much.

The rituals were shrouded in secrecy and men were banned from the proceedings, but that didn't stop Aristophanes's character Mnesilochus from dressing as a woman to spy on the events. He is caught and condemned to death, but saved at the last moment by another man, also dressed as a woman. As Deborah Ruscillo, an expert on the Thesmophoria, states: "The Thesmophoria were fertility rituals which are thought to be carry-overs from an older era...but given that piglets are symbols of female fertility (presumably because of the fecundity of sows) and snakes which are anatomically equated with male genitalia and fertility, this ritual must go beyond the mythical story."

Lesbos, also known as Mytilene, after the island's capital, is also where the poet Sappho was born around 620 B.C. and lived for most of her life. Born to an upper class family, she was exiled for a time due to her family's political activism. She was married (her husband had the inelegant nickname Kerkylas of Andros, which translates to "Prick from the Island of Man") and by some accounts, had a daughter, Cleis. But her attentions were lavished on the female students in her academy and her poetry belies the erotic love she held for her own gender.

Awed by her splendor

stars near the lovely

moon cover their own

bright faces

when she
is roundest and lights

earth with her silver

Whereas Homer was called "The Poet," Sappho had earned the title "The Poetess," and Plato called her "The Tenth Muse." Her language was derived from Aeolic vernacular and tradition and her terse phrasing is often compared to that of Homer. Her poems are filled with a depth of passion and delivered with a sensual and lyrical rhythm today known as a Sapphic meter:

Come back to me, Gongyla, here tonight,
You, my rose, with your Lydia lyre.
There hovers forever around you delight;
A beauty desired.

Even your garment plunders my eyes.
I am enchanted: I who once
Complained to the Cyprus-born goddess,
Whom I now beseech

Never to let this lose me grace
But rather bring you back to me;
Amongst all mortal women the one
I most wish to see.

Whereas the details of her life remain sparse, some accounts state that Sappho fell in love with a fisherman named Phaon. Widely held as a legend, it is possible the story was circulated to disavow Sappho's lesbian leanings. Supposedly her unrequited affections drove her to commit suicide by jumping off the cliffs of Lefkas, an island on the opposite side of Greece. Whatever the true story of Sappho's life or sexual orientation, her body of work remains today extraordinary and groundbreaking for its time.

For obvious reasons, Lesbos has become a destination for gay couples, but islanders don't pay much attention one way or another to their island's reputation. Tzeli Hadjidimitriou, the author of *A Girl's Guide to Lesbos*, suggests a visit to the island's many thermal springs, some of which, such as Polichnitos, you can book exclusively, and others, such as the women-only facilities at Gera and Lisvori, where you can swim in your birthday suit.

"Fortunately Lesbos is not yet an entirely tourist-oriented island. Particularly in the mountainous areas you will discover beautiful, still isolated villages and people who will captivate you with their kindness and warm hospitality. You...can sit down to eat in cafés next to the village elders and taste great food accompanied by the island favorite, ouzo."

Some of Hadjidimitriou's twelve commandments of visiting the island are:

"Watch the sun descending behind the rock that resembles Sappho's profile whilst enjoying a refreshing drink at the LGBT-friendly bar. Drink ouzo—responsibly! As the sun sets, try the fresh sardines of Kalloni at one of the restaurants you will find inside

Kalloni Gult, especially towards Skala Lisvoriou. Buy and try sweets and other delicacies from the many women's cooperatives on the island. Dip into the sea at night, with or without a moon, but not when you're drunk!"

Lesbos is an island filled with archaeological remains spanning millennia and studded with Christian temples, mosques, minarets, and churches. Visitors can explore the ruins of a Hellenistic theater in Mytilene that seated 15,000 spectators, a vast Roman aqueduct erected in the 3rd century A.D. and a massive Byzantine castle in the town of Molyvos that looms above the tangerine tiled rooftops that appear to sprout from the steep hillsides.

So whether you are here to enjoy a singularly feminine island, or explore a place far from the madding crowd, I suggest you pull up a table to the edge of the sea at Eressos Beach, ask for a pour of the island's lush, heady ouzo, and as you roll the chilled licorice taste over your tongue, contemplate these lines from Sappho:

You've come and you—
Oh, I was longing for you—
Have cooled my heart
Which was burning with desire.

✿

34 *Ithaka*

THE ODYSSEY, PENELOPE, AND SYLVIA BENTON

> *As you set out for Ithaka*
> *hope your road is a long one,*
> *full of adventure, full of discovery.*
> *Laistrygonians, Cyclops,*
> *angry Poseidon—don't be afraid of them:*
> *you'll never find things like that on your way*
> *as long as you keep your thoughts raised high,*
> *as long as a rare excitement*
> *stirs your spirit and your body.*
> *Laistrygonians, Cyclops,*
> *wild Poseidon—you won't encounter them*
> *unless you bring them along inside your soul,*
> *unless your soul sets them up in front of you.*

As an archaeologist who first set foot on Ithaka in search of the legendary palace of Odysseus, I have been returning to the island, like Odysseus, for more than twenty years. The poem, "Ithaka," by Constantine Cavafy, is for me an anthem of life, and when I heard that it was Jacqueline Kennedy Onassis's favorite poem as well, I smiled. For the words remind us that a place cannot make us happy; only we can do that. But it has taken more than two decades of returning to Ithaka for me to learn this.

Ithaka. Just the mention of the name brings up a kaleidoscope of male archetypes: Homer's epic poem, *The Odyssey*, and its hero Odysseus, sailing the seas for ten years trying to return to his beloved island after fighting for another ten at the Trojan War. But what of his long-suffering wife, Penelope? How did she spend her time when he was away?

Women waited a lot back then for their men to return from sea, and Penelope, trustworthy, steadfast—and stubborn—filled that role to a T. As queen of Ithaka, she had to put up with a hoard of gluttonous and lazy men living off her husband's land—competing princes from surrounding islands waiting for word that Odysseus was dead so they could marry his widow and inherit his kingdom. Yet how did she tolerate this situation for so long?

Even though she was mourning her husband's absence, she had no choice but to eventually accept one of the suitors in marriage. But Homer tells us that Penelope had a sly way of making them wait. Assuring them that she would surely pick a groom once her weaving was finished, she wove during the day, and when night fell, she secretly unraveled the work to delay the unbearable choice.

Archaeologists have searched for centuries, including the infamous Heinrich Schliemann, discoverer of ancient Troy, for the palace of Odysseus. As we sifted through the soil for evidence of a hero, inevitably we discovered countless loom weights that brought Penelope's story to life. As we dug in trenches I unearthed many of these, holding the familiar pyramid-shaped clay object in my hands during mornings when Gray-Eyed Athena's early morning mists crept over the site like earthbound clouds, and the wine dark sea of Homer glimmered hundreds of feet below our lofty perch.

This beautiful island was enthralling not only to Odysseus. Unfortunately, car ferries from the mainland no longer arrive in the main town of Vathy, but if you are able, charter a small boat and sail through its narrow headland where the largest natural harbor in Greece awaits you. The first time I sailed into the main harbor of Ithaka, I became dizzy. The ferryboat took an endless, almost 270-degree turn as it positioned itself outside the pillars of rock that bracket the harbor and keep it safe and placid.

As you glide along the mercury-colored sea, you will see a tower of balding, bluish rock erupting from the water, scrubbed with holm oak, olive, and staccatoed with cypress. Gaze around until you see the windmills atop the right-hand side. These look down both on the main harbor of Vathy as well as Dexia Bay, where Odysseus himself supposedly came ashore under cover of darkness so that he could plot his revenge against the greedy suitors and reveal himself, ultimately, to his beloved Penelope.

A mountain flanks us on one side, jutting straight out of the water to a soaring height, a thin scar along its face where a road must be. Soon enough the ship stops its endless rotation and a glimpse of what's beyond comes into sight. In the distance, the harbor's tiny islet of Lazaretto is fringed with pines, made lopsided by decades of stiff winds, a minuscule church nestled among the trees. Vathy is a symphony of light pastels and terracotta filled with sophisticated shops, boutiques, and small hotels; gripping the harbor's edge like a vice, their painted exteriors puddle the waters in a miasma of blue, pink, and white. The heights of Mounts Naiaon and Neriton rise like sleeping giants above the sea, intimidating, while distant, minute villages burrow tenaciously into the ancient soil, as if fearing becoming dislodged from the bosom of the earth.

Ithaka is an island good for goats, as Homer said—a hiker's paradise. With a copy of *The Odyssey* in hand, you can explore

Homer's reference points such as Raven's Crag, Eumaeus's farm, and the Cave of the Nymphs. The egg-sized stones on pebbled beaches create a shiatsu therapy for feet and the salt waters surrounding the island will make for an invigorating dip. Take a taxi or rent a car and drive to the small towns of Frikes or Kioni in the north for lunch of grilled local fish (go into the kitchen and pick among the pink- and saffron-colored catch) and admire the near-aerial views along the way of the Ionian and Kefalonia from dizzying heights. Inhale the sage, rosemary, and lavender permeated air and gather armloads to take back and perfume your room.

As an archaeologist, I was traveling in the footsteps of many who had entered this harbor in centuries and millennia past, including the German archaeologist Heinrich Schliemann, and Odysseus himself. But Schliemann wasn't the only archaeologist to excavate on Ithaka. Sylvia Benton, a British archaeologist, worked  on the island before World War II. When the sixty-six-year-old Benton returned to Ithaka post war, after having worked as a firefighter in London and being injured in a bombing raid, it was not on a traditional ferry, but on a minesweeper. It is said that this indomitable soul was so excited to see her beloved island that she dove off the prow and swam to shore before the boat could dock.

Born in 1887 in Lahore, India, to British parents, Sylvia eventually moved back to England where she studied at Cambridge. Determined to become an archaeologist, she traveled to Greece, where she studied at the British School at Athens. Resolute to explore the country as a single woman, Sylvia was banned from solo expeditions, such as climbing Mount Taygetos in the Peloponnese.

Stubborn and independent, she proceeded to do this on her own, and was promptly expelled for violating school regulations.

After a brief reprieve, she was readmitted to the school and assigned to an excavation on Ithaka. At the northern end of the island she worked to pump out a collapsed sea cave that revealed twelve bronze tripods, proving the significance of the island as a cult site. More importantly, her discovery of a potsherd inscribed with a dedication to Odysseus further advanced the theory that the island was indeed the Ithaka of Homer's poem. This along with her other discoveries brought worldwide attention to her work on Ithaka and fueled hopes that she had indeed discovered the long sought for place of Homer's *Odyssey*.

Sylvia's life was devoted to her loves: archeology and sports. An avowed athlete, she swam across expansive Polis Bay twice every evening after the day's excavations. As her friend and colleague Helen Waterhouse stated, "Domestic skills had no interest for her. She could not type either, and exasperation with those who reinscribed her manuscripts often delayed their publication. Her digs, on the other hand, were comfortably run; to live under canvas not far from the sea was no hardship in the Ithacan spring and summer. Sylvia prided herself on a hard-bitten no-nonsense exterior. Her Athens hairdresser complained that he was expected to cut her hair "as if round a pudding basin." Though seldom expressed, her attachments were "deep and long lasting, for Ithaca, for chosen works of art, for the beauties of mountain, sky and sea."

Unfortunately, neither Benton nor our excavations, some fifty years later, were able to locate the legendary Palace of Odysseus. After millennia of powerful earthquakes, some believe the remains of any settlement would have been knocked off the steep slopes and tumbled to the sea below, and the lack of palace period finds continues to fuel the debate as to whether Odysseus was a real person or a character of fiction in Homer's epic poem.

Whatever you believe, there is no questioning that Ithaka is a place full of magic. Friend and long time resident Kathleen Pepper told me, "As I entered the harbor of Vathy I remember smiling and saying to myself, 'This is the place—I no longer need to search elsewhere. Ithaka had embraced me and I, her. As simple as that.'"

Ithaka cast its spell on me, too, more than two decades ago, and while I continue to return, I have come to realize the truth of Cavafy's poem. Ithaka may be an unforgettable island, but it gently reminds you that life's beauty lies not merely in the destination, but in the journey itself.

❧

35 *Olympia*

THE TEMPLE OF HERA AND KALLIPATEIRA

Hera is one of those goddesses you don't hear about as much. She's not as sexy as Aphrodite, as tomboyish as Artemis, as warlike—or wise—as Athena. But she has her own temple, and it's well worth visiting. Olympia may be the birthplace of the modern Olympics, but the sanctuary is filled with some of the country's most beautiful 6th-century B.C. structures. And Hera's is magnificent.

Daughter of the Titans Rhea and Cronus, Hera is one of the twelve Olympic gods, and as the wife of Zeus, is considered the queen of the pantheon. Her sacred animals were the cow, peacock, and lion, and she was worshipped as the goddess of childbirth as well as marriage. However, as the consort of Zeus, Hera wasn't always successful in that department herself. Talk about dealing with a philandering husband! Their marriage didn't have the best start. After many unsuccessful attempts at seducing her, Zeus finally resorted to deception and took the form of a neglected cuckoo.

Taking pity on the creature, Hera tucked the bird into her bodice and Zeus, taking advantage of his situation, ravished the goddess. Ashamed, Hera agreed to marry Zeus but their marriage was tumultuous from the start. Zeus's indiscretions were legendary and Hera responded by taking out her anger not on her husband, but on his poor victims as well as Zeus's illegitimate offspring. Her most memorable revenge was wrought on Hercules, the son of Zeus and his lover, Alcmene, by forcing him into the legendary twelve labors.

Perhaps that's the reason her temple is one of the largest and loveliest at Olympia. Built in the Doric hexastyle, it has sixteen columns on each side and is oriented on an east-west axis. In antiquity, the columns were made of wood and were painted with portraits of the winners of the Heraian games. Yes, Hera had her own games! Sadly, the brightly painted portraits are long gone, ravaged by millennia of sun and erosion, but niches in which votives were attached remain. One of the oldest monumental temples in Greece, the Heraion was built around 600 B.C.

Huge statues of Zeus and Hera once stood in the temple's interior, with Hera in a seated position on a throne. Her head is preserved and is on display in the site's magnificent museum, which is well worth visiting. There you will find remains of sculpture from the Temple of Zeus, still marked with traces of bright blue and red pigment the ancients used to decorate the marble. Also in the museum is the famous statue of Nike, sculpted by Paeonius, a possible student of the famed Pheidias. Although her face is sadly missing, you can admire the exquisite carving of the gauzy fabric, which is draped around the figure's shapely thighs and billowing in the back as if blown by a Beyonce-force fan.

Postcards at the site abound with images of women dressed as ancient goddesses, lighting the Olympic torch. Actresses adorned in the robes of ceremonial priestesses use the sun's rays, focused in a parabolic mirror, to light the very torch that is flown to the opening ceremony of every modern Olympic games.

One of the most amazing facts about Olympia is that women were prevented from attending the males' events on penalty of death. Can you imagine not being able to watch Bode Miller ski the downhill without fear of losing your life? Young girls were allowed to witness the games, but if you were an adult woman, forget about it—and don't even bother trying to cross the River Alpheios on game days. Why? Because what awaited you was a fate worse than... well, actually, it was death. Any woman caught watching the games or even forging the river on days when the games were in session received the horrible fate of by being thrown off the cliffs of nearby Mount Typaion.

There are a few exceptions in which ballsy women managed to either compete or just witness the events, and one of them is named Kallipateira. After personally training her son Peisirodos, she wasn't about to miss his race. Eager to see the events, Kallipateira disguised herself as a trainer and managed to get into the stadium. Jubilant over her son's victory, she jumped the fence surrounding the training enclosure and her cloak slipped, revealing her gender. Facing certain death, Kallipateira received a pardon when it was revealed she was related to an athletically gifted family of Olympic victors, including her son, father, nephew, and three brothers.

Perhaps this is why women decided to create their own competition. Founded by Queen Hippodameia, Olympia is where sixteen noble women organized the Heraean games and left a woven gown known as a peplos dedicated to the goddess every four years. Ancient sources tell us that the Heraean games had only one event: a footrace in which maidens could participate. As in the men's games, female victors in the Heraean games were given an olive wreath crown and received a portion of the slaughtered ox for the patron deity. Men competed nude, but women wore a garment called a *chiton*, in which right shoulder and breast were bared. The footraces of the Heraia games were always run by virgins. They used a track similar to men but shortened by one-sixth to accommodate their shorter stride. Women judged and sponsored the games and had the right to dedicate statues inscribed with their names.

However, there is speculation that there may have been other events as well, including the javelin toss, chariot races, and nude wrestling specifically for Spartan women who trained and competed with their male counterparts. Supposedly women could only enter chariots and horses into races that were driven by men, but the website *Women's History Lost* tells us that Cynisca, a daughter of Spartan nobility, won the Olympic chariot race in the 4th century B.C. after entering on a dare from her brother. A courtesan and horse breeder from Ionia named Bilistiche, encouraged by Cynisca's win, proceeded to enter and win the four-chariot race in 286 and 284 B.C. Even though many scholars stubbornly maintain that chariots were always raced by men, Bilistiche received the honor of being made a goddess of Aphrodite upon her death. Not a bad consolation prize.

※

36 *Pylos*

GRAY-EYED ATHENA AND ROSY-FINGERED DAWN

When most people think of Greek beaches, they think of the islands. But one of the country's most gorgeous beaches is actually on the mainland. Since antiquity, this region has been known as Sandy Pylos, a name that comes straight out of Homer's epic poem, *The Odyssey*. When Odysseus's son, Telemachus, is sent in search of his father, who left his home of Ithaka many years before, he travels to Pylos to ask King Nestor about his father's whereabouts. Upon his return his mother, Penelope, begs him to share what he's learned. Book seventeen of *The Odyssey* opens with Rosy-fingered Dawn rising once again, followed by his reply:

> *We sailed to Pylos, to Nestor, the great king,*
> *And he received me there in his lofty palace,*
> *Treated me well and warmly, yes, as a father treats*
> *A long-lost son just home from voyaging, years abroad:*
> *Such care he showered on me, he and his noble sons.*

Pylos is the home of Nestor's Palace. Excavated in the 1950s, the archaeological site is one of Greece's most beautiful and intact royal residences, dating to the 13th century B.C. Take a day to walk through this astounding settlement, built to overlook Homer's legendary wine-dark sea. It may be difficult to imagine the site in its original glory, but if you take a moment to gaze at the remains of a gigantic round hearthstone you can imagine this room, known as the Megaron, encircled by four huge pillars supporting an open ceiling. The walls were decorated with brightly colored frescoes in primary shades of red, blue, and gold depicting images of palace life at its glorious height.

Pylos was home to one of Greece's five kings, but what about the queen? History isn't clear on this point; he was married to either Eurydice (not the same Eurydice associated with the god Orpheus) or Anaxibia. Nestor had six sons but only one daughter, Polycaste, who married Telemachus, and gave birth to their son, Persepolis. Book three of *The Odyssey* tells of their first meeting;

> *Then lovely Polycaste, youngest daughter*
> *of Nestor, son of Neleus, bathed Telemachus.*
> *When the bath was finished, she rubbed him with rich oil*
> *and gave him a tunic and fine cloak to wear.*
> *Coming from his bath, he looked just like a god.*
> *He went and sat by Nestor, the people's shepherd.*

Archaeology aside, one of my favorite parts of visiting Pylos is actually the approach to town. Driving from the north the road begins to snake along the coastline, high above the water, affording a fabulous view of shimmering Navarino Bay in the distance, where Greece fought for its independence from the Ottoman Empire in 1827. Locals still tell the story of the gory battle, the last fought with sailing ships. "The whole bay turned red with blood," a taxi driver remarked to me one day as we drove along this road, gesturing out the window and recalling the memory, burned into the Greek psyche as if it were yesterday.

Located about a four-hour drive along the gorgeous new Athens-Kalamata highway, this tiny town is tucked away at the furthest southwestern most point of the Greek mainland. The road dips steeply into the village, forcing you around hairpin turns past whitewashed houses and small businesses, while views of the green-blue sea flicker seductively between the buildings. Finally you reach the heart of town with its Italianate horseshoe-shaped town square, known as a *plateia*, facing the expansive bay spiked with a thin chain of islands called Sphacteria.

Pylos is one of the loveliest towns in Greece. In summertime the *plateia* is filled with families gathered around the park benches keeping a close eye on their children, who run free around the tree-lined park. Old men in baggy sweaters challenge each other to al fresco games of *tavli* and children laugh and scream, playing soccer and running to their parents for a handful of euros to purchase *pagota*—ice cream delicacies such as waffle cones and chocolate caramel bars—from the street vendor.

If you want to learn about the massive battle the area is famous for, be sure to visit the vast fortress looming above town. Built in the early 1600s by the Ottomans, this Neokastro, or "new castle," was erected to replace a Frankish fortress. History buffs will appreciate a short film describing the momentous battle that took place off these shores, and photography enthusiasts will enjoy views of the lapis-colored sea visible through niches cut into the fortress walls.

Pylos is also home to the country's largest freshwater preserve with some of the rarest birds and waterfowl. The Gialova lagoon, located a few kilometers from the town center, is home to 270 species of birds that inhabit these ecosystem wetlands. Osprey, heron, and bandy-legged ibis migrate in and out of this lush emerald network of marshes and reed beds year round. Grab a pair of binoculars and avid birders may spot graceful swans gliding through the lagoon's peaceful inlets or even flamingos, making a visit to this abundant sanctuary an exotic part of any trip to Pylos.

Cruise boats depart regularly for excursions out into the harbor and stop at the Spachteria, a lacy string of sharp vertical islands that shield the bay from wind and waves. Hike up on top of the largest for excellent views of Pylos and Mount Taygetos beyond. Curiously, a small Russian Orthodox chapel stands on one of the islets. Built of wood, its forlorn onion dome topped with a cross bears witness to the Russian contingent who took part in the 1827 Battle of Navarino.

Now for the sand—there is miles of it here, unlike other beaches in Greece, which consist of egg-shaped stones that give your feet an invigorating massage! Several beaches are located within driving distance from town, but my favorite is the hard to pronounce Voidokoilia, appropriately described by one visitor as, "a semicircular summer dream." This bowl of deep turquoise blue water is gripped by a perfect circular strip of soft white sand, putting it at the top of most beautiful beaches in Greece.

After spending your time exploring all of the glories of Pylos, from exquisite archaeological sites to Venetian castles and lush tropical lagoons, this is the perfect spot for some downtime. Pull up one of the chaise lounge chairs and order a Nescafe frappe *me gala* (with milk) from one of the hunky Greek beach vendors. With the sapphire-colored sea reflecting the midsummer sun, settle in for a late afternoon of sheer relaxation. Let the tranquil waters slurp at your feet and watch the sun sink like an overripe cantaloupe behind the lacy islets of Sphacteria in the distance.

❧

37 Delphi

ORACLES AND THE OMPHALOS OF THE WORLD

Perhaps you've heard of Oedipus, the fateful king who learned from a prophecy at Delphi that he would kill his father and marry his mother? Or the ancient priestesses who sat over a fissure in the earth, inhaling noxious vapors and went into a prophetic trance while heads of state awaited direction on how to marshal their armies? Far more than a mystifying place about which many tales have been told, the otherworldly site of Delphi is first and foremost a sacred sanctuary, and you can feel its power in your bones. A place of worship since the Mycenaean period (14th to 11th centuries B.C.), Delphi became a sanctuary to the god Apollo somewhere between the 11th and 9th centuries B.C. In the following century, the site became known internationally for its priestesses, known as Pythia, and their legendary oracular powers.

As you approach the site on the winding roads, passing elderly widows in black on donkeys weighed down with bundles of emerald green *horta*, you sense a majesty, a geomantic power of more than three thousand years that oozes from this valley with walls bristling with conifer and silver tipped ancient olive trees. The skeletal remains of columns, walls, and temples appear like a small human offering in the distance, matchsticks compared to the immense embrace of the cataract blue and dun colored mountains that ring this sacred enclave. An ancient hush comes over you and you feel as if, like the priestesses, you have been veiled. As it is said in Greek, "*Kalosorizo sto mysterio ton Delphon.*" Welcome to the mystery of Delphi.

I first climbed these steep trails as a child, visiting on a family vacation. On the taxi drive up from Athens, I recall mountain goats clinging to the sides of the road, posed like statues on clefts cut into the craggy rock. We arrived only to have to climb some more, all the way to the top, where the remains of the Temple of Apollo still stand, dominating the entire site with views to the Corinthian Gulf, shimmering like plate metal in the distance.

Delphi is known throughout the world as the *omphalos*, which, roughly translated, means "center of the world." A distinctly feminine word, it refers to the navel, and the new life through which the umbilical cord is attached. About a two-and-a-half-hour drive from Athens, you'll find the site sitting atop the slopes of Mount Parnassus on the Phaedriades, known as the "shining rocks" for their mirror-like reflection of light. The sheer cliffs surrounding the sanctuary, which is situated on a series of leveled areas down the slope, is a naturally dramatic setting creating the perfect foil for the ancient buildings, which includes a beautiful, spacious amphitheater burrowed into the mountainside. The area is seismic, with earthquakes occurring in this area of steep crevices and underground streams; not surprisingly, the site was originally dedicated to Poseidon, the god of the sea and earthquakes, as well as to Mother Earth. It was called the Pythos, a term used in Homer, and the Oracle was also named the Pythia, after the Python, who is the son of Mother Earth. The word Delphi comes from the ancient *delfys*, which means womb, further epitomizing the deeply feminine nature of this site.

There were multiple oracles in ancient Greece, but the Delphic oracle was the most famous of all. Leaders and generals from around the ancient world traveled from afar to consult her, bringing boars, sheep, or other animals to sacrifice. Directed to await their consultation in a room adjoining the Pythia's underground chamber, they wrote their questions on lead tablets. Most often the questions were about war, and the inquiry was posed in such a way that the questioner effected his own answer.

Before enacting the role of Pythia, the priestesses purified themselves in the Castalian Spring, located in the clefts on the slope beneath the site. The oracle would then ingest a laurel leaf and seat herself on the bronze stool called a tripod. Situated over a deep fissure in the earth, she would be exposed to gases that emitted from the earth's crust, become intoxicated, and then utter the response to the question. Most of the priestesses' responses were likely in the form of hysterical utterances, translated for the petitioner by the temple priests into graceful hexameter form.

Modern-day geological research has shown that the area is no longer prone to poisonous gases in enough concentration to induce intoxication, but locals have noted that birds flying into the caves surrounding the sanctuary still die from fumes. Testing has shown the gases to be composed of mostly methane, which can cause hallucinations in strong enough concentrations.

Starting at the lowest level, you will see the exquisite, carousel-shaped Temple of Athena Pronaos. Also called the *tholos*, this partially reconstructed circular temple was my favorite as a child, and is dedicated to the Athena of forethought. As you make your way up the path, you will arrive at a series of small buildings known as Treasuries. These tiny temple-like structures were commemorations built in honor of Apollo by the many Greek states, giving thanks to the oracle for her advice that led to victory in battle. The most famous is the Siphnian treasury from the island of Sifnos, known for its glittering gold mines in antiquity. Farther up the path is the museum, which contains statues of athletes, including the famous Charioteer, a bronze sculpture of a youth riding a chariot sculpted in the early 5th century B.C. in honor of a team victory in the Pythian Games.

Farther up the slope is a large level open area, on which sit the remains of the Temple of Apollo. Built in the 4th century B.C. in the Doric style, it stands on the foundation of earlier buildings erected on the same site. Only six of the bulky, muscular columns remain, towering like sentinels overlooking the ravine below. It was on this building that the following famous axioms *gnothi seauton*, "Know thyself," and *meden agan*, "Nothing in excess," were inscribed.

Just above the Apollo Temple sits one of the best-preserved ancient theaters in Greece, erected in the 4th century B.C. At this soaring height one can imagine the throngs of mesmerized pilgrims approaching this mysterious and intimidating site from below, filling the theater and awaiting a performance of Sophocles's Athenian tragedy *Oedipus Rex*.

Push through a final incline and climb the steps to an ancient stadium, erected at the very apex of the site. Built in the 5th century B.C., the 550-foot stadium seated 6,500 and was used for the Pythian Games, held every eight years in honor of the god Apollo's slaying of the serpent Python.

Apollo may have killed the serpent Python, yet the goddess is named after this creature. I've always been fascinated by the multiple meanings snakes and serpents have in our culture. The Adam and Eve story is the most famous, depicting the snake as evil, and there are numerous other references to the snake as a phallic symbol. While many serpent references are seen as evil, in Chthonic and earth centric traditions, the snake is actually a female symbol. Gaia is the goddess of Mother Earth, and the creature that inhabits her crust is not only female, but most definitely a positive and life-affirming influence.

Be sure to visit the entire site, including the Castilian Spring, if you are able. It's often closed to the public, but my sister Gael was lucky enough to explore this magical place. "It's gorgeous and you have the spring all to yourself!" she gushed after emerging from the wooded glen.

It's a strange anomaly that women were not allowed in the ancient sanctuary to petition the Pythia, yet it was women who ruled the site. Only females could be chosen to serve as oracular priestesses and were selected from peasant women who were of age fifty or older. At the height of the sanctuary's popularity, three Pythia shared the job. It must have taken a toll on the women, exposed to obvious toxins and sitting for extended periods on a tripod, bent over a deep chasm in the earth. While the role had its obvious prestige, it clearly also had its risks.

The site remained active until the mid 4th century A.D., when a Roman emperor, trying to revive the cult, was given the following and final response from the Pythia:

Tell to the king that the carved hall is fallen in decay;
Apollo has no chapel left, no prophesying by,
No talking spring. The stream is dry that had so much to say.

Most likely the time had come when the critical gases were no longer emitting from the earth's crust and the natural cycle of the site had come to an end. This last prophetic statement was the oracle's way of saying that the time for the cult had passed and Apollo was dead. Yet if you stand in the shadow of the Athena Pronaos and listen very carefully, you can still hear her voice from deep beneath the earth, as she hovers over a chasm and offers her unfathomable advice from a place beyond the veil.

❧

38 The Asklepieion of Epidaurus

AN ANCIENT SPA WHERE YOU SLEEP WITH SNAKES

Who doesn't enjoy a trip to a spa resort? You look forward to some health treatments, maybe a massage and facial, as well as time for relaxing in a beautiful environment and taking in the abundance of nature around you. Maybe it's a boot camp resort with early morning hikes in the countryside, or perhaps a yoga retreat where you spend your days bending your body into the shape of a pretzel. But if you live in the 5th century B.C., the notion of a spa is a long way from soul cycling and mani-pedis.

You have just arrived in Epidaurus, Greece. You spend your afternoon admiring the bucolic, thickly forested site as you watch handfuls of other patients move peacefully through the grounds, the temples casting long shadows beneath the towering Aleppo pines and arborvitae. As you prepare for bed that night, you are asked to sleep in a small confined area. Robed assistants, known as priests, are assigned to you. They tell you that you will have dreams in this small sleeping area called an *abaton*. If you've been struggling with some health issue, you confide your concerns to the priests. They take note of your problem, give you some herbal tea to drink, and before leaving you to relax into a deep sleep, they tell you to remember your dream in the morning.

When you awake, the priests arrive and you recall your entire reverie frame by frame. After consulting with one another, they turn to you and interpret the dream, then prescribe the treatment. An herbal remedy might be administered and you are sent to the baths for a therapeutic soak, or perhaps a surgical procedure is recommended. Little did you know that the dreams you have in this sacred place hold within them the treatment for your ailment. Miraculous cures were known to occur here for supposedly incurable diseases, because the ancient Greeks knew that there was much more to healing than just the administering of medicinal treatments. The soothing and salubrious effects of music, the arts, and a stunning natural environment themselves are a tonic for the soul.

Twenty-five hundred years later, Epidaurus is still a magnificent place. Located near the modern city of Nauplion, about a three-hour drive from Athens, Epidaurus was founded in the 6th century B.C. and developed out of an earlier cult devoted to Apollo Maleatas. While many visitors may not realize the deeper significance of this sanctuary and what it was used for millennia ago, they can certainly appreciate the spacious grounds with its magnificent amphitheater. Seating more than 13,000 people, it is one of the most acoustically perfect ancient theaters in the world. Every summer, hundreds of thousands of visitors flock from Athens to attend the annual Epidaurus Festival, in which ancient plays by Greek playwrights such as Aeschylus and Euripides are staged under a banner of pine trees and starry skies. Because of her political leanings, the famed Greek folk singer Nana Mouskouri was forbidden from singing at this epic theater in 1950. Decades later, she returned while filming a documentary with British actress Joanna Lumley. To the surprise and delight of a handful of delighted tourists, she performed an impromptu rendition of "Ave Maria," her distinctive, haunting voice echoing across the gleaming marble canyon of curved stairs, seats, and aisles.

The theater is set into a natural hillside and looks out over the rest of the complex, its bone-white marble seats deeply snugged into the cleavage of a hillside bristling with cypress, pine, and arborvitae. There is no need to witness a performance at this magnificent structure because merely standing at the top of amphitheater and listening to the wind flow through these ancient stones is music to the ears. Climb to the topmost seats and be amazed at how easy it is to eavesdrop on the visitors far below. If you can, have someone stand at the center of the orchestra and drop a pin. You will hear it, the tinkling sound echoing up the marble steps and into the whispering pines beyond.

The area adjoining the theater, known as the Asklepieion, is named after Asklepios, the ancient Greek god of medicine and healing. The symbol of the caduceus and the snake intertwined around the central staff, rooted in this ancient tradition, is the selfsame image associated with modern medicine. Asklepios's daughter, Hygeia, the goddess of good health, was an attendant to her father as well as a companion to the goddess of love and beauty, Aphrodite. Hygeia and her sisters, Panakeai (Cure All) and Iaso (Remedy), accompanied her in her duties, and focused on the prevention of sickness instead of the cure.

The Asklepieia, or temples built for the purposes of healing, contained special dormitories, or *abatons*, where the patients slept. The priests often used non-venomous snakes as part of the healing process, allowing them to slither along the floor during the night (one would think that would give some people nightmares instead of sweet dreams!). However, the snake is oft maligned as a symbol of evil, but in actuality, the serpent, as a creature who inhabits the recesses of Mother Earth, is an ancient symbol of the feminine.

Other important structures at the site include a stadium where games were held every four years, its marble stones now sinking back and being reclaimed by the green bosom of Mother Earth. A foundation exists for a temple dedicated to Asklepios, and a partial reconstruction of a temple dedicated to his daughter Hygeia overlooks the Roman-era Odeon. Wander through the vast space and see the remains of a Great Stoa, or marketplace, priests' residence, a Temenos of the Muses, and banqueting halls.

The Tholos, built in the 4th century B.C. by Polykleitos the Younger, also the architect of the theater, was a circular temple embodying five internal walls that formed a type of maze, and archaeologists believe this was used as a healing ritual for the patients. The Tholos also housed non-venomous snakes, similar to those used in *abatons*. Again, if patients could overcome any ophidiophobia (fear of snakes), the creatures, because of the shedding of their skin, were thought to symbolize healing and regeneration.

Modern medicine can trace its roots to the practices at this sanctuary, where physical as well as emotional healing was considered paramount—a place where not just the disease, but also the whole patient, along with any underlying psychological components, was treated. Here guests had access to theater, healing waters in the site's Sacred Well, shopping, good food, above all medical care and immersion into nature. With a Mycenaean sanctuary dedicated to a curative goddess located nearby, the area has been the site of healing since prehistoric times, and its popularity lasted well into the Roman period until the Goths raided and destroyed the region in 267 A.D. Two thousand years later, it's a pity we've lost the connection to this holistic model of health and to the model of a healing sanctuary that extends beyond the narrow parameters of pharmaceutical and surgical cures. As the god of health and of human happiness, Asklepios tended not only to the body, but also to the soul, an enlightened concept we would be wise to reintegrate into our modern world.

❧

39
The Temple of Artemis at Brauron

DANCE OF THE BEAR MAIDENS AND
THE SACRIFICE OF IPHIGENIA

Recently a friend had a layover at Athens's new international air-port. She asked if there was someplace interesting close by she could visit, since it was a forty-five-minute and thirty-five-euro cab ride into Athens. In an instant it came to my mind: Brauron.

Situated over the mountain range from Athens on the eastern side of the Attic plain, this lyrical and relatively unscathed site, nestled in a wooded glen near the Aegean coastline, is dedicated to Artemis, goddess of the hunt and moon. Traditionally overlooked by tour groups because of its remote location, it is now more popular since the new airport, located in nearby Spata, was built just prior to the 2004 Athens Olympic games.

With its multiple buildings, it is actually a sacred compound and is often referred to as the Parthenon of the Bear Maidens for its similar beauty to the Parthenon of the Athenian Acropolis. The precinct is organized around an ancient sacred spring, and the region was eventually flooded by the Erasinos River, making the site still a bit swampy. Located originally closer to the sea, silt deposits have in-filled the expanse, making the shoreline farther away than in antiquity. However, the remoteness of the site has preserved its idyllic character, and one doesn't need a powerful imagination to wonder at the festivities that took place in this wooded glen.

The complex's most notable structure is a large Pi-shaped (from the Greek letter Π) stoa, or open portico with multiple columns. This partially reconstructed building is the best preserved at the site, and contained multiple dining rooms for ritual feasting. Nearby the sacred spring are cave shrines and the remains of a small temple to Artemis.

The Athenian tyrant Peisistratos hailed from Brauron and made sure the worship of this site was a priority during his rule in the 6th century B.C. What is curious is that one would think a despot would prefer the worship of Ares, god of war, or Poseidon, the testy sea god, or even Zeus himself, the king of Olympus. Not this dictator. This cult didn't involve fighting and other manly things such as swords, harpoons, and tridents. The Brauronian cult, also known as the Cult of the Bear Maidens, involved something even more intimidating: little girls dancing—in bear costumes.

Every four years a festival called the Brauronia took place to honor the goddess, starting out with a parade of young girls, aged five to ten, originating in Athens some twenty miles away, and terminating at Brauron. The girls, called *arktoi*, wore bearskins, meant to honor the goddess, whose expertise was the hunt and whose sacred animal was, among others, the bear. The procession was a rite of passage for the girls from childhood to the age of marriage. Curiously, Artemis, known as a virgin goddess, is tasked with protecting women in childbirth, and ritual offerings of clothing, jewelry, and other items have been excavated in the area.

In Aristophanes's *Lysistrata*, (the play in which in which men play all the female roles) there is a part where the ritual duties of the young girls are chanted by the chorus, and the words have a wistful effect, as though an older woman is looking back on her days as a maiden at a coming out ball:

> *As soon as I turned seven I was an arrephoros,*
> *Then at ten I was aletris for the goddess;*
> *Then, shedding my yellow robe, I was a bear at the Brauronia;*
> *And once, as a lovely young girl, I was a kanephoros.*

The spot where little girls danced was also where a more tragic heroine met a heartbreaking end. Legend tells us that the goddess Artemis demanded that Iphigenia, daughter of Agamemnon, King of Mycenae, be sacrificed in return for her father's sacrifice of a deer, the goddess's sacred animal, or she would make sure the king's fleet would not meet with favorable winds on their way to fight the Trojan War. Iphigenia was summoned by her father on the auspices of marriage to the war hero Achilles, but when she arrived she was led to her death.

Other sources question this version, believing that Artemis took pity on the young girl. Substituting a deer at the last moment, Artemis spirited Iphigenia away to Tauris, in modern-day Crimea, to serve as her priestess. She later returned to Greece with her brother Orestes, and the wooden icon of Artemis. So identified with the cult of Artemis, she ultimately died and her grave is said to be at Brauron. From Euripides' *Iphigenia in Tauris,*

> *You, Iphigenia, shall hold her [Artemis's] sacred keys,*
> *and serve Her shrine at the Brauron steps.*
>
> *There, when you die,*
>
> *They shall adorn your grave with gowns of softest weave*
>
> *Left in their store by women who die in childbed.*

The sanctuary, ringed in silvery olive groves, weeping fig, and the milky blue, scrubbily wooded mountains, evokes an elegiac quality that transports you back in time more than two thousand years. If you listen closely, you can hear the sounds of little girls' voices in the wind and capture a glimpse of tiny maidens, dressed in saffron robes and bearskins, linked hand in hand and weaving their way in and out of this magical and sacred glen.

❦

40 *The Two Elenis*

A GRANDMOTHER'S AND GRANDDAUGHTER'S LIVES
INTERTWINE IN A WAR-TORN GREEK VILLAGE

After World War II, Greece was a country left in ruins, without leadership and the means to rebuild after the German and Italian occupations. Two rival factions emerged in this power gap, both intent on running the country and determined to eliminate the other. Communist guerrillas, set on dragging Greece behind the Iron Curtain, were locked in a life-and-death battle with nationalist forces that fought to keep Greece part of the West. In a small mountain village in the northernmost point of the country, one woman became caught in the grip of this war, and her heroic tale, as told by her son Nicholas Gage in the 1983 book *Eleni*, has become known worldwide.

In 1944, Eleni Gatsoyannis and her five children, barefoot and close to starvation, were struggling to survive in a remote settlement known as Lia. Located just a kilometer from the Albanian border, this is a part of Greece few people see. Perched on a sheer mountain face, the village is almost hidden in the thick foliage of springtime, and the Mourgana mountain range, a gray slash of rock, rises sharply behind, demarcating the border between Greece and Albania. This is not the Greece of postcards with gentle seas lapping upon silken shores; this is harsh country. Cobblestone paths line the mountainside, and the scenery belies the northern clime, with walnut and cypress falling under a gentle carpet of snow in the winter.

Eleni's husband, Christos, had moved to America, but her mother, threatening suicide if she left to join him, forced her to stay in Greece. Christos visited the family, bringing gifts and occasional financial support, which Eleni regularly shared with her fellow villagers, but ultimately she was left alone to raise her children under these brutal conditions. When the communist factions closed in on Lia, Eleni wrote to her husband, pleading for him to help them move to America. He wrote back, ordering her to stay put, assuring her that the New Democratic Party, or *andartes*, as the communists were referred to, were coming in support of the villagers and there was no reason to be afraid.

He could not have been more wrong. When the *andartes* arrived in Lia, they took over homes, raided the villagers' livestock and food stores, set buildings on fire, and forced people into labor. Known as the "Amerikana" because of her husband's habit of sending packages from America, Eleni became a target. Upon learning that the *andartes* were planning to conscript the older village children and train them as soldiers, Eleni desperately tried to prevent her eldest daughters from this fate. She hid them high in the mountains, but defiant and missing home, the girls eventually made their way back. One daughter was taken into the army as an *andartina*, or female freedom fighter, but thankfully was let go when she failed to pass the basic training. Eleni's life became one of servitude and pain, forced to feed, clothe, and house the *andartes* from dawn to dusk. Secretly she held out hope that the nationalists would eventually reach the village to rescue them, but when the government forces retreated, she realized she and her family were trapped.

Thanks to support from her husband, the "Amerikana's" house was the biggest in the village. In spite of her bottomless generosity to her neighbors and tireless service to the soldiers, the *andartes* kicked Eleni and her children out of her home to use as their headquarters, forcing them to live in crowded conditions with other villagers in the police station. When Eleni heard the communists planned a program to conscript the village's younger children between the ages of three and fourteen and take them over the border to Albania, she hatched a plan to escape. Jealous fellow villagers began to inform on her and, with a husband in America, Eleni was identified as a capitalist and taken into custody. The day before her planned escape, one of her daughters was put into labor in the fields, forcing her to reconsider her plans. With no intention of leaving unless she could take all of her children, Eleni stayed behind with her daughter, driving her other children to escape on their own.

Tortured and interrogated, she was tried with six other villagers and found guilty of helping her children escape. On August 28, 1948, at the age of forty-one, she was put to death in the village square by a firing squad. Before the shots were fired, she was said to scream out, "My children!" the words echoing hauntingly against the bleak Mourgana range. Her son, Nicholas, and three other daughters made their way through minefields to the port of Igoumenista, and eventually boarded a ship to America, where they settled in Massachusetts with their father.

In 2005, Eleni's granddaughter and namesake, Eleni Gage, returned to Lia. Warned by her aunts not to meddle and to leave the past in the past, Gage couldn't ignore a passionate desire to learn more about her grandmother and her history. In the lovely memoir, *North of Ithaka*, she chronicles a year in the village and her encounters with the inhabitants, most of whom were now over sixty, and her efforts to rebuild her grandmother's stone house, which had fallen into ruins.

As she reconstructed the home, stone by stone, the project became part archaeological dig, with key artifacts being unearthed, shedding light on her family's heritage and life. A Turkish coin dating to 1856 was discovered in the foundation, a custom meant to give the structure strength. Other households goods, parts of a bed and kitchen items were found, bringing Eleni into more intimate contact with her beloved grandmother, allowing her to more fully appreciate her life and not only the overwhelmingly tragic circumstances of her death.

Gage's hesitation to delve into the past is evident. "What if the villagers were offended by the house's reconstruction?" she writes. "I knew well that the home had the power to bring sorrow as well as joy. I was re-creating a building that was new to me but fearfully remembered by my neighbors for the tortures and killing that went on there. What if their pain and anger returned when they entered the gate?"

Eventually the family warmed to the idea of Eleni's yearlong project and the day of the house's blessing brought dozens of villagers to celebrate the resurrection of not only an exquisitely restored domicile, but also a newly formed bond between a granddaughter and her grandmother. From a pile of rubble, Gage had managed to painstakingly and lovingly rebuild her grandmother's home into a handsome and inviting two-story structure that once again melded seamlessly into the vale of trees and rock on this remote mountainside. A handmade keystone was erected over the doorway with the family's name and dates of its original construction in 1856, and Eleni's rebuilding date of 2002.

Even though her path was fraught with warnings from family members to leave the pain of the past behind, and fears that the locals might resent her efforts, Gage came to terms with her family's tragic history, and with the rebuilding of her grandmother's home, brought healing into the present. "The important thing was that the house had risen from a pile of rocks and would always call me back to Lia—and it would be filled with the specially chosen gifts of the villagers who didn't hold its tragic past against the house but welcomed it as they had me, and wanted to embellish the interior with pieces of their own past," she recounts, adding, "I knew I would visit the house often. But even if I never made it back, the fact that it existed would comfort me, making me as happy as all my memories of those villagers who came to celebrate its completion."

If you visit this remote corner of Greece, be sure to make a stop at the Vikos-Ooidos Gorge, on the road to Lia. Carved out by the Voidomatis River, this magnificent ravine, with its ethereally blue limestone cliffs, is Greece's answer to the Grand Canyon. Often referred to as the most spectacularly beautiful of the five canyon-like gorges in Greece, Vikos's wildlife sanctuary, replete with bear and wild boar, is a hiker's paradise. This is an opportunity to experience a refreshing alternative to the Greece of palm trees and beaches. A wide variety of deciduous trees, from oak, maple, and beech, sport a blaze of color in autumn and there's a ski resort for those with enough stamina after the seventeen-hour drive from Athens.

A maze of interconnected pathways cuts through this rugged terrain that characterizes the serrated and remote North Pindus Mountains of Greece. Walking between the small stone villages unique to northern Epirus, one can appreciate not only the region's majestic beauty, but difficult past; and in particular, marvel at the unforgettable memory of Eleni Gatsoyannis, whose undeniable courage, overwhelming love for her children, and singular voice still echoes through these sacred valleys.

❧

41 *Kassope Monument*

DANCING TO THE EDGE OF DEATH

In Greece, not all monuments erected in honor of women celebrate physical feminine beauty. There are some, such as one near the town of Preveza in the northern province of Epirus, that commemorate a bravery attesting to a much darker history in Greece's modern era. Some parts of Greece reflect the postcard view: the sunny skies, stark white dwellings, and searingly sapphire seas. But some parts of Greece reveal a more foreboding past. Atop this desolate plain overlooking the molten Ionian Sea, located on the western plateau of the province of Epirus, is such a place. It is where the wind speaks and tells a story of pain, sacrifice, and a staunch refusal to succumb to oppression.

The ancient settlement known as Kassope is located on the western coast of the Greek mainland. Sitting 600 meters high above the Ionian Sea, it looks out over the island of Lefkas in the distance, occupying a commanding position over the sea. In the early 4th century, the site was a vast network of buildings, including many in an ancient agora, or marketplace, which has an octagonal stoa with Doric columns, a theater and a chamber tomb.

Numerous sculptures dot the marketplace atop the plateau of Mount Zalonga, the city laid out in a format known as the Hippodamian system. Named after Hippodamos from the ancient

Greek city of Miletus, located in modern Turkey, this type of city planning was used in ancient Greece. Unlike some cities, such as Athens, whose urban sprawl took on a life of its own, Hippodamos envisioned a city planned on social order that would reflect and serve the needs of its citizens. The town occupies the southeastern slope of the Zalongo Mountains and is encircled by a polygonal wall that acted as a fortress.

Farther up the road is a monastery where locals took refuge when the region was attacked by forces of the Ali Pasha, an Ottoman ruler who dominated this entire region during the late 18th and early 19th centuries. Known as the Lion of Ioannina, after the main city in the region, he was immortalized in a poem by Lord Byron:

> *I talk not of mercy, I talk not of fear,*
> *He neither must know who would serve the Vizier:*
> *Since the days of our prophet the Crescent ne'er saw*
> *A chief ever glorious like Ali Pashaw.*

But what sets this ancient site apart from many others like it across Greece is a more modern event that occurred, not in past millennia, but in the past century. This event is known by the deceptively pleasing title *Horos tou Zalongou*, or Dance of Zalongo. During the early 18th century, the people of the region, known as the Souliot, grew tired of living under Ottoman rule. The Souliot men bravely fought against their oppressors, but could not overcome the might of the Ali Pasha's forces. As the wives, mothers, and sisters of these men watched their loved ones fall to the Lion of Ioannina's domination, they did not sit back and submit to whatever fate awaited them. In an eerily similar vein to the brave Jewish zealots who lived atop Masada and defied the Roman Empire in a shocking act, the women of Zalonga followed the same unfathomable path some two millennia later.

Escaping to the top of the mountain, they soon realized they faced the edge of a cliff, from which there was no other retreat. Legend has it that the women clasped hands at the verge of the mountainside, and, aware of the horrific fate that they would be taken into slavery, took their own destiny into hand and began to dance in a circle. Witnesses recall the awful spectacle that unfurled when each woman reached the edge of the cliff. First mothers threw their children off the edge, and then continuing this epic, sacred dance of a woman's ultimate sacrifice and defiance, waited their turn to hurl themselves to their own deaths on the rocks far below.

At the edge of this cliff today stands a monument dedicated to the inconceivable act of these brave women. Seen from a distance, the snow white, towering abstract figures clasp hands, recalling the dance of life itself, and not the death they chose. Their connected arms and strong upright profiles reach into the cerulean, cloudless sky as a testament to the ultimate choice of freedom.

Visitors today can walk along the precipice and imagine the dance of these brave women. The cliffs are fenced off, and the entire region feels lost in time and set apart from the rest of Greece, as if an important history is forgotten. Greece is many things: beaches, temples, sage-covered mountainsides, but its sacred spaces are not limited to temples with ivory columns and expansive theaters where the echo of ancient plays whisper in the breeze. Some sacred spaces are more modern, and hold more sadness; yet Greece has always honored the presence of both Apollonian and Dionysian sensibilities.

If you travel to this hidden region of Greece, make sure to take a moment as you stand in awe of this towering monument. Step into the wide pavilion-like space nearby, imagine you are holding hands, and recall the Dance of Zalongo, the sacred nature of this holy ground, and the ultimate sacrifice made by these fiercely proud and defiant women.

Farewell poor world,

Farewell sweet life,

and you,
my poor country,

Farewell for ever

Farewell springs.

Valleys, mountains and hills

Farewell springs.

And you, women of Souli

The fish cannot live on the land

Nor the flower on the sand

And the women of Souli

Cannot live without freedom

Farewell springs.
The women of Souli

Have not only learnt how to survive

They also know how to die

Not to tolerate slavery

Farewell springs.

III

The Blessed Virgin
Mary, Saints, Sinners,
and Mysterious Places
of Healing

42 The Snakes of Kefalonia

OF HEALING SERPENTS AND MUMMIFIED SAINTS

"Snakes," the locals whispered. "They come out of the ground only for a few days in August."

As an archaeologist working on the Ionian island of Ithaka, I had heard strange stories of people being cured from illnesses on the neighboring island of Kefalonia, a large and foreboding mass of land just to the west. Every August, locals told me, snakes crawled out of the ground into a small mountain church, and these serpents healed people from epilepsy, Parkinson's disease, and mental illnesses.

Healing with snakes? As a Catholic girl I had heard only of Lourdes, the shrine in France where people went in hopes of healing, bringing home with them little bottles of holy water. Yet this sounded more like a southern Baptist revival than something I'd find within the deeply conservative and devout Greek Orthodox Church.

I learned that the story of the snakes dated back to 1705. When pirates attacked a monastery in the tiny mountain village of Markopoulo at the southern tip of Kefalonia, the nuns prayed to the Virgin Mary and were transformed into snakes to avoid being captured. In the centuries since, villagers began to notice hundreds of small snakes emerging from the earth around August 15th, one of the most holy days in the Orthodox calendar, the Assumption of the Virgin Mary. The creatures would slither into the village church, eventually crawling across a painted icon of the BVM. Curious locals began to handle the snakes and soon news of miraculous cures spread, compelling pilgrims from around the world to flock to this Greek version of Lourdes.

Decades passed, until one late summer when I finally made my way to this mysterious place I had heard so much about. The night of August 15th, I drove up a dark mountain road to Markopoulo. My guide, Yanni, was eager to show me the festival. "Follow me," he said, warning, "it gets very dark up here at night and it's difficult to see." After parking the car at the edge of steep cliff, the coastline twinkling in the darkness far below, we followed a throng of locals up the dirt road to the village square. There, beneath strings of tiny white lights, a huge crowd spilled into the modest plaza; I watched as a line of pilgrims zigzagged down from a steep mountain path and gathered outside the church doors. Curiously, a pair of attractive blond policewomen flanked the entrance. When I asked about them, Yanni snickered, "On the night of the festival, they always put the pretty ones out in front."

Gazing through the doorway, I caught a glimpse of chandeliers, gold-filigreed wall paintings and flickering candles, casting an amber glow onto the crowd. Stepping inside, I joined fellow congregants as they filed down the aisle and circled around a table stacked with offerings of elaborately braided breads. Up on a podium, I watched as a bishop in the traditional black stovepipe miter, a large crucifix dangling heavily around his neck, extended his arms out towards the crowd, a staff in each hand. Upon closer inspection, I gasped as one of the staffs moved; in his left fist, a snake bobbed and undulated, mesmerizing the crowd.

For a moment, the sea of bodies parted and I could see the famous icon of the BVM, clutching the child Jesus. Arrayed in a blood red vestment over her iconic azure gown, the portrait was rimmed with a border of pink, white, and red roses. A pair of snakes, their bodies intertwined, lay draped across her crimson robes.

Stepping outside, the cool air was a refreshing relief. Another small crowd gathered around a man who stood in the middle of a courtyard. People pressed inwards to get closer, and I watched as he draped a snake over their heads, touching it to different body parts.

"Whatever part of your body you need healed, the snakes are put there," Yanni told me. A young girl, shoved forward by her mother, stood motionless, eyes wide and unblinking. The man laid the snake on her scalp and for a moment it languished, like a thick lock of hair, draped against her cheek.

"Don't worry," Yanni whispered in my ear as the old man lifted his hands to me. "It won't hurt you." The small, dark creature writhed anxiously between the folds of his aging, leathered palms. Gingerly, I reached for it with my fingers. No sooner than I was able to feel the coolness of its skin, a woman pushed in front of me. The gnarled hands clasping the reptile were absorbed back into the crowd and just as the throng closed around it I could see the snake's tongue flicker, an infinitesimal red fork in the night air.

The next day I followed Yanni over a mountain to another village. This time the source of healing was not from snakes, but from the 500-year-old mummified remains of the island's patron saint. Tucked into the bosom of the Omala Valley lay the church of Saint Gerasimos. Rising off the plain and dwarfing the surrounding monastery, its pale yellow walls and dromedary-humped dome reflected the midday sun in muted tones. I passed through a makeshift bazaar of *souvlaki* and *loukoumades* vendors, the smell of grilled lamb and fried doughnuts saturating the hot afternoon air.

In front of the church a cabal of priests, their robes inflating in the sluggish air like an infant's chest, huddled around a silver coffin; lifting the handles, they carried it like a litter towards a waiting throng. Suddenly, an onslaught of vertigo appeared to overcome the masses. Like a wave of cascading dominos starting to fall, hundreds of men, women, and children silently dropped to their knees and settled on the earth, heads in laps lying end to end, looking up towards the heavens.

Several men ran in advance of the priests, lifting errant arms and legs and braiding the line of people tightly together to give the narrow coffin ample room to pass over. The Bishop glided by next, his brocaded robes ballooning in the breeze like a blowfish. He lifted his golden staff, gesturing and pontificating in recognition of the multitude gathered on the sides of the road hoping to view the spectacle. Carefully, the priests started to pass the coffin over the line of people.

This motley collection of pilgrims—widows swathed in black, blond Scandinavian girls in halter tops, and bearded men in biker gear—was asking for healing, hope, or perhaps, redemption. For a moment, I questioned whether I should put my camera away and lie down too, but I realized, after being shoved back and forth by anxious hands, I didn't know what to ask for. The line of worshippers eventually became too wide for the litter and the priests abandoned their efforts, taking the casket to a clearing in the road and hurrying down towards the end of the processional route.

Years later, I'm not sure what kind of healing I expected to observe, thanks to snakes or the bones of a long dead saint. Yet after seeing the beatific expressions on the faces of the faithful, perhaps the fact that these elaborate rituals bring a sense of comfort to those who suffer is wonder enough. Even for those who don't believe in miracles, I would still recommend a visit to this remote Ionian island, just for the sheer beauty and history of this mysterious landscape. And if you happen to come around the late summer

holy day of the Virgin Mary and find your way up a remote mountain road to the village of Markopoulo, you can witness firsthand
the elaborate, unconventional, and sometimes inexplicable rituals
of those who do.

43 Tinos

CRAWLING ON HANDS AND KNEES
TO KISS A MYSTERIOUS ICON

Where in the world would women crawl on their hands and knees a quarter of a mile uphill to kiss an icon? There is such a place: the island of Tinos, which some call the holiest of Greek islands. As you arrive at the port, you will notice a red carpet that starts at the edge of the water and rises up a hill topped by a massive white confection of a church. Why the red carpet? It's not for VIP guests or movie stars. No—this carpet has a highly unusual purpose and destination: this is a carpet that women traverse to become pregnant.

All year round, but particularly on August 15, the Feast of the Assumption of the Virgin Mary, you can witness this incredible spectacle. One by one, women disembark from ferryboats and crawl, literally, on their hands and knees, a quarter of a mile uphill to the Panagia Evangelistria Church. Once they arrive, they wait their turn to kiss the holy icon, believed to be imbued with supernatural powers that will allow them to conceive.

The history of the icon dates to 1822. According to the legend, the Virgin Mary appeared to Sister Pelagia, a local nun from the Monastery of Kechrovouniou, instructing her to locate a buried painting with supernatural powers. Pelagia ignored the request on several occasions, fearing it was only her imagination, but she eventually sought help from a local bishop, who encouraged her to follow her vision. Excavations began and a 4th-century church dedicated to the Virgin Mary was discovered, along with an ancient well. Locals saw the location as sacred and began building a church on the very site; during the construction, the portrait of a kneeling BVM was uncovered. Soon inexplicable cures began to be attributed to the church and its icon, and as word got out, thousands began flocking to the church from around the world, hoping for healing or a miraculous pregnancy.

If you're not interested in making the long uphill crawl to visit the church, you can walk up the main road, which leads from the harbor to the top of the hill. Part of the street, covered in a rubberized strip, is dedicated for those who wish to make the journey on hands and knees, and even has a ribbon of lighting for nighttime use! Cars and motorcycles whiz past the crawling penitents as they labor up the hill, their backpacks and purses slung over their shoulders. Some choose to wear kneepads, some don't, but I would guess the BVM isn't going to discriminate!

The road spills into a large piazza of black and white pebbles in a series of geometric designs, bisected by the strip of red carpet. The final approach is up a series of stairs to the church, a lacy, white-hot layer cake of arched doorways and roofline studded with crucifixes etched against an impossibly blue sky. People pack into the interior, punctuated with black and white checkered floors and brass censers hung from barrel-vaulted ceilings. If you want to wait in line, the silver-framed icon is kept in a glass box and is covered with gold ornaments and votives, making it difficult to see the actual image.

Nearby the iconostasis is laden with *tamata*: images of feet, hands, eyes, arms, and even houses and cars, hammered into silver cards, which are left by worshippers asking for healing or other blessings. Several people have claimed miraculous cures from the icon and have left offerings, such as a Greek-American man who regained his sight and left the church a miniature orange tree carved of silver and gold. A holy spring at the site, with the improbable name of Zoodochos Pigi, is supposedly instilled with healing powers as well.

Tinos, like many of the islands in the Cycladic chain, is awash with snow-white cubist buildings, eternally gray rock and clutches of pine and cypress punctuating a landscape that is otherwise enfolded and caressed by an endlessly cerulean, undelineated sea. Once you've visited the church of the Panagia, there are many other delights that await you.

First settled by Ionians, Tinos became known in the 4th century B.C. for its sanctuary of the god Poseidon and his wife, Amphitrite, located near Kionia. Often described as a female personification of the sea, Amphitrite is the daughter of Nereus and Doris and one of fifty sister Nereids, or ocean spirits. As often occurs in mythological romances, Poseidon wooed Amphitrite but she initially refused his advances. After sending a dolphin to retrieve her, Poseidon rewarded the dolphin by making him a constellation, and the couple went on to have two children, a son, Triton, and a daughter, Rhode. The island's small archaeological museum, located next to the church, displays sculptures of Nereids and dolphins that were found at the sanctuary of Poseidon and Amphitrite.

Because it is so small, Tinos is easy to explore in a day. If you haven't had enough of a spiritual experience, head north of Tinos's main town and make a stop at the 12th-century walled Monastery of Kechrovouniou, one of the largest convents in Greece. This is where Pelagia had her visions of the BVM, and you can visit the actual cell and—not for the faint of heart—the chest where her embalmed head is kept!

One of Tinos's unique features is its *peristerionas*, or dovecotes. A drive through the interior villages of the island, peppered around the heights of Mount Tsiknia, will reveal about 1,300 of these elaborately decorated structures. All of them have two stories; the lower floor serving as a storage area and the upper level housing the doves. The exterior is often covered in ornate triangular and circular latticed designs and topped with stylized winged finials or faux doves.

Before heading back to the port, make a stop at Pyrgos, a little town in the northwest of the island, to see the area's unique green-veined marble. The stonework is considered among the finest in the islands and you can see evidence of the exceptional green marble in the church of Panagia Evangelistria.

Tiny and not overly populated, Tinos is essentially a spiritual destination, with more than 800 churches dotting the island. For those wishing to see another side of Greece, away from the nude beaches and crowded ruins, Tinos is a superb choice. Curiously enough, it can be reached for a day trip from one of Greece's most popular tourist destinations, Mykonos. In a country that appreciates opposing sensibilities, the Dionysian nature of the Mykonos experience is splendidly matched by the Apollonian tranquility of Tinos and its placid shores.

❧

44 *Rhodes*

JACQUELINE BISSET, RHODE THE OCEANID, AND A BLEEDING ICON OF THE BVM

Moonlight reflects off the water like molten pearls, and Jacqueline Bisset in her prime emerges from the sea to the slack-jawed astonishment of Kenneth Branagh in his first major film role. Most of you probably haven't seen the movie *High Season*, which was filmed on Rhodes, but if you have a chance to grab a copy, do. Seeing Bisset and Branagh's sexy tryst unfold against the stark beauty of this diamond-shaped island fringed with beaches, a central spine of peaks, and valleys studded with fig, pistachio, myrtle, and pear, is almost as good as an actual trip to this magical and historic place.

Floating serenely off the Turkish coastline, Rhodes lies within a stone's throw of Asia. I first visited Rhodes during the Thanksgiving holiday of my college junior year in Greece. Calling home, listening to the sounds of my family gathering around the table, I considered the curious coincidence of being so far away on this exotic soil, seeing Turkey and imagining my family feasting on the namesake bird, resting on its platter on my grandmother's Irish linen tablecloth.

The island is named after the Oceanid nymph Rhode. Hesiod, the Greek poet who lived in the 8th and 7th centuries B.C., tells us that Rhode is the eldest daughter of Tethys and Oceanus, who married the sun god Helios and became the protector goddess of the island, around which an important cult grew. Her name derives from the native island pink hibiscus that resembles a rose, from the Greek *rodon*. Mythology can get quite convoluted, and Rhode was also worshipped by the names of Leucothea, and more typically Halia, after her mother who threw herself into the sea. The towns of Lindos, Ialysos, and Kamiros are named after the daughters of Danoas, Linda, Ialysa, and Kamira, who died on the island and where their father founded a sanctuary to Athena.

✳ www.visitgreece.gr/en/greek_islands/dodecanese/rhodes

The largest island in the Dodecanese chain, Rhodes lies along major Mediterranean sea routes at the crossroads between Greece and the Middle East. Its history is a laundry list of conquerors, adventurers, and crusaders. The *Colossus of Rhodes,* a massive sculpture representing the sun god Helios, and one of the seven wonders of the ancient world, was erected over the harbor. Completed in 282 B.C., the statue took twelve years to construct and loomed over ships coming into port until its collapse into the sea, due to a cataclysmic earthquake that took place in 226 B.C.

In the early 14th century, the island was sold to the Knights of St. John and a medieval fortification and walls were erected in the port town. This crusader castle, which has been expanded and modernized over the centuries, still stands today and visitors can explore the numerous sections that were once used as a hospital, a church, knights' quarters, a synagogue, and market.

While most visitors to Rhodes arrive at the port town, they cannot miss the dizzying, lyrical beauty of Lindos, located on the opposite side of the island. Rising almost a sheer four hundred feet above the village is the soaring acropolis of Lindos, a spectacular thrust of rock that rises like a bishop's miter, towering imperiously over the gleaming white houses cluttered around its base. A cluster of ancient VIPs, including Alexander the Great and Helen of Troy, supposedly passed through this sacred site, atop which stands the temple of Lindian Athena. A portion of the 4th-century B.C. temple remains, its lyrical columns loom impassively, etched against an amethyst line where sky dissolves into sea. Ruins of 3rd- and 2nd-century-B.C. stoa, or marketplaces, dot the site as do the remains of a 13th-century church dedicated to St. John.

Saint Paul came to preach here, and the generous harbor expanding below the acropolis is named for him. Exploring Lindos town is easy, as traffic is banned, making an afternoon of wending your way along the narrow cobblestoned streets past lace sellers and bougainvillea-fringed pastel doorways a decadent treat. Have your camera ready, as many of the traditional houses, called *archontika*, have elaborate carvings in the stonework of ship's chains, and are built around intricately pebbled mosaic designed courtyards.

Sunbathing on your agenda? Plan to spend the day at Tsampika. This town with its wide sandy beach is a welcome change from Greece's largely pebbled shores; and if you get tired of sunbathing you can explore the Byzantine monastery atop an almost 1,000 foot peak. A legend states that an infertile couple found an 11th-century icon here and later conceived a child. Today, women wanting a baby will walk to the peak barefooted to pray to the Virgin and pledge that the child will be named Tsampika or Tsampikos, names found only in the Dodecanese chain of islands.

If you rent a car, circuit the island and wind your way up to Moni Skiadi, a monastery that houses a sacred icon of the BVM. When a heretic in the 15th century stabbed the image, it supposedly bled, leaving a bloody stain still visible today. The icon is carried from village to village during the Easter holy days, and finds its way to the island of Chalki, where it stays for a month every year.

On your way back to Rhodes town, make a stop at Skala Kameriou. Within site of the Turkish coastline, this charming fishing village makes for a wonderful lunch destination and place to sample the local dishes; don't miss the cyclamen leaves with a meat stuffing, a lush apricot paste called *kaysia*, and *pitaroudia*, chick pea fritters. Rhodian cuisine evokes its Eastern influence with hints of cinnamon and cumin, used in *karavoli giachnistoi*, snails simmered with onion, olive oil, tomato, and bay leaf. For the sweet tooth, the Rhodian pastries rule: *melekouni*, a local dessert made with sesame, almonds, honey, and herbs, and *mochopougkia*, a confection made from walnuts, almonds, rosewater, and grated nutmeg.

The evening isn't complete until you order a glass of *souma*, a heady and unique aperitif made from figs, but do as the locals do: make sure you eat something with it. Like ouzo, *souma*'s high alcohol content packs a punch, so no driving. Best to stay put, watch the sun sink into the lavender bosom of Asia and if you are lucky, the moonrise over the soaring 2,600-foot peak of Profitis Ilias, along the central spine of the island. While you're at it, lift your glass of *souma* and make a toast to Jacqueline and Kenneth for putting this dramatic, verdant, and lushly historic island on the map. While their cinematic romp may be memorable, there's no debating the truth: Rhodes is the film's undeniable star.

❧

45 The Athenian Agora

FOREIGNER, SLUT, INTELLECTUAL:
ASPASIA OF MILETUS

When Paul MacKendrick wrote the book *The Greek Stones Speak*, I'm
not sure if he had in mind a male or female doing the talking.
Many visitors pass through the vast space beneath the Acropolis hill
on their way to see the Parthenon, barely glimpsing at the expanse
of treasures that tell a story of Athenian history. This is the birthplace of democracy as well as a sacred shrine, and is shared by two
significant buildings representing each. The Stoa of Attalos was
basically a two-story shopping mall that was the commercial heart
of Athens from its erection by King Attalos of Pergamum in 150
B.C. until its destruction by the Herulians in 267 A.D. The modern
reconstruction, done by the American School of Classical Studies
in the mid 1950s, which accentuates the building's mesmerizingly
dense colonnade, is thanks to a grant by John D. Rockefeller, and
the building now serves as the Museum of the Agora.

The Theseum, built just prior to the Parthenon in 450 B.C.,
is possibly the world's best-preserved temple. It is unclear whether
the temple was dedicated to Theseus or to the god Hephaestus, the
smith-god, as well as the goddess Athena as patron of the arts; yet
its classical Doric construction of 13 x 6 columns is actually believed
to showcase sculptures depicting the exploits of Heracles. It's hard

to imagine, seeing tourists wandering through this dusty plaza studded with shrines and statues of writhing male figures, that this was a bustling center of activity more than two thousands years ago. Yet amidst these monuments to male gods and rulers, women also lived their day-to-day lives.

Athenian women could not vote, and those of the upper class were expected to stay home, bear and raise children. However, there is evidence that some females in antiquity lived lives outside the home. When it comes to the Athenian Agora, if you listen carefully, there are plenty of ancient women's voices to be heard; you can sense them echoing in the majestic pines that ring the site and imagine their figures passing by the towering façade of the Theseum, their flowing white *himatia* starkly contrasted against the original dazzling red and blue paint that would have decorated its sculptural panels.

Susan Rotroff, co-author with Robert Lamberton of *Women in the Athenian Agora*, explains the varied roles women held in this ancient space and how they changed through the ages. Describing a vase depicting women fetching water during the Archaic period of Athens, ca. 530 B.C., before the establishment of Athenian democracy in 508 B.C. she notes, "The women of these privileged families appear to have enjoyed great freedom and greater access to public space than the women of 5th century Athens, with its egalitarian ideology." During the classical period of the following century, women from wealthy homes were more likely to stay home, instead sending slave girls to the market to do the shopping. However, by the 4th century the Agora is described by sources as a place where women can purchase household goods.

Some sightings of women in the Agora were more dramatic than others. Sarah Pomeroy, author of *Goddesses, Whores, Wives, and Slaves*, tells the story of an Athenian named Alcibiades, whose wife, Hipparete, walked out and sought a divorce after he consorted with a prostitute in their house. Not willing to part with her large dowry, he chased her down as she approached the archon to register her divorce, and carried her bodily back home through the Agora, daring anyone to defy him.

Rotroff states that ancient writers such as the playwright Aristophanes cite public roles for women in the Agora, including innkeepers and merchants. Ancient sources tell us that certain religious festivals—specifically those devoted to female deities such as Athena—could only be performed by women. Girls also took part in the ceremonies; some were entrusted with carrying sacred objects between the Acropolis and the agora, others ground the grain that was used to prepare the honey cakes used in the festivals. The elite of young Athenian girls would parade through the agora carrying a basket on their heads, called a *kanoun*, containing a knife and barley that was used for sacrifices in sacred Greek religious practices. These young women, usually in their early teens, formed this procession annually in honor of Athena and in anticipation of marriage. Other young women, serving as priestesses of Athena, carried water jars, umbrellas, and other items.

As Rotroff states, "Women of all classes could also be seen making offerings at the small shrines that dotted the Agora," and the remains of perfume jars, loom weights, and infant feeders have been found. While it is thought that most women of means stayed at home where their husbands wanted them, and the majority of shoppers in the agora were men and slave girls, not all the women were nameless or invisible, and one in particular stands out.

Foreigner, slut, intellectual. A woman accused of starting a war, gifted with words and a "rare political wisdom." All of these have been used to describe Aspasia of Miletus. Born to a wealthy family in modern-day Turkey, Aspasia moved to Athens around 450 B.C. Outsiders were known as *metics*, resident aliens who, unlike Athenian citizens, did not share the same rights and had to pay

additional taxes. But something about Aspasia came to the attention of the ruler of the city, Pericles. Known as an accomplished
courtesan and educated in the fine art of conversation, she supposedly caught his eye at a party. Smitten with this lovely foreigner,
Pericles became her lover and divorced his wife. He was roundly
criticized for lavishing his attention on her, but Aspasia took the
brunt of the attack, being called a "dog-eyed whore" and dispar-
aged for her sexual charm. It seems not much has changed in more
than two thousand years. As with today's politicians and their scandalous liaisons with beautiful young women, little did Aspasia know
she was ahead of her time.

Ultimately she gave birth to a son, and a fierce debate ensued
over who was allowed the status of citizen. As N. S. Gill states, "That
she chose to enter into a relationship with the Athenian leader
Pericles put her, too, in a position of power, but also a position
particularly vulnerable to criticism." The Periclean citizenship
law, passed in 451/450 B.C. stated that no children born to a male
citizen and foreign-born woman could be a citizen of Athens.
Aspasia's role in society became that of a concubine. Yet Socrates
supposedly sought out her intellectual prowess and she became
known as a person to consult about public speaking.

For a woman who started off from a family of means and came
to be called a whore, she lived a big life. A foreigner who caught the
eye of a powerful leader and became influential in her own right,
she never was able to rise up in Athenian society. If the normal
aspiration for Athenian women was to bear legitimate children,
Aspasia was unable to fulfill this responsibility, and her son was
viewed as a bastard.

Regardless of how she was viewed by others, she persevered. She
raised her son, engaged in the political and intellectual discus-
sions of the day with the best minds. Aspasia's status as *metic*, as
painful as it was at times, also gave her freedom. Liberated from

the constraints of Athenian women, she was able to engage in a public life, as chastised as she was. When the intellectual elite came to hear her speak, they often brought their wives along. Where Aspasia endured the enmity of many—she was even accused by the playwright Aristophanes of starting the Peloponnesian War, and was held responsible for the influx of prostitutes into Athens—her potential influence on the lives of other women who came into contact with her can only be imagined.

Equally maligned and revered, Aspasia's life is a testament to any modern trailblazer fighting for women's equal rights. Perhaps, thanks to her, the women's movement started, not in the 1960s, but more than two thousand years ago. On any future visit to the Athenian Agora may you have a vision of her, seated on an ancient stone wall under a tree, mesmerizing her audience with her intellect, wit, and charm.

※

46 *Agia Marina Theseiou*

SLIDING DOWN A ROCK FOR PREGNANCY

Why would women slide down a sheer face of sloping rock in hopes of becoming pregnant? Or bring their children to touch a rock to bring them health? That's exactly what women still did, until the late 19th century, on an enormous outcropping of stone near the ancient agora of Athens. But what now stands as a church near this rocky slide was once an ancient shrine to a fertility goddess.

The late, great mythologist Joseph Campbell spent his career writing about the belief systems of earlier cultures that lived close to the earth and were assimilated into the Judeo-Christian system. To my knowledge, he never wrote about a small church sitting at the edge of the Agora in Athens, but if he had known about it, he would have likely enjoyed the story of how a small cavern in a rocky outcropping near the Temple of Theseus morphed into one of the city's major basilicas, and has been a site of worship for women for more than 2,000 years.

The church of Agia Marina Thesiou is named for both Saint Marina and its proximity to the temple of Theseus, a majestic sanctuary sitting in the corner of the Agora, beneath the Parthenon, curiously also known as the temple of Hephaestus—even archaeologists and philologists don't always agree on place names! The church itself, located in the neighborhood known as Theseiou, is relatively modern. Built in 1922, this impressive structure stands just beneath another large building that looms above on the Hill of the Pnyx, the scientific observatory of Athens. Encrusted with conifers and sitting on one of the huge marble outcroppings that rise above the plain of Athens, the first thing you notice about the church is its multiple terracotta domes and egg-white nave.

Carved into the hillside of the Hill of the Nymphs is a sacred shrine which classicist Gerald Lalonde refers to as an "early cave-church." Lalonde also states that this site, "is the only significant institution now known to have functioned on this spur since antiquity when the site was occupied by a shrine of Zeus." Until the 19th century, the church of Agia Marina was actually in a small cave in this rock, and the modern church has modified and built around what is essentially a grotto used for an ancient cult. According to the archaeologist and architect John Travlos, the church site was originally built on an ancient cistern, and the structure itself is in fact built directly into the rocky face of this massive hill. Caves are traditionally places where the divine feminine was worshipped, so one can see why this remarkable natural outcropping of rock, now so muted into the surrounding modern landscape of buildings, railroad tracks, and streets, was at one time an area that would have been highly noticeable and perhaps revered as a place of power.

Agia Marina, as many of her saintly sisters, had a difficult start in life, which got progressively more dreadful as time went on. Born in what is now southern Turkey in the 3rd century B.C., her mother died shortly after giving birth. Her pagan father gave over her care to a Christian nurse who taught her about her faith. When Marina came to embrace this new way of life, her father proceeded to disown her.

As with many tales of powerful men attracted to young and innocent women, Marina's tale also takes on a Persephone-like flavor. Marina caught the attention of a powerful governor who wished to marry her. After rejecting his proposal, explaining that she had devoted her life to Christ, she was subjected to an unending list of atrocities—beatings, stabbings, and being burned with boiling water—but her faith healed her from each attack. The ultimate test was being sent a demon while she was imprisoned. The tale tells that Christ appeared and helped her to beat the demon with a hammer, after which a great light appeared, illuminating the entire structure. Marina was once again healed from her wounds, but the insane governor ordered her to be killed once and for all, and she was beheaded at age fifteen in 305 A.D. Her right arm, encased in a golden sleeve inside a silver casket, is at Mount Athos, a monastery in northern Greece. Strangely, the relic of this remarkable woman is in the hands of a place where only men can go.

The church has a typical cruciform plan and is filled with murals depicting the life of the saint. Golden domes are painted with images of Christ and the Virgin, and the interior is filled with richly carved wooden benches and pulpit, as well as intricately patterned mosaic flooring. An enormous chandelier is suspended from the soaring ceiling, cascading a shimmering glow onto gold encrusted icons. But the most interesting feature is the most natural and simple element: a cave/chapel within the church, carved directly into the rock and dating to the 11th and 12th centuries.

Today Saint Marina is still petitioned to help women become pregnant and safely deliver their children. An old custom of leaving clothing behind at the church and exchanging it for other garments has likely roots in a smallpox outbreak, when children were brought in to heal and their clothing was taken and disposed of. Modern pilgrims who leave clothing behind return to collect it after a period of time, believing it to be sanctified by the Saint's powers and able to deliver a cure.

While Lalonde concludes, "there was no neat chorological cleavage between paganism and Christianity that would have facilitated the contact and syncretism of pagan and Christian religion," this area near the ancient agora is clearly still a place of power. This rocky corner perhaps is evidence of how that power has merely gone underground, managing to manifest in yet another form. Take a moment to ponder the energy of this place: have a seat on the ancient rock and listen to the bees, the sound of the wind whispering through the lacy pines and watch the light play on the ancient stones.

47 Mikri Mitropoli Church and the Metropolitan Cathedral

ELEITHYIA, SAINT FILOTHEI, AND THE VIRGIN MARY WHO ANSWERS PRAYERS QUICKLY

Do you want prayers answered quickly? Looking for a goddess to call on when it's time to go into labor? Then have I got a church for you!

One of the things I love about Athens is that every so often you come across a tiny church, shoehorned between a bakery and an apartment building. Some of them, such as the tiny Panagia Kapnikarea, literally sit in the middle of a busy pedestrian walkway. Yet the Panagia Gorgoepikoos is an especially big name for a miniscule church. Let me simplify things by saying this means "The Virgin Mary Who Answers Prayers Quickly." Built in the late 12th or early 13th centuries, the church, which used to be the cathedral of Athens, sits directly on top of another ancient site: a temple dedicated to Eileithyia, the goddess who protects pregnant women and women in childbirth.

Eileithyia's name means to "relieve" or "she who comes to aid." She is often depicted with her arms in the air as if to bring the newborn child into the light, and her Roman counterpart is named Lucina, or "light bringer." It is believed that she was born in the town of Amnisos, Crete, which is the root of the word amniotic. Although there are no visible remains, the ancient traveler

Pausanias tells us more about Eileithyia and her temple in his 2nd-century-A.D. travelogue *Description of Greece*:

> *Near the Prytaneion [or Town Hall of Athens] is a temple of Eileithyia,*
> *who they say came from the Hyperboreans to Delos and helped Leto in her*
> *labour; and from Delos the name spread to other peoples. The Delians*
> *sacrifice to Eileithyia and sing a hymn of Olen. But the Kretans suppose*
> *that Eileithyia was born at Amnisos in the Knossian territory [in Krete],*
> *and that Hera was her mother. Only among the Athenians are the wooden*
> *figures of Eileithyia draped to the feet. The women told me that two are*
> *Kretan, being offerings of Phaidra [daughter of the mythical King Minos of*
> *Krete], and that the third, which is the oldest, Erysikhthon [an early king of*
> *Athens] brought from Delos.*

It is said that the Empress Eirene, wife of Constantine, first founded this tiny, toy-like church in 787 atop the remains of the ancient temple, but it was destroyed and rebuilt in the following centuries, and many of the original pieces are still visible in the current building. Yet what Panagia Gorgoepikoos (also known as Mikri Mitropoli, or "little Metropolitan,") lacks in grandeur, it makes up for in charm. A series of friezes adorn the exterior walls, including a pre-Christian Panathenaic depiction, which was carved over in the Christian era with a Maltese cross. Other rich sculptures have been added and reused from other structures in an original recycling effort. Called a "puzzle piece" of reconstruction, approximately one hundred marble and limestone slabs date to a period of more than 1,500 years, and are inscribed with symbols and ornaments from ancient Greece, Rome, Persia, and Mesopotamia, as well as Jewish, Coptic, Catholic, and Islamic imagery.

What's curious about this microscopic church is that it sits amidst a huge city plaza in the shadow of another, much larger church: the main Cathedral of Athens. Known as the big Metropolitan

Cathedral, this building was erected between 1842 and 1862. After Athens became the capital of Greece in 1834, the city needed a new official cathedral where important ceremonies such as deaths of state officials and marriages could be performed. The whole process took more than twenty years, employing three different architects, and the remains of more than seventy-two churches were destroyed to use their marble to build the cathedral's majestic structure.

Whereas Mikri Mitropoli has both the Virgin answering prayers quickly and a goddess dedicated to mothers-to-be, Big Mitropoli has its own special woman. The tomb of Saint Filothei is located inside the Cathedral. Filothei's life is marked by the struggle of many female saints—protecting the rights and safety of women against the brutality of men, and eventually losing her life for what she believed in. Born to well-to-do parents in Athens, Filothei's mother, convinced she was barren, claims to have seen a light enter her womb, only to learn she was pregnant with her daughter, whom she named Revoula.

After capturing the attention of prominent citizens at the tender age of twelve, Revoula was forced into marriage with an abusive husband. After his death, she remained a widow and when her parents died she took up the life of monasticism. After building a monastery she took the name Filothei, which means "love of God" and spent her life rescuing women who had been taken into prostitution by the Turks. She faced beheading and narrowly escaped death only after Christians intervened and saved her from the Ali Pasha's verdict. With her wealthy inheritance she spent the rest of her life building shelters, monasteries, and poor houses all over Greece and became known as "Lady Teacher" by those who loved her. Filothei died in 1589 and her bones are encased in a silver reliquary in the Cathedral.

If you step inside the main cathedral you can admire the magnificent soaring central narthex, with the sky blue, gold-starred cupola over the altar. Richly decorated images of saints float above the faithful, as do soaring arches supported by diorite columns. An extravagant crystal chandelier hovers above the narthex and reflects the shimmering gold icons and brilliance of candles that light the holy sanctuary. Be sure to pay your respects to Filothei. A casket sits to the side encased in glass, and its elaborate nature seems less in keeping with her life than a small icon to the saint that sits nearby. Recalling her life of devotion and humility, it is the simplicity of the latter that best attests to this remarkable woman's life.

48 *Agia Irini Square*

THE CHURCH OF SAINT IRENE

Irene is from the word *eirini*, which means peace in Greek. It may seem a little implausible that a square located in downtown Athens would have this name, yet smack dab in the middle of this chaotic city of rich contrasts—timeless marbles alongside graffitied storefronts, stern-faced and black-clad widows looking on, perplexed, at a teeming youth culture—you will find the Apollonian amidst the Dionsyian. These contrasting elements cross paths at Agia Irini Square, at which the very center is the Church of Saint Irene.

Inside, pious housewives in sweater sets take a break from their shopping to light candles. Outside, lanky youths in hipster pants, multiple piercings, and tattoos gather in the cool cafés that line the square. Cliques of young students called *pareias* cluster around tables under the trees, smoking and sipping thick frappes, while a muted techno beat wafts out into the air, thick with a cocktail of incense, tobacco and coffee.

The Church of Saint Irene, or Agia Irini as it is known in Greek, was originally a medieval structure that was damaged in the Greek War of Independence in 1847. It was rebuilt in 1850 and is one of the largest churches in Athens. Enter through the paneled wooden doors and you are greeted with a sumptuous patterned floor of black and white mosaic. A row of golden fluted pillars line the narrow nave, topped with elaborated decorated archways supporting a screened gallery level above. Light filters in from the clerestory level, softly igniting golden stars in a pair of sky-blue painted domes that hover over a shimmering golden altar. Just in front, between the altar and the congregation, stands a large wooden screen known as an iconostasis, jammed with gold and silver *tamata*—small metal cards imprinted with images of hearts, ears, and other body parts used to petition God for healing, including one engraved with the word *efharisto*—"thank you" in Greek.

But what really catches the eye stands towards the entrance to the church: two mini altars side-by-side flanking the center aisle. Heavily embossed and gilded, they are topped with sky-blue half domes and a pair of slender pillars framing a painted icon. A widow dressed in black kneels in front of the left altar, and when she stands to leave, you see she was praying to a portrait of Saint Irene. A crown of leaves and flowers encircles the saint's head and she holds a single bloom in her left hand. Curiously, her right hand is not painted, but instead is inlaid with silver.

Who is Saint Irene? The story begins with a young girl born into a non-religious family who embraces Christianity. After she breaks all her father's idols he orders her to be trampled by horses. Instead of killing her, one of the horses rears up and kills her father instead, whom Irene miraculously brings back to life. Understandably, her father converts immediately! Irene spends the rest of her life devoting her life to God and performing miracles. One of the churches dedicated to Irene is on the iconic island of Santorini (which means "Saint Irene"), and her ancestor was the Greek goddess Eirini. Said to be the daughter of Zeus and Themis, she is one of the three Horai, goddesses of the seasons, whose sisters are Dike (Justice) and Eunomia (Good Order).

Before the main cathedral of Athens was built, Agia Irini was the city's primary church, and the surrounding square, known as

Plateia Agia Irini, was an important central meeting place. Today it is still a bustling hub filled with bars and restaurants that line the cobblestoned square covered in lacy trees, letting the Athenian sunlight filter through. Two of my favorites are Spollati (27 Aiolou), with its cool jazz vibe and two-story open interior space. Across the way is Tailor Made (Agia Irini Square), in an older building, a wedding cake opulence of rosy pinks and large, expansive windows in the style of old Athens. During a visit, my waiter pointed out a large mural of a man on the wall. "Ernst Ziller, a Bavarian architect," he explained, adding, "he designed the Parliament Building, the Archaeological Museum, and 150 other buildings in Athens including this one, which used to be a hotel."

In a city that has lost many of its original neoclassical structures to concrete apartment buildings, how lovely that what used to be a main center of Athens has seen a revival. Both the young and old share this space, along with Saint Irene and her goddess predecessor, whose name, Peace, continues to suffuse the air with tranquility, creating a welcome retreat in the city's hectic center.

※

49 Temple Prostitution at Ancient Corinth

SEX AND THE CITY

A flash of thigh, the sound of sandals hitting the earth. An attractive woman disappears over the top of the hill—you look down and see an imprint of letters left behind, pressed into the soil. Carved into the bottom of her sandals are the words: *Follow Me*. And you do. When you arrive at the top of this mound that rises singularly from the Corinthian plain, you are treated to a 360-degree view toward the desert-like Argolid to the south, the wasp-waisted isthmus of the Peloponnesian peninsula to the east and to the north, the sparkling, lapis-colored waters of the Gulf of Corinth.

Sitting at the intersection between two huge bodies of water and what was formerly a land bridge between mainland Greece and the Peloponnesian peninsula, Corinth was not only a bustling port, it was ground zero for the sex trade. Whether women were performing sacred acts or engaging in prostitution, historians disagree on the real purpose of the temple priestesses so often written about. Suffice it to say that Corinth, sitting at the crossroads of commerce for both land and water, was a happening place.

St. Paul preached to the Corinthians in hopes of reforming the residents of this ancient city from their wicked ways, and it was the worship of Aphrodite that caused him to denigrate the city as a center of licentiousness. In his famous sermons to the Corinthians during his eighteen-month stay in the infamous city, he was known to preach, "Evil communications corrupt good manners."

The cult of Aphrodite was all about the veneration of love, beauty, and, of course, sex. Every evening a gong and bell would ring out over the hillside, letting men know that business was open. If they needed any additional enticement, they just followed the footprints. At its height, according to the ancient historian Strabo, the metropolis housed one thousand sacred priestesses, but as a port city, some say this was not a cult, but a house of prostitution serving sailors.

Sarah Pomeroy, author of *Goddesses, Whores, Wives, and Slaves*, tells us, "Men were unlikely to marry before the age of thirty, and unmarried men had no opportunities for heterosexual activity except with prostitutes or slaves. Since there seem to have been fewer women than men in the general population at the time, shared women, or prostitutes, were a solution," adding, "Prostitution flourished in Greece as early as the Archaic period. Large cities, especially those on the west coast visited by sailors, supported vast numbers of prostitutes." Corinth, with its prominent positioning at the juncture of two major gulfs, would certainly apply.

As you approach from the distance, the hillock of Acrocorinth, or high Corinth, is easy to spot on the horizon, rising, almost breast-like, from the level surrounding plain. Settled initially in Neolithic times, the archaeological site is spread out over a large area and spans centuries. At the lower city of Corinth, the most prominent structure is the Temple of Apollo, a Doric-style structure that once had thirty-eight columns, of which seven, thick cigar-like pillars, still stand. Built in the 6th century B.C., it is one of the oldest temples in Greece, the remains of which are the most complete at the site.

Atop the Acrocorinth are the scattered remains of the celebrated Temple of Aphrodite. One can imagine the soaring quality of its columns at these dizzying heights and the magnificent 360-degree views available to worshippers on this towering limestone mountain, making it a natural fortress for succeeding waves of invaders after the Greek and Roman eras, including the Herulians in 267 A.D., the Crusaders during the medieval period, the Venetians, Turks, and ultimately the Greeks who won it back in the 1822 Greek War of Independence.

Later ruins include the Temple of Octavia, dedicated to the Roman emperor Augustus's sister. Three exquisitely carved Corinthian capitals with their signature fussily rendered acanthus leaves, remain on the foundation. Nearby, a small rock fountain is dedicated to Glauke, daughter of Corinth's King Kreon, who met an ugly end at the hands of Medea, wife of Jason, of Argonaut fame. Glauke's beauty so entranced her husband that he left her for the princess. Determined to put an end to their affair, Medea soaked a veil and crown in poison and, delivering them via her own children, managed to eliminate her rival.

Inside the city wall of lower Corinth are the remains of the Asklepieion. This sanctuary was like a combination spa and hospital and was dedicated to Asklepios, the god of healing. Patients hoping to recover from a variety of illnesses would visit the enclave and be treated by priests. Terracotta figures of body parts such as genitals, breasts, and legs, which the priests used in their rituals, were found in the excavations—many are on view at the museum.

A larger fountain, referred to as the "most famous fountain of Greece" by its first excavator Rufus Richardson, is dedicated to Peirene. Also situated in the lower city, visitors can get iconic shots of this elegant structure silhouetted against the soaring crag of Acrocorinth in the background. A natural spring that once supplied water for the ancient city around 500 B.C., the fountain was established in the Greek period. The Romans developed the site in successive waves starting in the 1st century B.C., resulting in the current elaborate façade, which was once replete with niched statues of sea creatures such as Scylla, the famed clashing rock Odysseus's ship had to steer past in the Straits of Messina. Four reservoirs once held water fed by an underground spring and were covered by a fountain house with a series of arches on the façade and the remains of two slender columns, one still topped by a delicate capital in the requisite Corinthian style.

As Annelisa Stephan, an editor at Getty.edu says, "Peirene was more than just a fancy waterworks, though. Ancient cities worshiped their springs and rivers, which were personified as gods or nymphs, and for Corinth, Peirene was both sacred and social, a source of life and center of society. It was famed across the Mediterranean as the place where the mythical hero Bellerophon tamed his winged horse Pegasus, and of the dramatic scene in Euripides's *Medea* where the tutor of Medea's children overhears news of their impending exile from old men gossiping around the water."

As happens with many women in Greek mythology, Peirene's fate was filled with sorrow. Peirene was a naiad-nymph and the daughter of the river god Asopos. Abducted by the sea god Poseidon, she bore him two sons, named for the twin cities of the region. The historian Pausanias tells us she met her ultimate fate when she was "turned into a spring of water by the tears she shed bewailing her son Kenchrias, whom Artemis has unwittingly killed." Frescoes of silvery-finned fish and crimson, spidery crabs, navigating a milky blue sea are still visible on this elaborate fountain that served as a meeting place for visitors throughout antiquity.

Located only a breezy hour's drive along the coastline from Athens, Corinth is a beautiful destination worth taking an afternoon to explore. Be sure to wear sturdy shoes to investigate the rugged archaeological site. After a day of ascending the craggy heights of Acrocorinth you'll be hot and hungry, so make a stop for freshly grilled fish and a frosty Mythos beer at one of the tavernas overlooking the glittering, wind-whipped waters of the Gulf of Corinth. On your way back to Athens, as you cross over the bridge, rubberneck the plummeting depths of the famous Corinth shipping canal and try to imagine the emperor Nero and his golden shovel, making the first attempt to excavate this vast expanse back in the Ist century A.D.

Priestesses, prostitutes, sacred, or profane: however you view it, as the settlement of ancient Corinth fades into your rear view mirror, it will undoubtedly give new meaning to the term sex and the city.

50 *Agia Kore*

BRING OFFERINGS OF UNDERPANTS
AND BRASSIERES

Beneath the heights of Mount Olympus lies a canyon with a mysterious history. A well-known tale from the Ottoman occupation of Greece, which existed from the mid-15th century to 1821, is the story of a young girl that captures the imagination—and horror—of the period. If you are interested in an abduction tale heavily laced with elements of the myth of Persephone, who was pulled into an underworld by its ruler, the god Hades, and whose modern shrine is laden with offerings of underpants, scarves, and brassieres, then the story of Agia Kore was tailor made for you.

The tale begins with a young girl from the town of Zagorochoria in northwestern Greece. Known not only for her physical beauty, but also her spiritual purity, Agia Kore caught the eye of the Ali Pasha, who in 1789 ruled the entire region of Thessaly, northwestern Greece, as well as parts of southern Greece, including sections of the Peloponnese and Evia. A kind soul learned of the Pasha's unseemly plans to capture Kore and force her into his harem, and warned the young girl she was about to be abducted. Kore did what any devout young woman of the time would do: she grabbed a portrait of the Virgin Mary as well as an image of Christ, and fled from her village across the treacherous terrain until she reached the area around Mount Olympus.

There are a number of different versions of what happened next. One is that Agia Kore, whose name means "Holy Maiden" in English, went to hide in one of these ravines. Exposed to the cold and elements, she died in the harsh environment trying to evade the Pasha's army. Another version tells she was chased to the edge of a deep ravine and fell to her death. Yet another states that as Kore approached a wall of rock in her desperation to evade her pursuers, it miraculously opened, allowing her entrance into a secret cave, and then closed behind her, preventing her capture.

All manner of healing stories abound in this strange, mysterious ravine in which weird sounds, lights, and visions have been witnessed over the centuries. A blind chieftain from Kontariotissa supposedly regained his sight after washing in the holy water, and he is accredited with building the first wooden steps that led pilgrims to this sacred site. Today the steps are metal and if you wish to climb down all 175 of them you can hike down into the canyon. At the bottom of the ravine sits a tiny church built in honor of Kore. The bubbling and supposedly healing waters of the Agia Kore River flow nearby.

Think of this as a trek in nature with a spiritual—and supernatural—bent. The canyon is gorgeous in itself, with sheer walls falling into the river valley below. Beneath the slopes of this mountain dedicated to the ancient gods and goddesses of Greece lie a series of ravines and canyons, an area of lush natural beauty including waterfalls, rivers, and streams. Sit on the terrace outside the church and gaze up at the rocky face of the dove colored canyon walls. Majestic pines, figs, and ferns tangle this moist, fertile valley and the sound of rushing water is a constant in the background.

The ancients believed that the ground around Mount Olympus was sacred, and it's not difficult to see why. A waterway running between Agia Kore and the nearby town of Brontou (literally "thunder") is called the "Thunderer" after the booming noise the water makes while passing over stony riverbeds on its way down from the heights of Zeus's Mount Olympus. This mystical cleft lies deep in the canyon, nearly hidden by the lush cover of evergreen, steep slopes, and the snow-capped mountains looming above.

Today the church stands empty and seemingly abandoned; however if there is a need for a marriage or baptism, a priest will come down to perform the ceremony at the site. Dust-covered gold-leaf icons lean against the plain walls, but as you leave the building and wander into the woods you will begin to notice more than the lush beauty of the ravine—you will realize that the sanctuary has moved into nature itself. Scan the trees and take note of the strange items tied to the branches. Pilgrims who brave the steps all the way into the ravine pay their respects to the memory of Agia Kore by leaving behind tributes, but not of the usual kind. Here you will find articles of women's clothing, eerily tied to the trees and hanging from branches, such as socks, underpants, scarves, and even bras!

"The hanging of gifts on trees is documented in ancient wall painting, and the custom persists in Cyprus (much disapproved of by the Orthodox Church), but this is the only instance I know of in Greece," my friend and colleague Susan Rotroff remarks. "I particularly recall an ordinary bobby pin, several strips torn from disposable diapers, and stockings, but the most common offerings were pieces of clothing, tied to branches or around the trunks of trees. Scarves and shirts were common, as well as occasional items of underwear; noteworthy was a baby's bib. Perhaps the oddest was a tape measure," she adds, concluding, "the thing not to miss is the grove of trees with its votive 'trash'—it's the trees with their gifts that make the place unique."

Before you leave, make sure to walk over to the small grotto, where the rocks miraculously opened to allow Agia Kore to escape her predators. A series of small embroidered rugs covers the rock floor and the grotto is filled with the usual apparatus of Greek orthodoxy: gold-painted icons of the saint, candles, vials of olive oil, alongside the more atypical offerings of women's blouses, sweaters, and other articles of clothing.

The similarities between Kore's story and Persephone's are clear—even her name, Kore, is another term for the goddess Persephone. Both were victims or near victims of abduction by men with dark intent, and both found transformation in the recesses of the earth, becoming sanctified with healing properties. The Greek Orthodox Church does not officially recognize Agia Kore, but her many devotees attest to her miraculous cures. For the nature lover, spiritual seeker, or aficionada of the unusual and arcane, a hike into the stunningly beautiful and curiously atypical gorge of Agia Kore will satisfy all of the above.

※

51 Lefkas

SAPPHO'S LEAP, SAINT MAURA, AND AGNES BALTSA

Millennia ago Lefkas was not an island, but an isthmus, connected to the mainland by a small spit of land. Brushing up against the coast, the island appears to dangle awkwardly off the western shore of Greece, a misshapen sibling to the rest of the Ionian chain, which seem to appear and disappear, submerged like sleeping bears in the molten seas that surround these remote and mystical islands. In centuries past, some archaeologists have argued that Lefkas was indeed the Ithaka of Homer; no surprise, as many of the neighboring islands in the Ionian chain clustered around modern Ithaka have also claimed to be the longed-for home to which Odysseus fought so hard to return.

Curiously, Lefkas shares a powerful connection with another island on the opposite side of Greece. Sappho, the godmother of all lesbians, may have started her life on Lesbos, an island lying in the shadow of Turkey, but she ended it in a brutal, frightening, and undeniable way on Lefkas. But why did our poor Sappho perish on an island so far from her beloved homeland? To find out you must take a winding road to the remote cape towards a lighthouse erected on the site where a temple to Apollo once stood.

The name of the dramatic cliff, known as Lovers' Leap, is thought to originate from a story about an affair Sappho had, not with another woman, but with a ferryman named Phaon. Although experts disagree on the story—some saying it is a homophobic attempt to reinvent her as a heterosexual, supposedly spurned by her lover—legend has it that she leapt to her death from the two-hundred-foot ledge. The Roman poet Ovid tells the tale of this doomed love affair in his epic poem, *Sappho to Phaon*,

> *One savage heart, or teach it how to love?*
> *The flying winds have lost them all in air!*
> *Oh when, alas! Shall more auspicious gales*
> *To these fond eyes restore they welcome sails!*
> *If you return—ah, why these long delays?*
> *Poor Sappho dies while carless Phaon stays.*
> *O launch thy bark, nor fear the wat'ry plain;*
> *Venus for thee shall smooth her native main.*

During Roman times this precarious ledge continued to be a spot where rejected lovers took their own lives, and during other periods, criminals were thrown off the cliffs to purify their souls, sometimes having birds tied to their legs to slow their fall. Today paragliders continue the tradition in a more sanguine way, using the cliff as a favorite spot to launch their Technicolor parachutes, sweeping like a painter's brush against the canvas of searing white cliffs. In fact, the island's name, meaning white, derives from this chalk-colored precipice that striates the southern tip.

Lefkas, like many of the islands in the Ionian, is a parfait of dense green rimmed with white-hot slices of beach foiled against a sea that shifts from deep turquoise one moment to bright jade the next. A violet haze seems to embrace the island and settles into ravines and valleys that are dotted with aspirin-white villages, the haze punctured by the dizzying heights of Mount Elati. The main town with its castle, built in 1300 by the Orsini family, is named after Saint Maura, an Irish saint and the sister of the better-known Saint Brigid. When the Ottomans came and ruled at various points throughout the 15th to the 18th centuries, the island was called Ayamavra.

Agnes Baltsa, a Greek opera singer, was also born on Lefkas. Thanks to the generosity of another great Greek singer, Maria Callas, Baltsa was able to study in Munich following her training at the Greek National Conservatoire. Known for her repertoire of classical operatic arias, Baltsa's heart is never far from her homeland, and she has recorded a number of popular songs including *From Greece with Love*, and *Songs My Country Taught Me*. Baltsa has been described as, "Greek in body and soul, and gives herself in her roles in the operas as Carmen, Fedora, Eboli or as Herodiade."

❋ www.greeka.com/ionian/lefkada

Just between Lefkas and the mainland lies a tiny island associated with a trio of famous women. Snugged in Lefkas's shadow, the

famed islet of Skorpios can be seen amidst its bigger siblings from as far away as Ithaka. This is where Jacqueline Kennedy married the Greek shipping tycoon Aristotle Onassis in the years following her husband, John F. Kennedy's assassination. As a private island, no one can visit, but you can easily see it from Lefkas and imagine Jackie and her daughter-in-law, Cristina, spending time at the Onassis estate. The animosity between these two women, as well as Cristina's untimely death, was enough to keep the tabloids fueled for years. After Cristina's death, her daughter, Athina, was willed the island. In recent years Athina, who has expressed no interest in her native country, sold Skorpios to a Russian oligarch, a shocking act considering her mother, grandfather, and other relatives are buried on the island. With all the sadness in the vicinity, it makes you wonder if the echoes of the Greek tragedy where Sappho supposedly took her life on Lefkas's notorious milky cliffs somehow extends out to Skorpios, beyond the time and space of these islands' gauzy and permeable borders, and recalls the words of the poetess herself:

and in my wild heart what did I most wish

to happen to me:
Again whom must I persuade

back into the harness of your love?

Sappho, who wrongs you?

52 Saint Theodora's Chapel

THE MIRACLE OF THE ROOFTOP TREES

Deep in the heart of the Peloponnese lies a tiny church that sprouts trees. It seems impossible that the frangible roof of this ancient, weathered stone structure could support the weight of not just one, but seventeen mature trees, but it does—and this "miracle" church has attracted the attention of scientists from around the country to study this inexplicable wonder. In 1993, Eleni Stavrogiannis-Perry, an architect from Kalamata, described the site: "The phenomenon is scientifically unexplainable. Considering the position of the church, its temporary construction and its age, the heavy weight and the winds should have gradually destroyed it. But it is still standing, after so many centuries, without any serious damage."

In a lush mountain gully near the town of Megalopoli lies the village of Vastas. This verdant, remote river valley is where thousands of pilgrims flock annually to pay their respects to the life of a brave young woman who lived and fought here during the Byzantine era. Saint Theodora was born in the 10th century, a time when a law stated that every family must send at least one male to fight as a soldier or be forced to pay a tax. Theodora's family was very poor, and as the only child, she agreed to serve so that her father, whom she loved very much, wouldn't have to.

When bandits raided the region, Theodora was called upon to defend her village. Since it was unthinkable that a woman would enlist, Theodora disguised herself as male and called herself Theodore. She not only managed to keep her true identity a secret, but she became a respected fighter, honored for her valor and strength. However, a young woman fell in love with "Theodore" and spread a rumor that she had become pregnant by him. Her commander gave her two options, either marry the girl or be executed. Revealing her true identity would have surely saved her life, but her father would have been subject to punishment, so Theodora did what saints do and took the retribution herself. On her deathbed, she uttered the fateful words, "Let my body become a church, my blood a river, and my hair, the forest."

The locals, moved by the bravery of this young woman, erected a chapel at the site of her grave. This small church, built sometime during the 11th to 12th centuries, honors Theodora and is intimately linked with her martyrdom. The single aisled, six-by-nine-foot chapel is relatively prosaic with one exception: The chapel's roof supports seventeen trees of different species, including holm oak and maple, each of which weighs over a ton and stands more than sixty feet high. Legend has it that a river re-routed itself to run beneath the chapel and that its holy waters nourish the miraculous trees that sprout from its roof.

During the devastating forest fires that ravaged Greece in 2007, 370,000 acres of land, including ancient forests, were destroyed, but the flames miraculously passed by Vasta, leaving St. Theodora's chapel untouched. Until recently, scientific investigation into the mystery of the trees remained unanswered, leaving devotees to believe that no other explanation for the mystery existed save for the power of God. In 2003, a geophysical report showed that the root system of the trees passes through the walls and reaches the earth, yet it still doesn't explain how the building withstands the considerable load of pressure from the trees.

Perhaps this is where science gives way to mystery. As some observers say, the entire site feels like a living, breathing, and indestructible relic, and the building has become "a living body." There are some who believe Theodora truly incorporated her deathbed promise and this tiny, remote church became her body, her blood the river that mysteriously rerouted itself beneath the building's foundation, and her hair a magical forest of seventeen trees that has been miraculously supported by this unique and extraordinary structure for more than eleven centuries. If you need an additional reason to visit this pastoral glen in the bosom of Arcadia, the Saint Theodora's Chapel is listed in the Guinness Book of World Records as a miraculous wonder.

⁂

IV

Favorite Haunts
in Athens

53 *The Plaka*

ATHENS'S OLDEST DISTRICT

Tucked beneath the dizzying heights of the Acropolis hill lies Athens's original neighborhood. With its narrow, winding streets and alleyways, this may be, second to the Parthenon, the city's most popular destination for tourists. Yet as crowded and crazy as it can get in the summer, with its shoulder-to-shoulder crowds and the fragrance of suntan lotion mixing with roasted lamb wafting out from vine-encrusted tavernas, it is well worth your time and effort.

Since much of the neighborhood was largely built in the Ottoman period, many of the Plaka's streets are paved in marble. When I lived in Athens, I used to walk around the district in flip-flops, unsteadily negotiating the slippery stone that has become warped and worn over the decades. These days I know better; wear only sturdy, rubber-soled shoes that can grip this unstable surface. Once you have gotten your footing on the slick cobblestones (ladies—heels not recommended!), look up and prepare to be dazzled by some of the city's most stunning antiquities, shoehorned between the narrow streets and seemingly around every corner of this labyrinthine borough.

✳ www.athensguide.org/athens-plaka.html

This teeming, lively neighborhood started as a village built high up into the northeastern slope of the Acropolis hill. This has been a place of refuge since the Peloponnesian War, where many have hidden from persecutors or dictatorial regimes in the caves that exist in this primordial rock. In 1841, King Otto declared Athens the newly independent country's capital and started a building campaign, attracting workers from the Cycladic island of Anafi. This small town became known as Anafiotika, and residents recreated the style and feeling of their former home, transplanting the island style houses and village feel to the foot of the Acropolis. Today, the island sensibility is evidenced by its narrow, vertical pathways, quiet cobblestoned streets, and whitewashed houses splattered with magma red and fuchsia bougainvillea. You won't find many shops or restaurants at this highest point in the Plaka, as this is the most residential part of the district, still largely inhabited by descendants of the original Anafi islanders.

Beneath peaceful Anafiotika, the rest of the Plaka seems to be dominated by tourists, yet the whole area is still a neighborhood in which locals live, work, eat, and drink, and was once the place where the working class called home. Charming, eclectic, and often maddeningly crowded, Plaka's collection of neoclassical buildings is actually erected on top of the ancient neighborhood of Athens, situated on the eastern and northern slopes of the Acropolis hill. In fact, archaeologists believe that Adrianou Street, one of the main thoroughfares of this popular shopping district, lies atop one of the original and possibly the most ancient streets of Athens and divides the district into two distinct sections: Ano Plaka, the area above the street leading up to the Acropolis, and Kato Plaka, the area below Adrianou and bordering Monastiraki and Syntagma Square.

Continuously inhabited since ancient times, the area wasn't called Plaka (probably originating from the Albanian word *pliaka*, which means "old") until the reign of King Otto in the early to mid-19th century. During the Ottoman rule it was the seat of the governor and, known as the Turkish quarter, it was also called Gorgopikos after a small cathedral. Its loose boundaries encompass several small churches after which the locals formerly referred to the neighborhood, and even earlier the area was divided into four districts of which the name Anafiotika remains today.

Back in the 1970s, the Plaka had reached its nadir of unpleasantness. As a college kid I would go disco dancing on the rooftops with my friends while on the streets below, plate smashing was all the rage in restaurants and on the steep steps leading up to the Acropolis. Car traffic was still allowed and tourist shops existed alongside stores where you could purchase authentic, hand-made embroidered coats, hats, and shoes from Epirus, Thessaly, and Crete.

Today cars are banned, but you will still find taxis and the odd person trying to squeeze their Honda or Range Rover between the marble curbs of the narrow lanes, so stay on the sidewalks! Hike up to the Acropolis and look down to see a jumble of terracotta rooftops stacked like a child's set of blocks, higgledy-piggledy up the steep slope. I've always envied the view of Athena's sacred temple that many residents have!

My friend and fellow hellenophile, Mary Lou Roussel, laughingly refers to the curved streets, blind alleyways, and steep lanes as "rabbit warrens." The entire neighborhood sinuously drapes itself around many of the major antiquities of Athens, including temples, monuments, ancient water clocks, and stoas. You can stroll down Byron Street, turn the corner, and be delighted by the appearance of the Choragic Monument of Lysicrates. Wend your way down Aiolou Street and suddenly you will find yourself in the Roman Agora, admiring the lyrical and perfectly octagonal Temple of the Winds. After wandering down Pandrossou Street with its cheek-by-jowl shops, curve onto Areos Street and you will come face to face with Hadrian's Library and its parade of bone white columns.

Whether you are admiring antiquities around every corner or getting fitted for sandals, remember the Plaka is primarily known for its endless array of shops selling everything from leather goods, rugs, clothing, reproductions of antiquities, and jewelry. Yes, shopkeepers can be dogged in their attempts to get you to come in and take a look at their wares, but this is the tourist section of Athens. Expect a circus atmosphere and revel in a clamor of calling hucksters, shrilling caged parakeets, and general hubbub of humanity passing by in a neon blur. Instead of decrying how it used to be, I enjoy it for what it is: a loud, crazy, and entertaining place that is the beating heart of Athens.

Some of my favorite shops:

- Yannis Michalopoulos, Fine Carpets, 6 Pandrosou Street
- Nikos Chalaris, Agora Ethnic Jewelry, 10 Pandrosou Street
- Gallery Demeter, Jewelry and Icons, 8 Vyronos Street
- Karambelas Brothers, Fine Leather Goods, 54 Adrianou
- Cotton Club Dimitris, Goddess-inspired dresses, 84 Adrianou

For thirsty shoppers, stop for a cool drink or bite to eat in Palea Agora Square:

- Ydria, Café and Restaurant, 68 Adrianou and Eolou
- Karyatis, Café and restaurant, 39 Kapnikarea and 55 Adrianou

And if you want an old-fashioned Greek plate smashing experience, just like in the old days:

- Adrianos Restaurant, Live Music, 4 Thespidos Street

54 *Kolonaki*

WHERE ATHENS'S ELITE LIVES, SHOPS, AND DINES

I recall the first time I figured out how to read a word in Greek. I was living in Athens, poring over a map, trying to find the address of my sister's old boyfriend and suddenly, like a string of Christmas lights exploding in my head, it made sense: the word *Voukourestiou*—Bucharest—emerged from the boxy, illegible Greek letters. Pounding the map in glee, I realized I had found not only his apartment with my nascent understanding of the Greek language, but I also had found my way to one of Athens's most desirable neighborhoods: Kolonaki.

✳ www.greece-athens.com/place.php?place_id=11

Every city has its tony section: Manhattan has the Upper East Side, Paris the 16th arrondissement, London has Kensington, and Athens has Kolonaki. Even though many wealthy Athenians have moved to the suburbs, this elegant quarter is still a destination for many locals as well as visitors who take in the area's many sites. My sister's ex-boyfriend, who arrived at our Minnesota home one Thanksgiving with the dessert baklava strapped to the back of his motorcycle in true bad-boy Greek style, lived in one of the many neoclassical buildings lining the streets that demarcate this lovely section of the city. After I spent weeks tromping up and down the steep, tree-lined narrow cobblestoned roads at the base of Athens's tallest hill, Lykavittos, the names began to roll off my tongue as if reading a who's who list of Loeb's Classical library titles: Ploutarchou, Pindarou, Iraklitou, Solonos, Kleomenous, Xenokratous, and Loukianou.

Years later, as an archaeologist, I spent a day visiting the American School for Classical Studies' Gennadion library, which is situated right in the heart of Kolonaki. The American embassy is nearby as are dozens of other embassies, as well as the major hospital of Athens. But what makes this neighborhood unique are not only the high-end shops and exclusivity, but the lovely squares around which it is arranged. Dexameni is my favorite. The word Dexameni refers to an ancient cistern built by the Emperor Hadrian, around which the square was built, at one point supplying Athens with all its water.

When I was a student, it was one of the first places in the city I visited on my own, and I recall the neatly dressed housewives in their fall tweeds pushing large strollers across the gravel walkways or well-fed toddlers on swing sets. Not much has changed in the intervening years. Grandmothers in widows' black still sit on benches ringing the park's perimeter as they tend to their precious cargo, one in particular watching a chestnut-eyed child riding a tricycle and yelling out *"Yiayia!"* as she breathlessly chased a butterscotch-colored tabby that had wandered into the park.

Nearby is the lovely Dexameni outdoor cinema. Located just beneath the towering heights of Lykavittos Hill, the venue is the perfect place to enjoy the warm breezes of an Athenian summer evening while watching the latest art house release (mostly English speaking titles) on a screen framed by towering conifers. Take a seat on the iconic blue-and-white deck chairs, inhale the jasmine blooming on the vine-encrusted walls, and order a glass of ouzo with your popcorn while watching under the stars.

There are multiple outdoor tavernas and cafés scattered among the mulberry, oleander, and bougainvillea-draped streets. All of Athens's parks serve as personal yards, so as the kids play soccer you can sit nearby and snack on little tapas-like plates, known as *mezes*. At Dexameni Café, located on the steep pedestrian walkway, choose delicacies such as *horta* (a seasonal green) with fist-thick wedges of lemon, delicately formed *keftedes* (meat balls) with almonds and basil, island dishes such as potato salad with Pestropha fish, marinated anchovies, and roast octopus in olive oil and herbs. After lunch, for those interested in getting a quick museum fix, the renowned Benaki with its Greek folk art, and Cycladic Museums are just a few short steps away. A popular hotel is the St. George Lycabettus, precariously cantilevered into the hillside and jutting out over the streets below.

While Ermou Street has become a popular shopping destination, the shops up and down Voukourestiou read like a who's who of luxury retail. Whereas Ermou caters to the younger crowd with H&M, Sephora, and Nike, you will be surrounded by all the luxury stores in Kolonaki. Dior, Louis Vuitton, Patek Phillipe, Tod's, and Ermenegildo Zegna are situated side by side with such high-end Greek brands as Delos, Eponymo, and the iconic Ilias Lalaounis, the Cartier of Greek jewelers.

For those wishing to check out a Greek department store, step into Attica, located on Panepestimiou Street at the bottom of Kolonaki. If you're like me and shopping is all about getting something to eat, be sure to take a break at the iconic Zonar's Café, adjacent to Attica. The steel, glass, and emerald marbled exterior belies this institutions' noble lineage. Zonar's used to compete with another famous eatery, Floka's, right next door. Floka's went out of business years ago and the family sold Zonar's. However the essence of this classic café lives on and this is the place to sample Greek desserts such as densely honeyed and cinnamon-studded baklava, lacy shredded wheat *kataifi*, and creamy squares of *galataboureko*. Sit outside next to the potted figs, order from the waiters and waitresses elegantly outfitted in black ties, and watch the who's who of Athenian society go about their day.

❦

55 *Gazi*

ATHENS'S CLUBBING AND ARTS DISTRICT

If you are seeking the new cool place to go in Athens, Gazi is your spot. The name comes from the Greek word for "gas" and refers to the above-ground gas reservoirs that stand just outside the Kerameikos cemetery and within earshot of the bustling Monastiraki marketplace. What was once a burned-out abandoned part of the city has been gentrified in recent years to become the hip destination for all of Athens, but primarily its youth and LGBT culture.

Gazi was founded in 1857 and was in operation until—unbelievably—1984, as the last urban gas factory in Europe. During the day, the two massive gas tanks give off a distinctly industrial air, but at night the whole place transforms, and the tanks, lit in neon blue and green light, at once invite you to enter this hip sanctuary and remind you that the spirit of rebirth is alive and well in a city that has seen its recurrence of decay and renewal over the millennia.

Any visitor to Athens will note that a lot of the city seems run-down or covered in graffiti. Don't let appearances deceive you—the thrum and spirit that has fueled Greek civilization since its inception is still operating, just underground. Instead of massive temples to gods and goddesses, today's Greek artists are engaged in a wide range of the arts, and a cool place to start is Gazi's Technopolis.

Known as an industrial museum, this massive complex covers thirty acres and is dedicated to the arts in a uniquely integrated sense in which the Greeks—some of the most imaginative people on the planet—excel. The ingenuity and insight that blessed the ancients is still with them today, albeit in a slightly different form. They are unafraid to blend artistic elements, and the industrial, cavernous space is a perfect foil for the incubation of poetry, visual arts, and music, and its eight main sectors are named after Greece's most adored poets, including Yannis Ritsos, Angelos Sikelianos and my favorite, Constantine Cavafy, author of the poem, "Ithaka," which was so beloved by Jackie O that it was read at her funeral.

The skeletal frames of the abandoned gas tanks appear like lace against the robin's egg-blue Greek sky, and at night the smokestacks become glowing towers of neon light. Technopolis is also a performance venue and has hosted the Athens Technopolis Jazz Festival for the past twelve years. The site's webpage best describes this hybrid space as only the Greeks can do: "The charm of a bygone era, conveyed through stacks, enormous cauldrons, chimneys and ovens, 'conspires' with reverence to establish the site as a 'factory' for the protection and production of art. Etymologically, the word 'gas' (derived from the ancient German *galist*, later *geist*) means spirit."

There is a bar in Technopolis, but don't limit your stay here without wandering around the rest of the neighborhood. Gazi is a strip of bars, restaurants, and clubs on either side of a green triangle of park. Bordered by the streets Persephonis and Voutadon, the area is easily accessible via the Kerameikos station of the city's pristinely beautiful metro system.

✳ www.technopolis-athens.com/web/guest/home

✳ www.hellenicfood.gr/butchershop

Take a stroll down Persephonis and stop for dinner at either The Butcher Shop (Persefonis 19) or Cartone (Persefonis 41 and Triptolemou 42). The Butcher Shop has a mesmerizing setting replete with threadlike birch trees magically embracing an intimate dining area. The menu offers delights such as organic wild boar sausage, *paidakia*—grilled tiny lamb chops—and potato, zucchini and spearmint salad. Farther down, Cartone's airy open space allows passersby and diners to both see and be seen and become part of this district's distinctly artsy and edgy vibe.

When dinner is done, cross the triangle of green space and choose among a number of unusual clubs. My favorite among them is Gazarte, a multicultural destination that is bookstore, cinema, concert venue, and rooftop bar wrapped into one. A bookstore on the entry level will lead up a staircase into an expansive wooden bookshelf-lined living space they call the library, but the action is all outside. With the smokestacks looming like Technicolor versions of modern columns in the background, the cityscape of Gazi is the perfect backdrop from Gazarte's expansive rooftop deck. Sink into one of the cushioned banquettes, savor the music as well as the view, and order an ouzo. You will be brought a glass of the licorice heavy brew complete with a side of ice. Drop the cubes in and watch the crystal liquid bloom into a milky stew, lean back and nibble on apps like a charcuterie plate and tiny triangular cheese *tiropitas*. In spite of the recent financial troubles, Greeks don't shy away from having a good time. The young crowd will stay up into the wee hours, dancing the night—and their paychecks—away with complete abandon. When you ask why, you will likely be given the same answer over and over again, "We Greeks, we live for today."

✳ gazarte.gr

In Athens, and particularly in Gazi, I encourage you to take their advice: Be Greek for a night and do just that.

❧

56 *Avissinias Square*

ATHENS'S OTHER FLEA MARKET

It's a place with a funny name, very easy to overlook. With its spindly, arthritic trees and sparsely shaded *plateia*, I wouldn't blame you. But you would be missing something. For Avissinias is a flea market and antiquer's paradise. Only after I rented an apartment across the busy main corridor of Athens's Ermou Street did I have a chance to walk by this mish-mash of collectors' items and jumble of shops every day.

Located adjacent to the main flea market of Monastiraki, Avissinias is a triangular piazza shoehorned with secondhand delights. I like to visit in the morning, when the vendors are setting up shop. There are two parts to this hobnob neighborhood. First take the time to wander through the square itself, ringed by antique stores; be sure to duck into each one. Bowling alley-like shops are deeply recessed and packed with furniture, paintings, and bric-a-brac, affording an opportunity to pick through at your leisure.

Don't let the metal corrugated garage doors splashed in luridly bright graffiti put you off. Men push three-wheeled carts beneath a canopy of mulberry and olive trees, locals stroll hand in hand, stopping to inspect stacks of furniture piled willy-nilly on the wide cobblestoned plaza. In one of my favorite shops (all are named *Paleopolio* or old curiosity shop), I was arrested by a jarring display of cerulean jadeite dragons, Harry Truman-era radios, stacks of Chinese-export porcelain platters, all dazzling the eye beneath a series of brass and crystal chandeliers suspended in the open marketplace.

Cherry wood barometers and statuesque grandfather clocks share space with porcelain samovars. Rolls of textiles and carpets lie gently against antiquary landscapes of Athens from previous centuries and portraits of stoic-faced individuals in a variety of Greek ethnic costumes.

Swing around the circumference of the square and peruse the vast array of furniture lined up in front of the stores. Chairs with brocaded seats and elaborately carved backs and legs are stacked two and three deep, just waiting for college students or newlyweds hoping to decorate their apartments on a budget. Cobblers sit in the shade, repairing items and polishing brass, and the sounds of hammers and scent of turpentine thickens the air.

Just outside the square, on Ermou Street, is yet another iteration of Avissinias's charm. For those looking for all manner of bric-a-brac and memorabilia, this is a must. Pickup trucks line up behind one another and goods spill out onto the sidewalks, making them virtually impassable. Instead of becoming annoyed, I take my time, stopping to ogle the boxloads of visual treats. Here you can find everything from the incomprehensible to the absurd: a poster of Rosy the Riveter jammed into a basket of luridly yellow tennis balls and an Impressionistic painting of women setting off on a sea journey, leaning up against a stack of car batteries.

Boxes of LPs are nestled against garishly embellished portraits of dour saints, staring impassively at passersby. Key rings, terrifying looking scythe-like blades, and swords with bejeweled handles share real estate with hand-painted icons of Christ, black-robed Archbishops, and cardboard cartons laden with antique telephones, linens, and car parts. Parakeets in cages lend their song to the rumble of traffic as it passes by and the hoards of tourists and locals alike, hoping to find a treasure among the mountains of relics.

Poking around Avissinias will make you thirsty—and hungry. Several places offer a sweet respite from the heat and charming clutter. Loukoumi Bar (3, Avissinias Square) is the perfect place to rise above the fray. Duck under the perforated leather canopy and make your way to the top floor for a glorious view of the Acropolis and city beyond. This funky bar offers bizarre cocktails with names like Pimiento Dark and Stormy, Bee Jam, and Bubble Gum, and is a favorite hangout for young Athenians. Pictures of Elvis and posters for Facebook and Twitter are scattered around the interior, and chessboards sit atop random tables for those with an appetite for the brainy sport.

For an evening you won't forget, make a reservation at the sumptuous Café Avissinia (7, Kinetou Street), located across from Loukoumi Bar. You can dine inside in the winter with elegant views to the ancient marbles of the Acropolis Hill, or in summer, head straight to the rooftop for incomparable views of the Parthenon, Mars Hill, and Lykavittos. Best to visit at sunset and watch as the lavender light reflects off the river of white buildings and bathes the Parthenon in an intoxicating blur of rosy and tangerine hues. Once the sun sets, watch for the moon rising behind Mount Imitos in the distance and set your watch for the sound and light display on Acropolis Hill.

If you're like me, order a plate of *halloumi* cheese, delicately pan-fried and a thick, savory wedge of *moussaka*. Have the waiter pour you a glass of crisp, pine scented *retsina*, and as he lights the tiny votives on each table, relish the shimmering effect of candles, moonbeams, and the dance of theatrical klieg lights as the Parthenon, Erechtheion, and Temple of Athena Nike emerge from a veil of darkness into a dramatic blaze that illuminates the entire Acropolis plateau.

❧

57 Syntagma Square

ATHENS'S MAIN PLAZA IS FORMERLY
THE QUEEN'S PERSONAL GARDEN

No matter how long your stay in Athens, you will likely pass through Syntagma Square at least once, if not multiple times. That's because this large open space, also known as Constitution Square, is not only at the center of a fundamental traffic crossroads, it is the core pedestrian hub of Athens and the starting point for the city's outdoor pedestrian mall, Ermou Street. Surrounded by hotels, restaurants, office buildings, as well as the Parliament Building, Syntagma was once the personal garden of Queen Amalia of Greece. It was originally connected to the National Gardens with its five hundred plant species imported from all over the world, and Amalia allowed citizens access to her private Eden until she felt her generosity was being taken advantage of. After banning entry to the public, not to mention diverting public reservoirs to water her plants, she managed to anger a lot of folks. She and her husband, King Otto, were ultimately deposed by the Greek populace in 1862 when they grew fed up with the opulent lifestyle of the queen—as well as with the idea of a monarchy in general.

Today, Syntagma is no longer a garden, but it is the beating heart and soul of Athens. Ever since the public took Syntagma back from Amalia, it has been in the hands of the Greek people, so if there is a protest going on, it will undoubtedly end up here. In the early 1970s, when Greece was under the control of the military generals, students demonstrated here regularly, as Syntagma is located directly across from the Parliament Building. I regularly witnessed protests when I was a student living in Athens, and in 2011, at the height of the economic crisis, I observed daily demonstrations while police stood watchfully nearby. However, Greek protests are largely peaceful, and once the rally is over the city cleans up the signs and opens up traffic, restoring the Square to its hectic pace.

As Matt Barrett says, "The Square has a long history. It seems every major event in Greece has either been mourned or celebrated here. It has held some of the biggest political pep rallies that have ever been seen on the planet."

At the end of World War II, the British arrived in Syntagma to liberate the city, only to find the Germans had already left, forcing them to battle communist partisan forces. In December 1944, Syntagma became a combat zone where British military were forced to protect wealthy citizens against the poor and working class. Barrett goes on to add, "This led to civil war throughout the whole country. The resistance and heroism of the Greeks against the Italians and the Germans had been an inspiration to all the subjugated people of Europe. You could say that the events on December 3rd in Syntagma were the beginning of the Cold War. Though these events are known to few people outside of Greece, when you consider the effects that the policies of the Cold War had on the entire world, it is a wonder that there is not some kind of international recognition of the importance of that day in Syntagma Square in the last half of the twentieth century. It was a defining moment in history."

It is in some ways ironic that this hotspot of political activism is surrounded by the most luxurious hotels in Athens, among them, the King George, the Meridien, and the grand dame of them all, the Grande Bretagne. In the old days, several cafés operated on Syntagma's sleek white marble surface, but today the cafés are gone. However, you can buy an ice cream from one of the *peripterra* (kiosks) and bring it to the center of the square and sit, people watch, and feed breadcrumbs to the flocks of pigeons that descend on visitors. Even though cars, buses, and taxis whiz by the circumference, the array of arborvitae and mulberry trees cast welcome shade on hot Athenian afternoons. With all this pristine marble reflecting the ferocious bright light, you will need to wear sunglasses!

In recent years, the city has undertaken a massive remodeling effort and the entire square has been refurbished, its vast surface clad in shimmering white marble. Benches and light posts have been replaced, a large fountain has been updated, and small ponds have been added along the sides. Part of the reason the square was under construction for so many years was due to the building of the city's metro system. The Syntagma station is one of the most beautiful, with its own mini-museum of artifacts found during the excavation, exhibited in gleaming cases throughout the station.

A set of huge, theatrical marble stairs leads up from Syntagma towards the Parliament Building located across Amalias Avenue, named after the tyrannical queen. Originally meant to be installed atop the Acropolis hill, the Tomb of the Unknown Soldier is located in front of Parliament and is protected by those tall hunks in tights and clogs called *evzones*. Engraved into the tomb is the funeral speech of the 5th century B.C. ruler Pericles, which surprisingly ends with a dedication to women who lost a husband or loved one in battle:

On the other hand, if I must say anything on the subject of female excellence to those of you who will now be in widowhood, it will be all comprised in this brief exhortation. Great will be your glory in not falling short of your natural character; and greatest will be hers who is least talked of among the men, whether for good or for bad.

"*My task is now finished. I have performed it to the best of my ability, and in word, at least, the requirements of the law are now satisfied. If deeds be in question, those who are here interred have received part of their honours already, and for the rest, their children will be brought up till manhood at the public expense: the state thus offers a valuable prize, as the garland of victory in this race of valour, for the reward both of those who have fallen and their survivors. And where the rewards for merit are greatest, there are found the best citizens.*

"*And now that you have brought to a close your lamentations for your relatives, you may depart.*"

58 *Choragic Monument of Lysicrates*

A TROPHY TO END ALL TROPHIES

We've all received awards in our life, right? Maybe a badge for learning how to build a fire in Girl Scouts, or a ribbon for winning a three-legged race? What about that debate cup you won in college or that trophy you were awarded at a swim meet? They're all nice, but they've got nothing on this, because the biggest trophy I've ever seen is sitting at the intersection of Tripodos and Lysicratous Streets in Athens's Plaka district.

You might be heading down Byron Street, admiring window after window of jewelry and handicraft shops, staying out of the sun, and minding your own business when you turn a corner and—boom—there it is. Ringed by terracotta tile-roofed buildings, shops, and restaurants, a tiny, exquisite round temple-looking structure sits just off to the side of the street. Surrounded by leafy trees and ringed with a wrought iron fence, the elegant looking artifact seems out of place with motorcycles and cars squeezing by on the narrow lanes. Yet more than two thousand years ago, this was an intersection of the arts, and this is no tiny temple: this is the Choragic Monument of Lysicrates.

In the 4th century B.C., Lysicrates was a wealthy patron of the arts who sponsored a prize for music performance at the Theater of Dionysus, located just around the corner at the base of the

Acropolis hill along the Makriyanni pedestrian walkway. Choragic monuments are decorative edifices that commemorate the victory of the leader in the choral dances that competed against one another. In antiquity, chorus leaders such as Lysicrates were wealthy citizens who underwrote the dance choruses, who performed and competed in dramatic productions of the time. The word chorus means a group of singers or a choir in ancient Greek, and the *choregos*, or theater sponsor, would today be called an angel. He or she over-saw the selection, training, costuming, and financial support for a team of musicians and dancers. Three types of theater required three different groups of choruses: for tragedy the least amount, fifteen, was necessary; for comedy, twenty-four were required. For a dithyramb chorus, performances devoted solely to Dionysus and which were wild and riotous in nature, a group of fifty performers was necessary.

To the victor come the spoils, and every time an angel would win a competition he was allowed the opportunity to erect a monument at his own expense to assure his name would be immortalized. In honor of his chorus's victory in 334 B.C., Lysicrates had this stunning rotunda erected that served as a base for a bronze tripod given to the best performance.

Nine feet in diameter and more than twenty-one feet high, the cella, or cylindrical core of the monument, is decorated with six adroitly fluted columns topped with lavish Corinthian-style capitals. While the columns appear to be engaged, or half columns, they are actually whole columns separated by panels in between. The bottom of the structure is carved in marble imported from the island of Poros, and the cupola, carved from a single piece of marble from Mount Hymettus, which can be seen looming in the distance over Athens, is patterned in a dizzying display of laurel leaves—appropriate since the leaves were used to crown victors in athletic contests as well.

Gracing the topmost portion is a lacy acanthus finial that was used as a base for the Dionysia contest's winning bronze tripod. It is no longer there, but you can admire the ornate, bucolic carving and the substantial floral scrolls that bracket the finial, most likely crowned originally with sculptures of bronze dolphins. The entire monument sits atop a square platform topped by stairs formed from three cylindrical bases. Between the columns, just beneath the cupola, is a carved frieze of tripods as well as images of pirates being transformed into dolphins by the god Dionysus. Satyrs cater to the god, serving him wine, while he caresses a panther (shades of Doctor Evil with his cat!) and enjoys the entertainment of his pirates being driven into the sea.

An inscription, still legible today, reads,

Lysicrates, son of Lysitheides, from the deme of Kikynna, choragus. The Akamantid tribe carried off the victory in the boy's choirs, Theon was the flute-player, Lysiades of Athens the choir-master, Evainetos the archon.

We have some interesting art lovers to thank for this monument's preservation. In 1658 an order of Capuchin monks built a monastery on this site and in 1669 incorporated the monument into the building, supposedly using it as a library. Later, in 1810, during his second visit to Athens, Lord Byron was a guest at the monastery. Impassioned as ever, his heart aflame with love and inspired by the beauty of Greece and its women, he wrote his poem, *The Maid of Athens*, here.

Maid of Athens, ere we part,
Give, oh give me back my heart!
Or, since that has left my breast,
Keep it now, and take the rest!
Hear my vow before I go,
Zoë mou sas agapo.

By those tresses unconfined,
Woo'd by each Ægean wind;
By those lids whose jetty fringe
Kiss thy soft cheeks' blooming tinge;
By those wild eyes like the roe,
Zoë mou sas agapo.

By that lip I long to taste;
By that zone-encircled waist;
By all the token-flowers that tell
What words can never speak so well;
By love's alternate joy and woe,
Zoë mou sas agapo.

Maid of Athens! I am gone:
Think of me, sweet! when alone.
Though I fly to Istambol,
Athens holds my heart and soul:
Can I cease to love thee? No!
Zoë mou sas agapo.

59 Temple of Olympian Zeus

A COLOSSAL TEMPLE FIT FOR
A GOD OF ENORMOUS APPETITES

Where else in the world could you be walking down a busy metropolitan avenue, with buses, motorcycles, and taxis whizzing by, and suddenly be stopped in your tracks by a small forest of five-story Corinthian columns? That's exactly what you'll find in Athens, for standing right in the middle of downtown is the largest temple in Greece. Constructed on three levels, or a stylobate of three steps, the Temple of Olympian Zeus, also known as the Olympieion, took more than a whopping six hundred years to build. The foundation, which was laid by the tyrant Peisistratos, has the same curved feature as the Parthenon, tilting each of the columns slightly and giving the structure a springy vitality.

Each of these Sequoia-like, fifty-five-foot columns had to be constructed in sixteen sections and the elaborately carved capitals in the Corinthian style were each created in two parts. Originally there were 104 columns, 48 in triple rows under the pediments and 56 in double rows at the sides. Only 15 columns remain standing, as the 16th blew over in what must have been one hell of a storm in 1852, pancaking the pillar like a child's giant stack of blocks across the temple's floor.

The temple was erected on the banks of the ancient River Ilissos, which ran through this area southeast of the Acropolis hill. A series of rulers worked on the structure sporadically, with great gaps of time when nothing was done due to despotic rulers, the deaths of kings, and occasional sackings of the city. Aggressors like Sulla used the building as a quarry and removed some of the columns to rebuild the Temple of Jupiter Capitolinus in Rome, which had burned to the ground.

Construction on the Olympieion, a Greco-Roman temple, began in the 6th century B.C. and was not completed until the 2nd century A.D. under the rule of the Roman emperor Hadrian. In the 15th century, twenty-one columns were still standing. In 1759, one was knocked down and used for lime in the construction of a mosque. The offender, a Turkish governor of Athens during the Ottoman Rule named Tzistarakis, was fined for his vandalism and later poisoned. During the medieval period, an earthquake brought down the remainder of the building, a fate shared with many ancient monuments in Greece, and its contents were quarried and reused to construct other monuments.

A temple of this size was meant to honor the king of the Olympian pantheon as well as a god with massive appetites—and Zeus's were legendary. Some of his most bizarre sexual conquests include his first: the seduction of Metis. This cunning Titaness managed to evade Zeus's advances for a time, but eventually he was successful in impregnating her. Upon learning a prophecy that she was to bear a son greater than the father, Zeus swallowed Metis whole. Unperturbed, Metis knew her child was not a son, but the goddess Athena, and proceeded to hammer away at a set of armor for her daughter, causing Zeus great discomfort. Upon pleading with Hephaestus, the smith-god, to relieve his pain by cracking his skull open, he gave birth to his daughter Athena, who emerged fully formed from his forehead and ready for battle.

Zeus's other memorable conquests were those of Leda, Danae, and Europa. A first rate master of disguise, Zeus transformed himself into a swan to woo Leda and a shower of gold to seduce Danae. For Europa, he shape shifted into a bull and encouraged her to climb onto his back. Swimming across the sea to Crete, he ravaged her there, where she gave birth to the famous half man, half beast, the Minotaur.

When he wasn't busy disguising himself, he managed to transform the objects of his affection into a range of creative camouflages, which came in handy if they happened to be, like Io, a priestess of his insanely jealous wife, Hera. Zeus changed Io into a white heifer in order to hide her among the herd, but Hera wasn't fooled. She put the heifer under the exceptionally watchful guard of the one hundred-eyed shepherd, Argus. With the help of the messenger god, Hermes, Zeus had Argus killed, and a furious Hera took her final revenge by sending a stinging gadfly to torment the heifer, which still manages to plague the beasts today.

A colossal ego must be honored with an equally colossal statue. Temples typically had cult statues within them, such as the Parthenon, which housed the immense image of Athena constructed in gold and ivory by the famed sculpture Phideas. The statue within the Olympieion was believed to be equally massive, and most likely it was made of gold and ivory like its counterpart in the Parthenon. We only have accounts of such statues in modern times, because thieves looted and dissembled them in antiquity, selling off the precious gold and ivory. A similar statue in Olympia of a seated Zeus was more than forty feet tall. Constructed on a base of wood with thin layers of ivory and gold applied all over the surface, the statue held an image of a winged Nike, or goddess of victory, in its left hand, and was so magnificent that it was said to make Roman emperors weep in veneration.

The temple is very close to all downtown attractions. It lies only 500 meters southeast of the Acropolis and 700 meters south of the main square of Syntagma, and Hadrian's Arch, the Zappeion, and the modern Olympic stadium of 1896 are all located nearby. I like to walk to the eastern end of the complex, where you can take in the full glory of the monument as well as the heights of the Acropolis and the Parthenon looming above in the distance. Lest anyone forget, in spite of the gargantuan scale of this temple to the king of Olympian gods, it's ultimately Athena who rules this town.

❧

60 Kerameikos Cemetery and Museum

CITY OF THE DEAD

One of the things I love about Athens is that, in the midst of a city teeming with traffic and millions of people, you can find an idyllic spot right in the center that makes you feel like you're a thousand miles—and a thousand years—away from it. Within the gates of the Kerameikos, the ancient cemetery of Athens, you can wander through the stands of pines and meadow-like grasses and, leaving the city with its teeming lines of tourists behind for a few precious moments, admire the exquisitely carved funerary monuments that punctuate the undulating terrain. Of course the cemetery is replete with the graves of military and political heroes, but interspersed between are monuments offering a tantalizing peek into the lives of everyday women.

The name Kerameikos derives from the ancient Greek word *kerama*, which means pottery, and refers to the community of ceramists that once lived on the banks of the River Eridanos. It also refers to the hero Keramos, the son of Ariadne and the wine-god Dionysos. Most are familiar with the tragic story of Ariadne and Theseus, who had come to the Palace of Knossos to kill the fabled Minotaur. He married Ariadne, the King's daughter, who had left a trail of yarn, helping him find his way out of the beast's famous lair, the Labyrinth. The love affair was short lived; Theseus dumped his bride on the island of Naxos, where she promptly rebounded with Dionysus. She bore him a number of mortal sons, one of whom is Keramos. Mythology tells us that Keramos was important to Dionysus because of the ceramic cups used to drink wine.

All cities have their main thoroughfare, and cities of the dead are no different. The Street of the Tombs, begun in 394 B.C., runs the entire length of the Kerameikos. On either side of this generous, twenty-six-foot roadway are the tombs of the Athenian elite. Stroll among these elegant headstones, each a sculptural triumph, and you will see the classic manner in which the ancient Greeks said goodbye to their loved ones and the uniquely human touches, such as the Aedicula of Eukoline, a portrait of a little girl and her pet dog. In the 5th century B.C., it was common to portray women in scenes from everyday life, not to mention highlighting their status as Athenian citizens. Due to a law invoked by the leader Pericles, from 450 B.C. on Athenian citizenship was passed down through the female line, and sons of these women in particular were keen on displaying this prized inheritance.

Among the male-dominated graves of soldiers lies the monument of two sisters, Demetria and Pamphile (ca. 350 B.C.). Not much is known about their lives, but there is elegance and timelessness to this portrait of two women, fingering their veils and looking out towards the viewer with impassive gazes. Nearby is the tomb of an unmarried bride, which is marked by a *loutrophorous*, a type of water jar, used for a bridal bath. Next to this is the Stele of Hegeso, from 410 B.C., of which the original is in the National Museum. As all who are buried in the Kerameikos, Hegeso was from a leading Athenian family. She is shown selecting a necklace from a small box, held by a servant. Their clothing tells a tale of status: Hegeso wears the flowing himation, chiton, and gauzy headdress, the gathers and folds lovingly captured by the sculptor's hand, while the servant girl wears the shapeless and simple dress of her status. Her hair is wrapped in a simple snood, while Hegeso's elaborate head-gear signifies her priestly office. Regardless of status, the expression of deep sadness on the two women's faces compellingly portrays their emotional connection and sense of loss.

In the southeast corner are the remains of the sanctuary of Artemis Soteira, dedicated to the worship of the goddess Hecate. Known as the third goddess in the triumvirate of Persephone and her mother Demeter, Hecate is the crone of the maiden, mother myth cycle and represents the natural endings of things in life. Her caul-dron is where matter goes to be broken down into its basic components so that it can once again be reincarnated into life.

The entire expanse of the cemetery, known as a *deme*, or neigh-borhood, was divided into two sections: the inner Kerameikos, from the Greek *agora* to the Dipylon and Sacred Gates, which served as the "potters' quarters," and the outer Kerameikos, which ran from the city walls to the Academy of Plato. The site lies at the juncture of some notable architecture: the Themistoklean wall, a fortification that was built in 479 B.C. by the ruler Themistocles, surrounding the entire ancient city following the Persian invasion, but more importantly by the Dipylon and Sacred Gate. The Sacred Gate was constructed over the Eridanos River and the Sacred Way, a road that initiates followed from Athens all the way to the site of Eleusis, some twelve miles away, to attend the annual Eleusinian mysteries.

The Dipylon, whose name means double gate, was the main and larger entrance, and welcomed the greatest volume of visitors to the ancient city. The Dipylon was erected in 479 B.C. on the site of the former Themistoklean gate, and was the favored route to the port of Piraeus. It led all the way up to the Acropolis hill and was known as the Panathenaic Way.

Take some time to wander around the enclosure, which includes the remains of gates, walls, and the tombs of warriors and citizens alike. For a moment you can forget the sounds of the train rumbling by and the busy pedestrian traffic on nearby Ermou. Skinny cypress pines punctuate the site, creating a pleasant boundary from modern-day Athens and frame a view of the Church of Aghia Triada, its carrot-colored terracotta dome hovering above the meadow-like grasses that tumble across the sanctuary. Perhaps take the unique opportunity, as I've seen happen with many visitors, to lie down on the enclosure walls and take a nap in a cemetery. Breathe in the rosemary- and pine-scented air and be lulled to sleep by the insistent drone of the cicadas, complaining crows, and mourning doves.

Before you leave, be sure to visit the small museum. Most of the older finds are in the larger Athens National Museum, but there are gems here. As the name implies, there are large amounts of lovely ceramics on display and a description of Greek pottery types. Just to the right after the entrance is the stele of Ampharete, a portrait of a deceased woman holding her infant grandchild, dated to 410 B.C. These scenes of parting are tender and moving, depicting the small and affectionate moments that make up life. As a photograph today might convey the same instant and freeze it, few do more so for eternity than this touching portrait of a grandmother holding the grandchild she loved, and will miss the most.

꙳꙳

61 *National Archaeological Museum*

LOVELY LADIES IN STONE, FRESCO, AND GOLD

The National Archaeological Museum in Athens is a rather intimidating and cavernous building; filled with treasures from all periods, it sometimes feels stark and formal by nature. Established in 1829, this neoclassical structure, one of many Athenian buildings designed by the German architect Ernst Ziller, contains one of the largest collections of Greek archaeological artifacts in the world. Located next to the Athens Polytechnic University, the museum is in the Exarchia neighborhood famous for its student-friendly bars, restaurants, and clubs. There are many museums in Athens, but this magnificent collection, housing some 20,000 artifacts, is a must see for any visitor to Greece. To make your sojourn through the labyrinthine rooms and massive selection of artifacts a little more user-friendly, I've curated a handful of lovely ladies that offer a peek at Greek art through the ages, and more to the point—from a feminine perspective.

Sculpture of Aphrodite, Pan and Eros

In all your nightmares about being accosted by a creepy old man, none of them would probably come close to this. In the National Museum you will find a statue that will keep you busy for hours, if not incite lurid dreams. This gorgeous, if not somewhat unnerving, sculpture, was discovered on the Cycladic island of Delos in 1904, found in the somewhat verbose Hall of the Guild of the Poseidoniasts of Beirut, which in plain English means worshippers of the sea god Poseidon. This threesome is one of the strangest in antiquity; here is a hideous beast accosting our poor goddess of love and beauty, Aphrodite, and all she has to defend herself is her sandal! Upon closer inspection, however, something tells me she really isn't too concerned about her devilish pursuer.

Aphrodite is the Greek goddess of love and beauty. Many myths abound regarding this powerful goddess, who famously hooked up with many a god and mortal in her romantic encounters. However, she was equally known to be the active agent in breaking up relationships, starting wars, and turning family members against one another in a series of episodes with often-disastrous consequences. But sometimes the goddess found herself in a more playful mode, and in this piece the artist wanted to showcase her sense of humor. What I like about this statue is that it shows Aphrodite in all her curvy glory. Not quite the depiction of dimpled thighs, but neither is it idealized. Ample hips and a roll at the midsection show that the artist appreciated the female form in a guileless way.

Take a close look at this group. Here's Pan, our resident lewd guy, trying to pull the goddess's hand away from her genitals, which she is intent on keeping covered. Pan's leering stare is only heightened in its creepiness by his ersatz horns and fur-covered and hooved legs. What he doesn't know is coming is the imminent whack of a sandal by Aphrodite, whose demeanor seems more amused than fearful of this annoying half-man, half-beast. And Eros, too, has a sly grin on his face as if enjoying the theatrical fireworks.

In the official museum description, scholars state that the sculp-ture reflects the tastes and culture of the tradesmen of Asia Minor. Indeed, the playful, somewhat erotic and almost naughty mood of this piece is in stark contrast to other sculpture from this period, which conforms to the more prevalent severe nature of classical Greek sculpture. Just be sure not to miss this piece, rather on the small side, as you leave the main galleries. It will be guaranteed to put a smile on your face after a long day of ancient art fatigue.

Relief from Eleusis

To the uninitiated, this scene looks like two women standing pas-sively and gazing down beatifically at a young man. Take a closer look and you will see they are handing him a shaft of wheat. This seemingly unremarkable view actually depicts one of the most ancient and mysterious religions: the Eleusinian mysteries. This annual ritual, known as a mystery cult, attracted participants from all over the ancient world, hoping to partake in a nine-day ritual that was designed to free its initiates from the fear of death and release them to a full life. The two women depicted are the main figures in the cult: Demeter, the goddess of agriculture, and her daughter, Persephone, or Kore, the queen of the underworld. When Persephone is abducted by the god of hell, Hades, her mother weeps and nothing grows, which is how ancient mythology explained the seasons. When Persephone is finally returned to the above world, all of nature rejoices and spring returns to the earth. However, because Persephone ate three pomegranate seeds, she was forced to return annually to the underworld, and once again, her mother lets nothing grow one month for every seed, otherwise known as winter. This elegant frieze shows the goddesses handing the all important wheat shaft—symbol of the renewal of crops—to the boy, Triptolemos. Through the gesture of offering wheat to the son of the King of Eleusis, the goddesses are in fact bestowing the gift of agriculture to all mankind.

The Mycenaean Lady

The flowing, diorite-colored locks, curled around the forehead and bound into an elaborate chignon. The saffron and brick-red colored robe, kohl penciled eyes, and graceful curve of the wrist. This could be a portrait of any woman throughout time, dressed for an important event and decked out to the max. Yet this woman lived in the 13th century B.C. in Mycenae, an ancient royal kingdom located in the Peloponnesian peninsula, and this stunning fresco would have been one of many decorating the expansive palace walls. The slate blue background, serene profile, and aristocratic stance all testify to the royal birth of this woman, who is shown receiving the gift of a gold necklace. There is a slight smile on her face, which indicates that she is pleased by the gift, but the slyness of the grin suggests perhaps she was just expecting a little trinket and that, like many women of all ages, suspects she is well worth it.

Boxing Girls

So are they boys or girls? This is the eternal question when gazing at this lively and playful scene from a fresco excavated on the island of Santorini, which was destroyed in a catastrophic volcanic explosion sometime between 1650 and 1550 B.C. Some archaeologists state that the darker coloration of the skin denotes a male figure, but the Minoan culture that produced this lyrical fresco was a playful and largely matriarchal society where women held roles of equal importance to men. I prefer to think of the pair as tomboys, their flowing locks braided into tight ropes, braceleted arms and thin waist garments, duking it out for fun. In fact, just outside this exhibit as I was leaving the museum, I saw a pair of bored preteen girls sitting on a marble bench and slapping it out in an elaborate game of patty cake. Just goes to show you some things don't change in thirty-six hundred years.

Glorious Gold Jewels

✽ www.namuseum.gr/wellcome-en.html

A leafy, golden myrtle wreath peppered with berries from the 4th century B.C. A golden hairnet from the 3rd century B.C., with the bust of the goddess of the hunt, Artemis, and her quiver of arrows. A pair of glimmering serpentine bracelets that would give a snake charmer fits. Golden necklaces, earrings, and an almost pliable-looking braided strap of gold punctuated with a Herakles knot that would have been fitted diagonally onto a woman's chest. These are but a few items of the magnificent gold jewelry collection in the National Museum's collection. I could stand in this hall for hours and gaze at these stunning objects, imagining the glory of the women who wore them and wondering what occasions might have warranted such finery. Even though I'm a silver girl at heart, I'd make an exception for these gleaming treasures—and if I had to choose between wreaths, rings, snoods, and braided belts, I wouldn't have any trouble. Those snake bracelets with their ruby-jeweled throats and tails had me at hello.

❧

62 The Athens Metro

ARCHAEOLOGICAL SITE AND
SUBTERRANEAN MUSEUM

If you told a visitor to New York that the subway was a beautiful and tourist-worthy destination right up there with the Statue of Liberty, they would probably look at you like you were crazy. But in Athens, it's true. Ever since the labyrinthine network of underground tunnels was painstakingly carved out of the bowels of this archaeologically significant city, the result makes you wonder if the underworld of Athens is almost more beautiful than the above-ground city.

Ever since my school days in Athens, I never got tired of coming upon pieces of temple foundations in drainage ditches, grave stelae in restaurant basements, and sections of the ancient Themistoclean wall that surrounded Athens in the lower levels of parking garages. All had makeshift fences around them, barely shielding them from wear and tear. So when the excavations for the subway system began, workers had to stop almost every day because they ran into archaeological material everywhere. Representatives from the Greek Archaeological Service were tasked with overseeing the excavation and the subway has been a long time in the making. Fifty archaeologists and hundreds of workers labored ten long years to create this state-of-the-art subterranean and aboveground railway system.

But for that, we are grateful. Today, the subway stations are some of the most pristine, beautiful, and archaeologically significant in the world. But the project was not without its problems. During construction, sinkholes would open up and "swallow" items, such as street kiosks, and part of an ancient wall located in the National Gardens started to sink, thanks to the tunnel boring machine, or TBM, a gigantic claw-like contraption that burrowed its way under the streets and buildings of downtown Athens. Hawk-eyed archaeologists deduced that sticking to a depth of sixty-five feet would bypass the most critical areas of archaeological remains, but ventilation shafts had to be dug nonetheless, and when artifacts were found, the TBM was stopped and the tunnel was hand dug, earthful by earthful, sharply reducing the probability that any remains would be overlooked or worse—damaged.

In a city of too many cars, the efforts of the TBM and a few lost kiosks were worth the trouble. Athens's pollution has been so famous it has a name: *to nefos,* or "the cloud," a filmy haze that, in past decades, surrounded the city like a ring around the collar of dirt. With the metro in full operation, car use has dropped off dramatically, leaving Athens with a shot for improving its notorious air quality.

This first time I went underground with my friend and long-time Athens resident, Katharine, she prepared me for the many wonders I was to witness. "It's absolutely fabulous. The excavators left portions of ancient water pipes in place and you can see them behind glass panels." She was right. As an archaeologist, I was almost shocked to see the pristine state these clay pipes were in. Abruptly cut to make way for the station, their original purpose had long since been rendered ineffective, yet behind the huge plate-glass cases they almost appear as works of art. Earthen walls are thickened with blush-colored stone, interlaced with brick-colored clay pipes that recall a Louise Nevelson sculpture, or one of Georgia O'Keefe's bone-stark compositions.

✳ www.athensinfoguide.com/gettingaround.htm

For a short tour, start your trip at Monastiraki Station. After buying your ticket at one of the self-serve kiosks, pass through the gates and descend the gleaming escalators to a true underworld. Deep beneath the bustling marketplace of Monastiraki lies a veritable playground of pipes, conduits, waterways and other archaeological wonders. Gaze at a giant slice of glassed-over wall of ancient Athens or climb stairs to walk directly over an ancient road, still in situ. I marvel at the juxtaposition of ancient and modern pathways, the fluidity of water that once coursed through ancient clay pipes and the modernity of commuters flowing through huge earthen pipes in metal tubes.

Change trains at Syntagma Station and take time to admire the steel and marble central hallways. As you pass along your way to the Acropolis line, make note of the huge photograph taken from excavations, showcasing a veritable river of ancient pots lying, unfettered, in an ancient underground space, just uncovered by workers.

Arriving at the Acropolis Station, leave the underworld via the gleaming escalators and once again you are greeted at the ground floor by a showcase of ancient pithos jars, earthenware pots and sherds of black-figured vases that were recovered from the excavations. The dazzling display as you exit the main area of the station is a welcome and tantalizing prelude to the treasures that await you aboveground in the new Acropolis Museum.

As one journalist stated, "The metro is like an art salon under the city turning the journey around Athens into a unique and pleasurable experience." Considering that aboveground the journey often entails heat, graffiti, and traffic, don't miss a chance to head into Athens's underworld where hallways of marble, archaeological treasure, and efficient transport await.

❧

63 *Athens's Pedestrian Walkway*

ARCHAEOLOGICAL UNIFICATION PROJECT
AND OPEN-AIR MUSEUM

When I lived in Athens years ago, there were no pedestrian-friendly walkways in the city. Ermou Street was just one of many chaotic, taxi-clogged arteries leading away from the city's central heart of Syntagma Square, as were the busy main thoroughfares that wound around the base of the Acropolis hill. I can still remember the plumes of exhaust and noise that accompanied a taxi ride around the circumference of the Parthenon. Trying to crane my neck out the window to look up at this magnificent building was seriously hampered by swerving traffic, impatient drivers, not to mention the insistent chatter of the dispatch and nerve-jangling music on the radio.

Today all of this is different. Thanks to the 2004 Olympics, Athens decided to banish automobiles from the long winding roads around the base of the Acropolis hill and transform them into a pedestrian walkway, and the results are nothing less than magnificent. What was formerly an unattractive stretch of asphalt is now completely free of traffic, creating an archaeological zone around Athens's most important monuments and offering visitors a chance to approach and appreciate these glorious ruins from an intimate and peaceful perspective.

The genesis for the Grand Promenade, as this archaeological unification project has become known, was to create an ostensibly open-air museum around the city's most prominent sites, all gathered in close proximity around the base and summit of the Acropolis hill. Billed as perhaps the country's largest outdoor museum, the promenade encompasses all the sites between the Temple of Olympian Zeus, Hadrian's Arch, the Acropolis monuments, and the Hill of the Nymphs, passing neoclassical architecture, state of the art museums, and culture-rich regions filled with cafés, shops, and transportation.

Anna Kafetsi, curator of a former exhibition along the Grand Promenade, states the importance of this archaeological space in a way only the Greek mind can elucidate:

"As experience and metaphor the Grand Promenade allows unexpected encounters and ties, stories and within history, new relationships between the local and the universal, and an open conceptual narrative incorporating the Elsewhere and Others."

Depending on where you're staying, you can start this promenade at either end. My preference finds its genesis at Anafiotika, near the Acropolis Subway station. Anafiotika is one of the loveliest sections of the Plaka neighborhood and is chock full of quaint tavernas, shops, and antiquities, such as the Choragic Monument of Lysicrates. The eyesore of asphalt that used to be the city's most busy street has been replaced by a veritable Wizard of Oz yellow brick road, paved instead with silvery tinged square cobblestones. Lined on one side by a stretch of sidewalk friendly trees, the other is nothing less than an up close tour of Athens's hit parade of sites.

Starting at the Acropolis Metro Station, you will see the new Acropolis Museum to your left as you set out on what was formerly known as Dionysiou Aeropagitou Street. Snugged into a neighborhood of posh neoclassical buildings with killer views of the

Parthenon, this modern glass structure somehow shares real estate comfortably with its more staid neighbors, reminding visitors once again of Athens's unique character to blend the old with the new.

A few steps farther on you will come across the Theater of Dionysus. Built into the south slope of the Acropolis hill in the late 6th century B.C., this amphitheater was dedicated to Dionysus, the god of wine and pleasure, whose statue was prominently displayed in the front row so he could enjoy the performances in his honor. In the 4th century, stone seats were added and the site could accommodate an astounding 17,000 spectators. In the following centuries the site was renovated, altered, and improved upon until its destruction by the Roman emperor Sulla. Take a moment to wander among the ruins and imagine the thunderous applause that would have rung out after performances by such tragic poets as Euripides and Aeschylus, reverberating against the ancient sheer rise of the Acropolis on an ancient Athenian evening.

Directly adjacent to the Theater of Dionysus is the Herodus Atticus Theater. This structure was erected under the Roman Emperor Herod and is easily recognized by its lacy multi-tiered façade, what remains of a massive three-story *skene*, or wall behind the stage. While this theater presents a more dramatic façade than its neighboring theater of Dionysus, it only seats 5000.

Continue down the walkway as it gently curves to the right and becomes what formerly was Apolostolou Pavlou, or street of Paul the Apostle. To the left you notice a fork that leads you into a densely wooded area up to the Hill of the Nymphs. The main pedestrian promenade continues to the right where you will see entrances to the Acropolis monument itself. It's difficult not to swoon as you stroll along this portion of the promenade. As the Parthenon and the Temple of Athena Nike come into full view, you can't help but come to a full stop and stare as well heeled Athenian dowagers walking their pampered terriers bemusedly pass you by, leaving you to your reverie. Once you come to your senses, you have a choice: enter a pathway to the right that will lead you to the ancient Greek Agora, or continue on the promenade. Eventually you will arrive at an intersection of tony cafés that offer both outdoor seating and rooftop dining with sublime views of the Acropolis hill and Aeropagitou or Mars Rock, the smooth balding plateau of rock just beneath the Acropolis.

Active social life is evident in this area. Lovers lean against fences, mothers push twin strollers, old men walk arm in arm on their way to a game of *tavli* and glasses of *café metrio* at a local taverna. As you draw closer to the Theseion Metro Station, the walkway becomes an outdoor market and you come upon tangled displays of shadow puppets for sale, ice cream vendors, and crowds gathering around spray paint artists who create their masterpieces wearing gas masks. Athens is a city of stark contradictions and one needs a sense of patience and humor to navigate its often frustratingly confusing streets and often-incorrect directions by well-meaning locals. But it is also a place of seduction; if you take a moment to stroll along this epic promenade you will catch a glimpse of this city's powerful urban heart and soul.

☙

64 The Panathenaic Olympic Stadium

FEMALE ATHLETES NOT ALLOWED

As modern Olympic stadiums go, we normally think of vast concrete and metal leviathans that loom around the track competitions, or the immense halls erected for the skating exhibitions. But imagine if the main stage Olympic events were held outside in a sunny clime and you were seated in a huge stadium, fashioned entirely out of shimmering marble? Well, such a stadium exists—right in the middle of downtown Athens.

As we all know, Greece is the birthplace of the Olympics. Established in 776 B.C. in honor of the god Zeus, the ancient Olympic games were held every four years at the site of Olympia in the Peloponnese, and attracted the best male athletes from the Hellenic world. The games continued every four years—a time period that came to be termed as an Olympiad—until the 4th century A.D., when they died out.

After some 1,500 years, the Olympics were revived in the modern era back in the country of their origin: Greece. A special stadium, known as the Panathenaic Stadium or Kallimarmaro (beautiful marble), was carved into the hill of the Pangrati neighborhood and constructed entirely of creamy marble from Mount Pentelis. This glimmering icon, as beautiful as it is, had a design malfunction. With corners so sharp that track athletes had to slow down at the curves, it made the races difficult to negotiate. But the 1896 games were a rousing success for everyone involved, with the exception of women, who, as they had been since antiquity, were not allowed to compete.

✳ www.visitgreece.gr/en/culture/monuments/
    the_panathenaic_stadium

Originally the site of a natural valley between two hills, an ancient stadium previously stood at this site, erected in 330-329 B.C. by a politician named Lykourgos. During the Roman period it was expanded by Herodes Atticus, a Greek philanthropist and Roman senator who funded other buildings, such as the epony- mous theater at the base of the Acropolis. The modern restoration of the stadium began in the late 19th century using Pentelic mar- ble—the same material used to build the Parthenon some two mil- lennia before—and the venue was expanded to accommodate some 60,000 spectators.

In 2004, the Olympics came back to Greece, and the stadium, while not used for the track and field events due to its incongru- ous design, did serve as the finish line for the much anticipated marathon event. The marathon was first introduced to the Olympic games in the 1896 Athens event, and was won by a Greek, Spyridon Louis, bringing great glory to his home country. As history buffs may know, the original marathon was no sporting event; it was the personal race of a messenger bearing news of war.

Marathon is a real place, a town by the sea about twenty-five miles northeast of Athens. In 490 B.C., the Athenians won a great victory in battle against the Persian army. Long before the Internet or television, news still had to travel, and this critical information was vested to a messenger named Pheidippidis. Taking off from Marathon, he covered the near twenty-five miles in record time to deliver the news. Upon arrival, however, exhausted and depleted from his exertion, he reportedly collapsed on the spot and died, having the strength to utter only one word to his fellow Athenians: "*Nenikikamen*—We Won." To commemorate his heroic efforts, the marathon event was first introduced with the modern games. The race remained at 25 miles, until the 1908 Olympics in London, when the distance was lengthened to the requisite 26.2 miles. According to legend, the royal family wanted to view the event, so the course was stretched to commence on the lawn of Windsor Castle to accommodate Queen Alexandra and the youngest royals, who watched from their nursery's balcony. The race finished up in front of the royal box at the Olympic stadium in London, and the additional mile plus has remained a part of the race since.

In 2004, huge crowds witnessed the return of the marathon to Greece, which began at the town of Marathon and finished in the Panathenaic Stadium. The world record holder, Paula Radcliffe from Great Britain, heavily favored to win the race, ended up quitting at twenty-two miles due to a leg injury, a deep disappointment to many fans who had expected her to win. She was overtaken by Mizuki Noguchi, who won the gold, and Catherine Ndereba, who took silver. But it was Massachusetts-born Deena Kastor whom Americans cheered on as she entered the massive stadium for her victory lap and the bronze medal in this hallowed event.

The stadium is located just off the main artery of Vassileos Konstantinou (King Constantine) Avenue and across the street from the National Gardens, where I often see joggers making their leisurely way around the track while busloads of tourists disgorge to take shots of this still striking venue. If you have a chance, take a moment to admire this vast expanse of precious marble, an architectural feat in itself. Then climb the risers, take a seat high up in the stadium, and imagine the roar of the crowds as the athletes from both 1896 and 2004 were crowned for the marathon events.

65 The Grande Bretagne

THE GRAND OLD DAME OF ATHENS

Lady Gaga slept here...and so did Sophia Loren. In this world there are elegant old grand dames of hotels, and of them all, the Grande Bretagne in Athens is the reigning queen. Perhaps the Excelsior in Rome, the Cipriani in Venice, and the Georges Cinque in Paris all rank up there, but there is an old school vibe to the GB, as locals call it, that you can't find anywhere else.

If only these walls could talk. The sheer number of celebrities who have graced these halls is astounding. After all, when in Athens, there really is no other place to stay for the well-heeled and well-connected. The neighboring King George and NJV Athens Plaza are both spectacular hotels, but this neoclassical designed structure, built by architect Kostas Voutsinas, is an original. To this day it stands, like the queen it is, towering over Athens's main Syntagma Square.

Condé Nast Traveler lists the GB as one of the world's best 100 hotels. As Matt Barrett of Matt Barrett's Travel Guides states, "the Grande Bretagne is not just a luxurious hotel in central Athens. It is an historic landmark that has hosted the world's most well-known dignitaries and has been the scene of some of the most remarkable moments in Greece's history." During World War II when Greece fell under German control, the GB became a Nazi headquarters for three years. After the war, heads of state such as Winston Churchill met with Greek government leaders at the GB to discuss the communist resistance.

Barrett goes on to list a number of updates done for the 2004 Athens Olympics, including a rooftop pool with killer view of the Parthenon, and a state-of-the-art spa. Wander through the reception area and admire the gold-painted coffered ceilings, silver candelabras and silk settees. The design scheme offers a mixture of Ionic and Corinthian capitals on columns and pillars, rich period furnishings, paintings, and elaborately decorated marble flooring.

✳ www.grandebretagne.gr

My friend Shelley Sarver recently stayed at the GB and raved about the hotel services. "The restaurant on the roof and the view were definitely the highlight of the hotel," as were "the Hermes toiletries in the bathroom!" adding, "The view of the Acropolis day and night was its most unique feature and never gets old."

Some famous broads who have slipped between the multihundred thread count sheets of the GB include icons of past and present. Sophia Loren and Elizabeth Taylor have graced the GB with their exquisite presences, as have Maria Callas, Ursula Andress, Rose and Ethel Kennedy, Natassja Kinski, and Joan Collins. More recent guests include Tracy Chapman, Grace Jones, and Paris Hilton, who once dated the incredibly same-named Paris Latsis, the son of a Greek shipping tycoon. In 2014, Lady Gaga stayed at the hotel during the Athens leg of her European tour and her entourage included her mother, whom Shelley sat next to while enjoying a pedicure in the GB's spa.

Yet the most notorious cinema goddess on the Grande Bretagne's guest list has to be Brigitte Bardot. This sex siren stayed at the GB at the height of her career, during the leather bustier, thigh high boots, and whip phase. According to Matt Barrett,

Bardot rode a motorcycle down the Grand
Stairway of the GB in 22.8 seconds, a record
"likely to remain unbroken." For the rest
of us lesser mortals, we can still feel like a
cinema queen just walking through the GB's
lobby and imagining the heads of state such
as Indira Ghandi, Dwight Eisenhower, Yassir
Arafat, Jimmy Carter, and Lyndon Johnson,

all whose heels have clicked down these marble hallways.

At the end of the Ottoman occupation in 1842, the structure
was built as a private home for businessman Antonis Dimitrios.
In 1874 it was purchased by hotelier Savvas Kentros and Efthasios
Lampsas and opened its doors to visitors. One of its most important
early moments came during the first Olympics of the modern era in
1896, when it hosted visiting heads of state, diplomats, and royalty.

In 1956 four stories were added to the hotel at the end of
Greece's bitter civil war, and witnessed several decades of political
instability. After the military occupation of Greece ended in 1974,
the GB was headquarters for Constantine Karamanlis, who formed
a new government in the confines of his fifth floor suite. The year
2003 saw the hotel undergo a complete renovation just in time for
the 2004 Olympics, where the hotel once again saw a parade of
athletes and other modern Olympic luminaries.

Any major event involving heads of state takes place in the
GB's dining rooms, which offer the kind of banquet facilities one
would expect to pass muster with royalty. Heavy swag drapery, gilt
mirrored walls, lacy chandeliers, and the finest china, crystal, and
silverware are definitely old school with a nod to Versailles.

I have to admit, when I was a student living in Greece, my
friends and I enjoyed visiting the Grande Bretagne for reasons
other than the chic bar or the swank dining room. In these pre-cell
phone days the only way to phone home was to locate enormous

red public phones that were installed in bars or movie theaters. A favorite place to ring up friends was the red phone in the basement of the GB, where we snuck away from school to spend a few private moments calling family, friends and most of all, my boyfriend (and now husband) just to hear his voice. These bulbous, cherry red phones have become relics from the past, but I can guarantee you that, no matter how many decades pass, the Grande Bretagne will never go out of style.

66 Greek Shadow Puppetry and Karaghiozis

FIGOURES AND KOUKLES AND HARIDIMOS
WORKSHOP AND MUSEUM

Don't be fooled—people may say this is for kids only, but if so, I'm a big kid. I love shadow puppets. Ever since *The Year of Living Dangerously* starring Mel Gibson and Sigourney Weaver became one of my favorite movies with its Javanese shadow puppets, I've been mesmerized by these storytelling figures. Java may have Semar and Gareng, but Greece has the most famous shadow puppet character of all: Karaghiozis.

Shadow puppetry probably originated from Wayang Kulit in Indonesia, and came to Greece during the Ottoman rule in the 19th century from the Turkish shadow play Karagoz and Hacivat. Called Karaghiozis in Greek, which means "dark-eyed," this comical character depicts the common everyman with his human faults and tribulations. Portrayed as a poor hunchback, Karaghiozis's right hand is always depicted as longer than his left. His feet are bare and his clothes scruffy and ragged. He lives with his wife, Aglaia, and their three sons in a hovel across from the Ottoman Palace and his escapades depict the social and political struggles of life in 19th-century Greece.

Karaghiozis and his host of fellow characters are portrayed by colorful paper cut-outs manipulated by a puppeteer behind a white screen. The cozy theater, Figoures and Koukles, located at 30 Tripodon Street in the Plaka neighborhood of Athens, is one place to see this ancient art from, but shadow puppetry is prevalent all over Greece. Popular with both children and adults, Karaghiozis appears in the summertime in village squares, as well as theaters and festivals, such as the Wall Festival in Thessaloniki.

Shadow puppet expert Dorina Papaliou explains what the character represents to the Greeks. "The carnivalesque element...could be what makes Karaghiozis and shadow theater so appealing. Carnival is characterized by role and situation reversal. Through the use of masks and fancy dressing, everyday hierarchical order is temporarily suspended...emphasis on food, sexuality, the insatiable desire for material satisfaction and transformation are characteristics present in Karaghiozis performances, providing the audience with something like a temporary liberation from the prevailing system of laws and control. Shadow theater is part of the Greek cultural inheritance. The Karaghiozis shadow theater is an oral art form, and it is through its talented performers that it will stay alive."

✳ https://www.cityofathens.gr/en/haridimos-shadow
   -puppet-museum-theatre-1

Children and adults alike can relate to this comical character, who appears in a vast array of guises, including sea captain, icon painter, prophet, and doctor. With his bulbous nose and extra long arm, the scrappy hero is always trying to impersonate some professional with the aim of making money, but his antics inevitably get him into trouble, much to the delight of audiences who watch him try to worm his way out of his difficulties. This hard luck characteristic appeals to the Greeks, who have struggled for centuries with foreign occupations, wars and political juntas.

Another favorite spot is the museum of Karaghiozis, located in the Melina Mercouri Cultural Center, also in the Plaka district. Here children on field trips can try their hand at puppetry and admire the intricate designs of the dozens of characters that appear in these shadow dramas. Visitors from two to one hundred and two can enjoy the more than nine hundred images depicting sets and characters of the work of Sotiris, Christos and Giorgos Haridimos, a trio of puppeteers famous in Greece. The exhibition traces the growth of the art form during the 20th century, showcasing the different techniques and materials of various masters.

While the museum doesn't offer regular shows, visiting school children are often treated to impromptu performances. If you are lucky, you might catch a glimpse of Mr. Haridimos himself, a lead figure in the art of shadow puppetry and historian in his own right. Although his own theater was closed and transformed into a café, his craft lives on through his teaching, which is supported by the Greek Ministry of Culture, to ensure this delightful storytelling art form does not die out.

❧

67 Athens Graffiti Tours

ONE PERSON'S SCRIBBLE IS ANOTHER'S ART

Seen the Parthenon already? Tired of one too many Corinthian capitals or heroic statues? How about a graffiti tour? What some disparage as urban blight, others see as an art form in its own right. As you walk through the streets of Athens you will see your share of walls covered in a rainbow of colors, particularly in the Psirri neighborhood, where this old red-light district has been repurposed in recent years to become a destination for people seeking a different kind of pleasure: bars, clubs and restaurants.

If you prefer, wander through the narrow, labyrinthine streets of this tangled part of town and take in the panoply of designs that cover apartment buildings and shop walls—you could take all day, just weaving your way through these narrow lanes and getting lost in the process. Or you can take a graffiti tour, courtesy of several outfits in Athens that offer a new way to see the city. Graffiti is not a new thing—the word itself comes from the Greek *grapho*, which means to write. The ancients themselves carved their initials into buildings and even more modern visitors have done so, such as Lord Byron, who purportedly scraped his name onto a column at the site of the Temple of Poseidon at Sounion, located at the tip of Attica.

✳ www.alternative-athens.com/streetarttour.html

When I lived in Athens, graffiti had a primarily political bent. Everywhere you would see scrawls consisting mostly of black and red inscriptions for the communist party KKE, with its iconic hammer and sickle symbol, and PASOK, the socialist party. However, today, young Athenians have found new ways to express themselves. No longer tethered to just red or black lettered political jargon, artists often create huge designs, sometimes retro in nature, showing women with a fist raised in a power gesture and the words "Never on Sunday" next to them, alluding to the famous movie starring Greek icon Melina Mercouri. Or you can find existential quotes, such as the eye-grabbing *Where is My Mind?* hovering, inexplicably, above a black-and-white image of a bicycle.

As I have said, graffiti is controversial. An apartment building gets freshly painted and it doesn't take long for some kid with a spray can to put his mark on the wall. Is this the work of aimless youth or an artistically inspired generation of artists? You come to Greece to see works of art, and the ancient types hardly ever disappoint (although I did once hear a loud American bellow out, after huffing and puffing his way to the top of the stairs to the Parthenon, "I came 8,000 miles just to see a pile of rocks?")

Cartoon characters, spaceships, and geometric designs...the possibilities are endless. Yes, there is a share of really unattractive stuff—someone out to merely mark up a building. But the choices of colors, and the level of artistry for many of these wall scenes is remarkable. It runs the gamut from the sacred to the profane: some walls are covered in Japanese-style manga angels, many quote famous writers and philosophers and some are jarringly, if not hilariously, pornographic. It's not unusual to be walking down a maze-like series of streets in Psirri, turn the corner and be confronted by a corrugated shop door, closed for afternoon siesta, emblazoned with a kissing couple and a cherub floating nearby, or a huge diorama with the words: *Dinatos o Laos* (Power to the People) suspended over a toddler in sunglasses wearing a shirt with the logo: *I love life*. Sometimes the art is not limited to graffiti; near Agia Irini Square a cobalt blue mask of a human face is embedded into the wall above a sun gold image of a cartoon character and a smiley face.

Some of the images are on a huge scale and are artistic achievements indeed. A pair of praying hands, painted by graffiti artist Pavlos Tsakonas, descends from a wall towering over Pireos Street, appearing to bless passersby with a God-like benediction. On a five-story elevator shaft near the Kerameikos Cemetery is a pair of superimposed—and thoroughly imposing—images of the ancient Athenian leader Solon by the artist iNo.

Some people fail to see the beauty even in traditional forms of art. So after a tour of Athens's graffitied walls, you decide: defacement, or art? It is images such as these that remind you of the fluid nature of a city that hovers between past and present, eternally attempting to maintain a creative link between its ancient and modern realities.

≈✗≈

68 Outdoor Cinemas

WHERE OUZO AND POPCORN MEET HOLLYWOOD

It's a slow summer evening. You rack your brain, thinking of things to do, and then it comes to you: a cool drink, popcorn, and air conditioning—let's go see a movie! But if you are in Athens, you won't be heading to the local suburban multiplex to see the latest chick flick. Oh no, we can do much better than that, ladies: we can all head to the Thission.

Imagine you are waiting for the lights to dim. You hold a cold drink in your hand; a cool breeze ruffles your hair. Wait a minute—did I say cool breeze? That's exactly right; while you wait for the projector to light up, you tilt your head skywards, and instead of a foam-insulated ceiling you see—the stars. And then you turn your head to the left and to your astonishment, there's the Parthenon, lit up and glowing. As the opening credits appear on the screen, you can hardly tear your gaze away from the other show in the room: the entire top of the Acropolis hill in Athens, lit up and glowing like an enormous Roman candle on a hot Athenian summer night.

The first time I went to an outdoor cinema like this, I was a student, living in Athens. My Greek friends asked if I wanted to go to a movie. Thinking they meant the local Odeon, I was thrilled to find we entered a gate, and, crossing the crunchy gravel beneath our feet, seated ourselves in the metal chairs. Back then, everyone in the theater smoked, because it was outdoors! Today is no different, so if you're a non-smoker, consider yourself warned. Greeks smoke outdoors everywhere, so you'll have trouble getting away from it.

There is more than one outdoor cinema, but the Thissio is probably the most famous, with its amazing view of the Parthenon and the adjoining Agora. Built in 1935, the theater has a retro feel to it, with images of Bogey and Bacall stenciled onto the cocktail tables scattered throughout the theater, and bougainvillea vines crowding the open-air screen. Located near the Thisseo metro station along the Grand Promenade walkway near the ancient Agora, and open April through October, the Thissio is number one on CNN's list of ten of the world's most enjoyable movie theaters. But if you feel like cinema-hopping, there are a number of other theaters scattered around the metropolitan area.

✳ www.athenskey.com/open-air-cinema.html

The Cine Paris is located nearby in the Plaka neighborhood. Opened originally by a hairdresser, this movie house occupies another prime location in downtown Athens. Built in the 1920s, the hairdresser once lived in Paris, hence the name. The theater shut down for almost twenty years in the 1960s, when Athens was undergoing a building boom. Anxious to take advantage of the opportunity, more than one thousand cinemas were shut down when owners sold their land. Yet Cine Paris managed to survive, and was re-opened in 1986, where it occupies a rooftop setting situated just beneath the Acropolis hill.

Generally there are two showings a night, one at 9 P.M. and another at 11 P.M. Recall that Greeks are late night folks, especially in the summertime, when this is the coolest time of day to be out enjoying yourself. Savor a handful of popcorn or a glass of anise-flavored ouzo, and inhale the fresh jasmine growing alongside as you watch the latest Hollywood releases.

Dexameni is one of the toniest parks in Athens, located in Kolonaki where some of the most expensive real estate is located. This is the neighborhood where many embassies are based, as well as the American School of Classical Studies and other foreign archaeological schools and their libraries. Dexameni's open-air cinema was created on the site of one of the city's old reservoirs, so it has the double effect of repurposing an abandoned structure and creating an enjoyable and entertaining destination in one of the city's fanciest neighborhoods. The large screen, lush vegetation, and bespoke blue-and-white lawn chairs provide a serene respite for the theater's loyal clientele.

Nearby is Cine Psyrri. Built in a transformed warehouse and parking lot, this cinema screens both the favorite classic black-and-white films (a nostalgic favorite among locals) as well as new releases. In the heart of the Zappeion garden, located within the city's national gardens and just off Syntagma Square, is the Aigli. This large cinema with its ornate outdoor screen and walled enclave shows blockbuster films and offers unique treats; instead of snow caps and gummy bears, order up some souvlaki and sangria.

If you're in Athens during the summer months, consider taking in a movie at one of these historic outdoor cinemas. Even if the film isn't on your favorites list, go anyway for the ambiance, the eclectic food choices at the concession stand (some theaters offer meatballs, *tiropitas* [cheese pies], and *moussaka!*) and a chance to view not only the stars on the screen but those sparkling overhead.

❧

69

Doctor Fish, Hammam, and the Grande Bretagne Spa

PLACES TO GET PAMPERED IN ATHENS

The first time I walked by this place, I couldn't believe my eyes. Women were lined up against the walls, traditional beauty shop style, but there were no hairdryers over their heads. Instead, their feet were all plunged into what I could only describe as...aquariums. Fish were nibbling at their toes! What was this, some miniature type of piranha torture? I approached a mother-daughter duo sitting side by side and asked how it felt. "Sort of weird," said the daughter, gingerly lowering her feet into the tank. The mother hesitated, and then bravely plunged in her candy-pink-painted toes. I waited for a moment when she suddenly shrieked with laughter and cried out, "It tickles!" I asked the shop's manager if this was where Kim Kardashian had been filmed on her reality TV show's Greek family odyssey, famously shrieking after dipping her toes into the fish-laden waters. The shop manager rolled her eyes and replied, "No, that was another shop on Santorini."

❋ www.doctor-fish.gr

Apparently having fish nibble on your toes is all the rage in Greece. I watched as the fish—actually they are a breed of tiny carp—worked away at the mother's and daughter's feet. Their electric-painted toes shimmered in the water and created a surreal scene as the fish zeroed in, nibbling away at the dead flesh. Just the slightest bit gross? Maybe. But if you're the kind who wants to knock yet another to-do item off your bucket list, then an Athenian fish pedicure might be just the thing for you. Doctor Fish is located in the heart of the Plaka district, so if you're tired after packed days of sightseeing, shopping, and eating, take a break and enjoy this cool, serene respite from the nonstop pandemonium of the city.

If fish are not your thing, there are several different kinds of spas to choose from in Athens. For the younger crowd, Hamman is your bet. Located just beyond the Monastiraki district, this little gem is the spot to book massages. Hamman is a Turkish word for spa and you are warmly greeted and led to one of the private rooms for treatment. I felt immediately relaxed upon entering the hushed, darkened space shimmering with candles, in sharp contrast to the blinding Athenian light just outside. Take an hour—or two—and treat yourself to a variety of treatments.

✳ hammam.gr/en

A hot room dominates the spa, built in the style of the traditional hamman in Istanbul. This domed ceiling, decorated with moons and stars, hovers like a magical sky over a round central platform, and is supplied with metal bowls to dip in water and pour over your head. There are hot and dry massage areas, beautiful changing rooms lined in serene blond wood and a relaxation room where you can cool down and enjoy mint tea and Turkish delight after your treatment. One women gushed that the owner himself, "who resembled Leonidias in *300!*" offered them towels, tea and candles after their massage. What better way to end a day of beauty than having a hunky Greek god escort you into a relaxation space!

If your travel budget is a little heftier, you might want to indulge in the grandmother of all Athenian spas, the GB spa at the Grande Bretagne hotel. Bone-white marble walls, crystal chandeliered ceilings, orchids, blond wood saunas and tessera-tiled walls will greet you. A central courtyard is dominated by a fountain and towering palms beneath a glass skylight, and the spa has state-of-the-art massage tables, a tiled Jacuzzi known as the amethyst grotto, and a gold-tiled herbal steam bath. It is described by one website as "decadent," and you can indulge in a variety of treatments including Thai, Balinese, Ayurvedic or even-wait for it...an ouzo massage!

✳ www.gbspa.gr

A full range of exercise equipment awaits you in the gym, and personal trainers—in the land of the Olympics—are on standby to help you get into gold medal form. Get your hair done or treat yourself to a mani-pedi; the price may be hefty (the spa is open to non-guests for a fee of 45 euros) but is worth the indulgence. Film stars, entertainers, and heads of state are regular customers, and who knows whom you might bump into?

My friend Shelley Sarver recently stayed at the Grande Bretagne and reported a brush with celebrity. "Lady Gaga was performing in Athens during our stay and we could barely make our way out the front door every day to get a taxi." One afternoon Shelley decided to treat herself to a spa break and was seated next to a woman who was allowing her pedicure to dry. "My manicurist, whose English was poor, told me that she did not like Lady Gaga at all, and I commented that she actually has a beautiful voice. The manicurist continued to criticize until the other client replaced her shoes and said, 'Gaga is a very nice person, and I should know, as I am her mother!' With that, she left." Moral of the story: if you're lucky enough to pamper yourself with a spa treatment at the Grande Bretagne's GB spa, be careful what you say, as you may be seated next to a superstar...or her mother!

✤

70 Street Food of Athens

KOULOURAKIA, SALEP, AND ROASTED CHESTNUTS

One of my favorite things to do in Athens is to wander the streets... and eat. Not stopping into restaurants, but dining to my heart's desire on some of the best street food in the world. In my mind, Athens is the capital of street food. Now I realize New Yorkers will disagree, as will probably those living in Paris and other foodie-centric places. But since I first lived in this city, weathering a gray, overcast winter, I will always remember Athens for its street food.

Specifically, roasted chestnuts. I identify my college year in Athens with this saving grace. About the time the first winter winds set in, a semblance of fall in the October air, I detected the scent of something unforgettable as I walked through the downtown streets. There on the street corner was a vendor. Standing over a little grill, I forked over a handful of drachmas and he handed me back a warm paper envelope filled with heaven. On a chilly gray afternoon, the mountains of Pentelis and Imitos looming like lavender leviathans on the horizon, there are few things nicer than sitting in an Athenian park, watching kids on the playground and peeling the husks and devouring these warm, nutty confections.

That is, unless you want a souvlaki. Suvs, my friend Suz referred to them, when I first moved to Athens. She had directed me to a literal hole in the wall down the street from my apartment and she knew a good thing when she saw it, for Suz was an earth mother known for her sarcastic comments. Before I left for Athens my junior year, she showed me a photo of her Adonis-like boyfriend leaning against his motorcycle and vamped in her best Lauren Bacall accent, "Is that a banana in your pocket or are you just happy to see me?" Late at night after club-hopping with my friends, I often took her advice to order a suv with fries at one of many kiosks around the city, and have to admit an Athenian gyro beats a Sabrett's hotdog by a long shot.

After dinner you need dessert. Go no farther than a few more steps down Ermou Street, where vendors clog this pedestrian alley. You see a man hawking something odd. A small fountain spritzes a flume of water and you see glistening confections underneath. What exactly is this mountain of white pastry in cylindrical and rectangular shapes? Naturally, this is the coconut candy vendor! His cart is filled with all manner of delicacies made with the nutty and flaky treat, and the water fountain is to keep the slices of fresh coconut moist and tasty for customers.

Thirsty? Look for the man carrying a large Middle Eastern-looking samovar around. For a couple of euros he will hand you a small shot glass and fill it with an unusual-tasting beverage. I had to get up the nerve to try this strange concoction, called *salep* or orchid tea. An herbal beverage known to be a medicinal potion containing glucomannan, it is thought to heal bronchitis and digestive problems, and washes down well. A foamy finish tops the brew with a dash of cinnamon, and I detected the most exotic scent. Take a sip and you will be treated to the strangest but most satisfying mixture of nutty and sweet citrus.

Maybe you are familiar with Greek cheese pies known as *tiropitas* and perhaps cheese and spinach pies called *spanakopitas*? Other fillings can be put into this delectable phyllo dough pastry shell. Resembling doughnuts, these soft chewy rings called *bourekia* come in a variety of flavors. Try them with a filling of cheese or ham, or if you are feeling more adventurous, perhaps apple, olive, or even chocolate! Other types of treats are called *bougatsa*, also stuffed with sweet or savory fillings, such as minced meats, custard or feta cheese. Greeks love their pastries in all shapes and sizes, and the gold standard comes in the form of loops, rings, twists and pretzel shapes. Called *koulourakia*, this crisp biscuit is served with morning coffee, crumbled on top of creamy yogurt or eaten alone. Sprinkled with sesame seeds, they come in anise flavor or the more exotic grape must-flavored version known as *moustokouloura*.

If you're in Athens during the winter, keep any eye out for yet another savory treat. Some vendors offer roasted corn on the cob during the cold months, another delicious way to warm a chilly Athens day. When I lived in Greece, I never saw corn used in any foods, as it was referred to as "pig food." However I've noticed an upsurge of its popularity over the years and a cob of roasted corn, salty and delicious, is a great new addition to the Greek street food scene.

Keep one ear open for the ring of a calliope, and perhaps you will be fortunate enough to experience the entertainment portion of Athenian street food. An old man strolls the Ermou pedestrian mall with his music grinder, pushing the elaborately decorated, ancient music box up and down the cobbled streets. Festooned with red velvet and gold brocade, the ornate wooden calliope frames a portrait of a Gibson girl era woman, her photo reverently flanked by two white gardenias. Drop a couple of Euros in the basket and then take a seat in front of the tiny Panagia Kapnikarea church in the middle of the street, where you can savor one of those chocolate or olive-studded pastry rings, and listen to the vapor trail of the child-like, heartrending music retreat into the distance.

⁂

71 Bairaktaris

BEST GYRO IN TOWN—JUST ASK NAOMI CAMPBELL!

I admit it. Sometimes when I am in Athens I don't even go to a restaurant for dinner. In fact, recently, for three nights in a row, I didn't go at all. It's not that I don't eat—I just eat while sitting on a bench in Monastriaki Square, people watching...the best people watching in the world. Because everyone else is eating what I'm eating: the best gyro in the world.

That's right—I'm throwing down the gauntlet on a subject about which I'm sure there are a million opinions. When I lived in Athens, my favorite stop on the way home from clubbing was a hole in the wall in my neighborhood of Ano Ilissia. The proprietor would be open at goddess-awful hours and I'd shell out a handful of drachmas for a warm blanket of pita bread wrapped around juicy slices of lamb-pork mixture, cherry red tomatoes, a dollop of tsatziki—a garlicky confection of yogurt and cucumber—with a handful of French fries bristling out the top of the greasy wax paper cone.

In the intervening decades I have been hunting for this same warm, satisfying late night snack. A few years back I was having trouble finding my favorite meal in Athens: a simple roast chicken with French fries. Every restaurant was touting nouvel Grecque cuisine and I was tired of eggplant stuffed with weird cheese and chicken flambéed like we were in Paris. I wanted roast chicken—regular

286

old-school roast chicken—and I found it, delectably oven-baked in lemon, oregano, and olive oil, at Bairaktaris. Actually there are two sections of this venerable establishment at the corner of Monastiraki Square and Ermou Street restaurant, straddling the street and making it very confusing. But that's Greece; pick a side in the sun or shade and settle in for a great meal, or do what I do—skip the table altogether and line up by the corner of the 17th-century Pantanassa church at the restaurant's very own gyro stand.

I realize Bairaktaris is old school. Folks whom I respect, like Matt Barrett of *Matt Barrett's Greece Travel Guide*, have recommended many smaller, off-the-beaten-path tavernas in Athens, and I appreciate his thoughtfully pointing out these worthy establishments. But on any given day I'm apt to mix high and low brow with no compunction, so I don't hesitate to admit when I like something even if it's considered touristy. Apparently I'm in good company: in a recent *Parade* magazine article, celeb chef Andrew Zimmern named Bairaktaris the best gyro and souvlaki place in Athens.

Part of the fun is the dramatic serving flair of the gyro guys and gals, who assemble the sandwiches in lightning fast pace and periodically tumble their knives together to sharpen them, and I find myself mesmerized by the towering spinning vertical spits of meat called gyro, from the Greek word for "to rotate." Dressed in chef's whites, the smiling gyro barista is happy to pose for your camera as you capture him expertly slicing succulent wedges of roasted pork, chicken, or lamb off the *doner kebab*, and stacking them onto a warming plate.

In a skillful, almost seamless motion, he snatches up a warmed pita, loads it with the glistening meat, asks if you want tomato (yes) *tzatziki* (yes please) and smiles when you ask for a topping of fries. If you're dining al fresco, he will cradle it in wax paper and napkins and hand it back. I walk to the long bench surrounding the church and sit along with the rest of humanity. With the Parthenon seemingly suspended in the violet late afternoon sky and the lonely marbles of the Agora visible across the crowded market square nestled amidst the jade colored Aleppo pines, I watch how others devour their gyros; some wolf it down in huge mouthfuls, others nibble at the edge, careful not to drip the copious amounts of garlickly *tzatziki*, now melting from the warm meat.

Sometimes I rent an apartment in Athens, and when I feel like dining in with my gyro, the Bairaktaris boys and girls will bundle it up for me to take home. With one eye on the BBC and the other waiting for the lights to come up on the Acropolis, I sit back with an Amstel beer and unfold the deliciousness waiting inside the foil. The gyro literally fills the plate and I can sit happily for the next half hour, keeping abreast of the day's news while seeing the lights begin to glow on one of the world's most gorgeous ancient monuments.

✳ www.facebook.com/pages/Bairaktaris-Restaurant /145744818789760

If you choose to dine at the restaurant, Bairaktaris is a haven for celebrities. Admire the walls of signed photographs in this old Athens establishment. Fellow goddesses such as Queen Sophia of Spain have sampled Bairaktaris's wide array of traditional Greek fare, including *moussaka*, *stifado* (a savory stew), *papoutsakia* (stuffed eggplant "shoes") and of course, the old standard, chicken roasted in lemon and olive oil. Another goddess of the fashion world, Naomi Campbell, loved the food here so much she returned three nights in a row! So whether you're a monarch of the old school type or modern runway royalty, at the very least drop by Bairaktaris, if just to watch the meat baristas at work. And if you're feeling hungry, remember; even top models went off their diets for Athens's most delectable gyro!

❧

72

Pass the Pastitsio

EXPERIENCE HOME-COOKED MEALS IN ATHENS

Because I have lived and worked in Greece over the decades, I've been lucky to experience a huge variety of home cooked meals. Some of my favorite food memories are *kolokithia* (zucchini) blossoms stuffed with a mixture of ground lamb, pine nuts, and mint, crisply fried, offered from the kitchen of a local village woman in the mountains of Crete, where I lived for a month. I watched as my Greek hostess slaughtered chickens, then helped her pluck their feathers and roast them, and used our fists to beat the batter for a huge almond cake in preparation for the August 15th festival of the Assumption of the Virgin Mary.

I have been offered gaggingly sweet glasses of *vissinada*, a cherry flavored mastic spoon sweet served in a glass of water, as well as hair-on-chest-inducing glasses of *raki*, a potent Greek brandy. An old boyfriend offered me sea urchin roe straight out of the waters of the Aegean (definitely an acquired taste) and I've had the pleasure to sample bread fresh out of a community oven, where women from all over the village came with their kneaded dough in the morning, pushed it in with long wooden paddles and returned a few hours later to collect their loaves. Often housewives would bring along pans of chicken surrounded by a scattering of potatoes, doused in lemon, fresh olive oil, and sea salt to be put in the ovens along with the bread.

If you've ever wanted to try a real home-cooked Greek meal but you don't know anyone in Athens, now you don't need to! Savvy Athenian businesswoman Tina Kyriakis has come up with some fantastic ideas for visitors to experience the cuisine of this ancient country in ways most tourists will never encounter. The geniuses at Alternative Athens, a team of friendly and knowledgeable women and men, can put you in touch with some of the city's best cooks so you can taste this exquisite cuisine for yourself. Founder and CEO Tina says the best part of the home-cooked meal experience is "entering a real Greek home and having a warm, authentic lunch or dinner with a Greek family. It's a very rich and intimate approach to understanding a lot about the Greek culture in a few hours only. Greeks pride themselves on being very hospitable anyway!"

If you are gastronomically curious and tired of eating in restaurants every day, then Alternative Athens offers you the opportunity to choose your chef/host, your menu, and book a date convenient to your itinerary. Your potential hosts are as creative and as interesting as the eclectic cuisine they offer.

✳ www.alternative-athens.com/

Eleni, whose apartment is in the Lykavittos neighborhood with sweeping panoramic views of the city, offers a more traditional menu for those wanting to try some fabulous standards in the Greek culinary repertoire. Start with *melezanosalata*, an eggplant dip, or *taramosalata*, a salty cured fish roe spread. Follow that up with *Imam Bayidi* (literally "the priest fainted" in Turkish—so named after a priest offered this dish purportedly swooned at its sheer deliciousness!)

A standard both in Italy and Greece—*bakala*, salt cod, is prepared *skordalia*—with a thick rich garlic dipping sauce. Savor the leg of lamb in tomato sauce or a thick wedge of *pastitsio*—what I like to call *moussaka* with pasta instead of potatoes—a rich confection of layered noodles, ground lamb simmered in a tomato sauce and topped with a creamy béchamel. Eleni finishes her meal with a lighter touch, either fresh fruit or yogurt topped with a fruit preserve.

At Lena's home in the Gizi district, you will be offered a taste of the old and new cuisines, including stuffed red peppers with feta and dill, baked artichoke hearts stuffed with cheese, and *psari plaki*, haddock baked in tomatoes, garlic, and olive oil. Chicken with quince, and a beef stew in a lemon and thyme sauce round out her meat selections, and for dessert you can try the *kormos*, an unusual chocolate cake made with Metaxa, a Greek brandy.

All hostesses offer a variety of beverages with their meals, including local wines, coffee and herbal teas. If ouzo is your pleasure, just ask Eleni for a shot. Savor a glass of my favorite beverage, *mastiha*, an after dinner digestif similar tasting to ouzo, or if you are feeling brave, *tsipouro*, a whopping 40 percent alcohol brandy made from the residue of the wine press. But diners beware: make sure you have Lena call a taxi, because the walk home might be difficult!

Tina says to expect "a relaxed evening at a friend's home, enjoying good food and wine, chatting laughing and enjoying Greek hospitality." One of the nicest compliments she has received is that "the meal has been the highlight of all the activities they did in Greece," and underscores the reason for giving Greek in-home dining a try on your trip to Athens. "I think people that choose to have a home cooked meal are very open to meeting people and exchanging on their culture, and what cannot be conveyed in a word is the warm feeling that is developed between hosts and guests."

❧

73 *Brettos Ouzo Bar*

THE MOST COLORFUL BAR IN ATHENS

The wrought iron sign over the doorway, the quaint location down a side street in the northernmost end of the Plaka district, its proximity to elegant restaurants and satisfying gyro joints, as well as some of Athens's most prominent ancient monuments, such as the Choragic Monument of Lysicrates in the shadow of the Acropolis. All would be reason enough to visit this venerable Athenian institution. But what brings them in, and catches the eye of the passerby in this cobblestoned neighborhood street, are the towering floor to ceiling back-lit walls of bottles in a riot of neon colors.

Even if you don't drink ouzo, *tsipouro,* or any of the other spirits Brettos sells, it's worth a stop at this unique bar just to ogle the colorful walls of bottles and take a photo for posterity's sake. If you haven't ever tried ouzo, now's the time to taste the distinctly licorice flavored beverage. Made with anise, this cocktail packs a stiff 40 percent alcohol, so it's best to drink the way the Greeks intend—with *mezes.* Greeks never consume alcohol without something to eat along with it, so *mezes* were born. Delight in the wide variety that can be offered at different bars around town, most typically a *meze* which consists of a plate of bite-sized tomatoes and cucumbers, freshly made sausage, and hunks of feta cheese.

If anise isn't your thing, then try the equally strong *tsipouro*. This alternative beverage to ouzo offers all the fun of the original version without the anise, thus eliminating the strong, and for some, disagreeable licorice taste. Sample some *mastiha*, a smooth, syrupy liqueur flavored with resin from the mastic tree. My favorite comes from the island of Chios, and for those on a health kick take heart: mastic has been known since antiquity for its salubrious benefits and its anti-inflammatory, anti-oxidant, and anti-bacterial qualities, so drink up!

There is one beverage at Brettos that I can't imbibe: Metaxa. The first time I drank this potent brandy was at a baptism party in Crete that went on—literally—all night. I could barely get down one glass of this stomach-challenging beverage. But ouzo has my heart. My favorite moment is taking a cube of ice and dropping it into the glass and being mesmerized by the bloom of cloudiness that results when it hits the liquid. This drink is best enjoyed after siesta time or around 5 P.M. when Athenians wake up from their afternoon naps. After digesting the largest meal of the day at midday, an ouzo is the best way to start a long Greek evening.

The oldest distillery in Greece and the second oldest in Europe, Brettos has been around for more than a century since its founder, Michael Brettos, began distilling ouzo, brandies, and other liqueurs in 1909. The business got its start in the first floor of an old Athenian grand mansion; this is what the Plaka once looked like before developers tore down the neoclassical city estates and replaced them with rivers of concrete apartment buildings. Maybe the owners didn't realize it at that time, but they built their monument to all things Greek alcoholic by erecting it a mere stone's throw from the first Greek university!

Brettos specializes in not only traditional ouzo, but experiments with flavors, offering thirty-six, including pomegranate, banana, mint, and apple, using original family recipes from Smyrna, a Greek community located in modern-day Turkey. If you happen to find yourself in this neck of town, wander in and take in the room. On a typical hot summer day in downtown Athens, the interior of Brettos is a veritable haven from the penetrating Greek sun. Pull up a stool at the bar, admire the floor-to-ceiling wooden barrels full of spirits and let the old ceiling fans douse you in cool air while the barkeep pours you an ice cold glass of raspberry flavored ouzo.

Brettos has a small shop, so you can take home your very own souvenir of one of Greece's most famous exports; this distinctively licorice liquid treat will remind you of those gorgeous Greek sunsets with every glass. Just remember when packing your bottle of ouzo that you wrap it well (several layers of plastic bags should do the trick) and place it in your checked luggage!

᠅

74 Athens's Central Market

PRODUCE, FISH, SPICES, AND A WHOLE LOT OF MEAT

"You don't eat no meat?

Remember that scene in *My Big Fat Greek Wedding*? Nia Vardalos's character, Toula, has just gotten engaged, much to her father's dismay, to her hunky but decidedly non-Greek boyfriend Ian, played by John Corbett. At the first meeting with her family, Toula introduces her fiancé to her aunt, played by Andrea Martin, who invites him to dinner. When Toula informs her that Ian is a vegetarian, the incredulous aunt pauses for a moment after uttering her famous rejoinder, then settles into the obvious solution: "That's O.K. I make lamb."

If you head over to Athens's central market, located between Omonia and Monastiraki Squares, just off Athinas Street, you will see a lot of lamb...a whole lot. If you're the squeamish type, this stop may not top your favorites list, but for anyone who is into organic and locally sourced product, this is the place for you.

Until the late 19th century, meat and produce vendors hawked their wares outdoors, just like in the old days, in the vicinity of the ancient Agora, which means marketplace. In 1875, the city got its own sparkling new market, a spacious neoclassical structure with rows of lofty, arched windows and room for fishmongers on the one side and meat vendors on the other. When I lived in Athens, I first visited the market—known as the *Dimotiki* or *Nea Agora* (municipal or new market)—in the heat of summer. Wearing flip flops (unaware this was a big no-no) into the fishmonger side of the building, I skidded all around the floors, made slick by vendors spraying water to keep the iced seafood cold and glistening.

Once I adjusted to the floor (note: walk slowly and carefully to avoid slips) and the fragrance (let's just say the aroma of the sea) I found myself fascinated by the heaps of all manner of seafood. Lumpy octopus squatted with tentacles curled into their beds of ice, buckets of eel beckoned with silvery skin. Low hanging light bulbs sparkled like fireflies, illuminating plump sea bream, pink mountains of shrimp and sinewy stacks of sardines. One vendor had sliced and displayed his salmon, fanned out on the ice like a deck of rose-colored cards.

Do you like squid tentacles or bodies? You can have either, as well as anchovies, mackerel, red mullet, and *bakaliaro*, dried and salted codfish. If you haven't yet had your morning coffee, this place will wake you up. With 30,000 people visiting the market each day—and that's 150 fishmongers, more than 100 meat stalls and 80 produce stands—vendors yell at the top of their lungs to garner attention and the air is pierced with shrieks and shouts as merchants call out their wares and prices.

✽ www.athensinfoguide.com/wtsmarkets.htm

Turn the corner and you will be in the meat hall, a vast corridor of individual booths each manned by about five people. Many of these stalls have been in the same family for decades and everybody knows everybody in this micro culture. This is no American super-market with pork chops shrink-wrapped in plastic and foam con-tainers—this is the real McCoy. Expect to see whole lamb carcasses and even boar's heads (Greeks use every part of the animal). The rabbit stalls are particularly curious. Suspended from the racks and lit by the same low bulbs, the critters are completely skinned, except for their furry little ears, feet and bunny tails, still attached in their black, white, and gray pom-pommed glory.

Whole pigs hang, suspended from metal hooks, just waiting for the butchers to do their jobs, and the sounds of blades hacking against wooden blocks, saws, and meat grinders scrape the air. Cases nearby are filled with tripe and innards, often used to make a dish known as *kokoretsi*. The first time I tried it—intestines filled with organ meats, wrapped in twine, basted in olive oil and lemon and roasted on a spit—I was a bit unsure. But like a sausage, each section, hot off the fire and sliced into bite sized portions, was salty and delectable. Mixed in with the innards display are pigs' feet, lined up at the edge of the case, multiple protruding toes with extended nails, reminded me of ladies awaiting a pedicure. If you're feeling adventurous, make a stop at Ipeiro, one of the restaurants located directly inside the market. With the meat so close by, you are assured of the freshness, especially in the *podi* and *patsa*, soups made from the foot of a cow and tripe.

If it weren't for the gamey aroma, and shouts of "Lamb! Pork! Wild boar!" the atmosphere resembles a science fair with the butchers milling about in their white coats; either that, or some weird space-aged set with specimens lit up behind glass cases. Be aware that, along with more than five hundred workers in the meat section alone, you are literally walking shoulder to shoulder with the thick crowds. This is where all of Athens shops, and during holy days such as Easter, the numbers can swell to ten times the normal rate as people gather to purchase their holiday meals.

Just across the street is the produce vendor where hills of ruby cherries, fragrant *peponi* (melon) and ripe, bursting figs beckon in season. Admire the banks of blood-red tomatoes, glossy amethyst eggplant, and saffron squash blossoms. Thump bulbous yellow peppers, stroke the baby-skin-smooth peaches, and Everest high peaks of *fassolia* or green beans; the sheer colors and textures will bring out the photographer in you, as will the letters and numbers squiggled on signs designating variety and price. Instead of becoming flustered if you can't read the words, just go with the flow and enjoy the general confusion that seems to reign, bringing truth to the axiom that it's "all Greek to me." Be on the lookout to dodge housewives dragging their roller carts behind them and people swinging plastic bags filled to the brim with grapes and onions. Because this is a working market and people are making purchases, it's best not to pause too long to take photos as vendors don't want buying customers to be blocked from their stalls.

Be sure to make a stop at the olive vendors, with lustrous mounds of almond-shaped Kalamata, picholine green cracked Tsakistes, large oval Amphissa or wrinkled black olives called Thruba from the island of Thasos basking in tall metal containers or white plastic buckets. Nuts and dried fruit abound nearby, including the tasty red *arapika* peanuts, quail egg-sized walnuts, and neon orange dried apricots.

The Miran salami vendor is a revelation—as you walk inside, a benediction of roped and bundled sausages and braids of garlic dangle suspended in the air above your head, and displays of *pastirmas* (air cured beef from Turkey) beckon from gleaming cases. Nearby shops bulge with selections of loofahs hanging in Christmas tree-like formations, jars of liquid-gold Hymettos honey, and homemade candles and soaps. Spice merchants near Evripridou Street with their small satchels and packets of dried herbs look like Chinese apothecaries; the doorways are framed with twists of capsicum and other neon-colored herbs, and the air is thick with lavender, rosemary, and fennel. Cheese shops have ample amounts of feta—multiple varieties, in fact, from hard to crumbly—as well as zesty *mizithra*, *kefalotiri* (similar to Italian parmesan or pecorino), and *kasseri*.

As you head back to your hotel, purchase one of the many Greek desserts for sale; shredded wheat-like *kataifi*, clove-studded pans of baklava or *galatabouriko* (a pudding-like dessert), and check out the tropical bird and pet stores nearby. Munching on one of these thickly honeyed treats and admiring the teal-colored parrots, chipmunks, baby rabbits, and exotic monkeys is a sweet way to end your market day.

75 Church Things

A MYSTERIOUS ICON VENDOR IN THE PLAKA

The first time I entered this store I thought I had stepped into just another artifacts shop in the touristy Plaka district of Athens. It was a cool haven from the grease fire spattering rays of the sun, yet I felt myself surrounded by incense and eyes staring at me from all the shelves. Its name, Ekklesiastika, translates to the more amusing Church Things in English, and ever since my first visit, when I was on a quest for *tamata*, I realized this peaceful oasis was far more than a mere tourist shop.

Perhaps, after wandering through one of those tiny island churches, you've seen those shiny silver votives attached to the altar screen? Known as the iconostasis, the screen is the dividing line between the sacred and the secular. If you are praying to heal a body part or asking for protection for your home or car, you purchase a silver plaque—known as a *tamato*—with the corresponding limb, house, or automobile, and you hang it on the screen and ask God to heal and protect it.

Fascinated by these tiny works of art, I stopped in my tracks one day when I saw this store. Located just around the corner from Agora Square at 29 Pandrosou Street, directly in the heart of the Plaka district, I saw a window full of beautifully painted icons of saints, their faces staring out dourly through the glass. But there, in the corner, was a glinting pile of silver. I pushed open the door and was welcomed into the world of Anastasios Vobirakis. Tall, with a Fuller brush head of hair, his face has a way of melting into a smile; he oozes calm in an almost Benedictine monk sort of way. If I didn't know I was in a shop in the middle of Athens I would almost imagine myself in a cloisters, the smell of incense hanging in the air and the golden-eyed glinting of stoic faces glaring at me from around the room.

I told him of my love of the tiny silver icons, and he called out in recognition, "Ah-*tamata!*" He pulled out a stool and asked me to sit at the messy desk. Darting into the back room, he disappeared for a moment into the darkness. I had a moment to glance about the room—shelves were piled high with saints: Dimitrios astride his horse, George triumphant with his dragon. When Anastasios reappeared, he held a small paper bag. As he dumped the contents onto the desk, another customer who had just entered the shop, a French tourist, let out a gasp. "Ahhh, *c'est magnifique!*" she cried out and gathered up a handful. I too collected some and fanned them out like a deck of cards.

Anastasios runs his shop like a tiny monastery. I have sat in there for hours, and if you are lucky, he might treat you to stories about his life. Anastasios believes in the curative power of icons, and told me a very personal story of how one healed his family. Some years before, he and his wife had tried to have a child. Unable to get pregnant, a friend told them she should travel to the island of Tinos, where there is a magical icon of the Virgin Mary. If a woman wants to get pregnant, she needs to crawl on her hands and knees to the church and kiss the image.

So Anastsios and his wife made that journey. She crawled from the harbor to the church, located about a half mile from the port. Weeks later, he told me, after they returned home, his wife reported feeling funny. She proceeded to visit the doctor, and tests results showed that she was indeed pregnant.

At that point, he confided that his wife and now ten-year-old son lived at home, but he slept at the shop. When I asked him why, he replied that his wife is so protective of their son that she sleeps with the child, so he sleeps at the store. He looked up at the ceiling, his eyebrows bristling with concern. Sometimes, he told me *sotto voce*, he wakes up because he hears things. "Between two and three in the morning," he whispered, his eyes beaming bright and his voice filled with awe, "the heavens open up."

Every time I come to Athens I drop by to visit Anastasios. On occasion I buy a few more of these silver cards, but by now I own one of every kind of image: hearts, arms, legs, eyes, houses, cars, man, woman, child,...and *Efharisto*, which means "thank you" in Greek; it is my favorite. Over the years prices have gone up for precious metals, so the tiny silver *tamata* are more expensive. Instead of buying handfuls of them as I used to for friends as gifts, I can afford them now only for very special occasions.

So if you are in the market for some Greek icons or *tamata*, or just want to hear an extraordinary story, drop by Church Things. Just being in this serene environment for a few brief moments is a welcome respite from the hustle and bustle of the Athenian marketplace, and, after hearing Anastasios's miraculous tale, you will feel you have indeed entered a sacred space.

❦

76

Melissanos the Poet Sandal Maker

WHERE THE STARS BUY THEIR
ONE-OF-A-KIND GREEK SANDALS

SJP (that's Sarah Jessica Parker for those non *Sex and the City* fans), Lily Tomlin, Jill Biden, Kate Moss. Then there are those who need no last name: Sophia and Barbra. Finally there are two—Jackie O and Maria Callas—whom we thought only shared the same lover: Aristotle Onassis. What do they all have in common? The same man crafted the most elegant, goddess-worthy sandals on earth for their celebrity feet. And he has the most ludicrous, Greek god-worthy name: Melissanos, the Poet Sandal Maker to the Stars.

Yes, you heard that right. He's a shoemaker to the stars who spins out a variety of sandals that are *poli oraio* (that's "very beautiful" in Greek) and he also serves that muse in charge of poetry, Calliope. Not surprising for a guy whose shop is a stone's throw from the Hill of the Muses.

Melissanos, located at 2 Agias Theklas Street, can be found in the hip, graffiti-covered, former red-light district known as Psirri. I had recently rented an apartment on the next block and, dodging the blistering August sun by ducking into side streets, I came along Melissanos's place quite by accident. Seeing a line of people waiting to get in, I had to stop and find out why. I was greeted with a waiting room filled with mostly women, while a host of men measured, cosseted and tended to their feet. The walls were literally overflowing with all manner of leather, and owner and lead sandal maker Pantelis Melissanos, with his flowing, Zeus-worthy gray hair and beard, moved back and forth from the front to the rear of the shop, passing through a Scylla and Charybdis of leather sandals cascading from the ceiling like so many snakes from the head of Medusa.

A photo shows Lily Tomlin posing with Pantelis, a third-generation shoe aficionado, along with her impassioned caption, "I walk in Cleopatra's shoes!" Pantelis's father, Stavros, inherited the business from his father Georgios, who founded the business in 1920. The tale goes that Giorgios created a pair of sandals for a visiting choreographer, who ordered several more. Giorgios decided to make a few extra pairs just for kicks and hung them in the window of the shop, and American tourists promptly snapped all of them up that same day.

✳ www.melissinos-art.com

The Melissanos family knows a good thing when they see it. These are the folks who outfit those sylph-like priestesses of Apollo who light the Olympic torch every four years, setting it on its world circling journey. Clad in white flowing gowns, the women wear custom made sandals from Melissanos. One of the flame-lighting goddesses gushed, "I'm honored that your hands' creations embraced my feet when I walked on the sacred land of Ancient Olympia. May the Flame always light you on your way."

Just looking at the sheer variety of sandal types I never knew existed, my head began to spin (I have a thing for sandals). Feeling a bit prim? Try on a pair of "Cyclades" and you morph into Audrey Hepburn in Sabrina. Maybe you're channeling Jackie O with the relaxed hip tourist look? Then none other than the eponymously named "Jackie O" sandal—a classic single strap across the arch—will do. Feel like doing some butt kicking? The nine-strapped, all-the-way-to-the knee Amazon warrior-style is just for you. (I used to wear a similar style of sandal, which my friend Mary Lou still refers to as Spartacus boots!) Pantelis churns out twenty-eight different styles, but if you don't like what you see in the shop, he will custom make a pair just for you *grigora* (on the spot). Choose to embellish them? How about encrusted with faux jewels, brightly painted leather strips to match your toenail polish, or opt for gold-toned straps?

You could spend all day in this tangled vortex of sandal production. After fighting my way past the boudoir scene of women, feet extended, being tended to by men and swashbuckling through a jungle-like vine of leather straps, I imagined I'd have dreams of leather-like serpents undulating through dense forests of psychedelic colors. For Pantelis not only makes sandals, he writes poetry, and his shop is an atelier of his other art: wildly colorful graphic chairs, zebra prints and florid jungle themes. Pantelis's play, *Bacchus*, a musical comedy, stars Princess Semele, "a totally dumb bombshell from Thebes, (who) hooks up with Zeus, gets pregnant and turns the entire Universe upside-down. Hera, the jealous wife of Zeus, takes the whole thing as an insult to her own femininity (and who wouldn't?), and turns to the bottle (of ambrosia) to ease her pain and vows revenge."

There is a bygone era feel to the place as well. The Melissanos family has been shoeing royalty of all types—not only Jackie O, Ari and Maria Callas—but the Beatles and the Queen of Spain. John Lennon looks hip in a shot with Yoko as he trods an English country path in his Melissanos originals.

So the next time you're wandering through the old red-light district of Psirri and feel like getting out of the sun, duck into Melissanos the Poet Sandal Maker to the Stars. Even if you don't feel like purchasing sandals, the sheer entertainment value of this crazy, one-of-a-kind atelier will be well worth your visit.

‰

V Active and Cultural Adventures

77 Sailing Holidays

EXPLORING GREECE FROM THE WINE DARK SEAS

I was young, wide-eyed, and knew only a little about boats. My family had a small dinghy, and I used to sail it around the lake near our house on weekends while my dad, tired after a long week at work, napped on deck. But as a junior in college, living in Greece, I had never seen a boat like this one.

Exploring the island of Skyros with my friend, Georgia Norris, we spied a group of fit and tanned men all sporting the same t-shirt emblazoned with the word, "Soledad." Thinking it was some kind of cult, we quickly realized as they congregated at the wharf, they were crewmembers for a yacht. When Georgia asked one of the men what Soledad meant, he replied in a sexy, sauerbraten-thick German accent: "Solitude." As they scrambled above deck, readying the yacht for departure, they shouted to us to join them. We stared at each other for a minute, and Georgia finally nudged me, whispering breathlessly, "Look at that gorgeous boat—not to mention the guys! How often do you get a chance to crew on a yacht?"

For about a millisecond, I did entertain the idea, fantasizing about taking turns at the helm, raising sails, savoring fresh caught seafood dinners atop decks...and those super cool t-shirts. But being a bit less adventurous than my impetuous companion (and cognizant of the fact that school started in Athens in a few days) I nixed the plan, much to Georgia's chagrin. But I still think of *Soledad*, gazing at her cobalt blue hull and her hunky Chippendales-worthy crew, casting their ropes and sailing off into the chartreuse and tangerine sunset.

During my many years of returning to the island of Ithaka in the Ionian Sea, the sounds of the wind whipping through the rigging of sailboats has been the lullaby that rocked me to sleep at night. Walking past the sailboats lined up along the wharf of Vathy harbor on my way to our excavation hotel, I would often admire the blis-teringly white and chrome boats with their colorful flags of nations whipping in the breeze, and sleek forms reminding me of Olympic athletes. Sailors would come into our small pension and pay a fee to get a hot shower. At night, the voices of people atop decks, talking, drinking, and often singing  and carousing late into the night wafted down the wharf and in through the windows of our pension. We often took bets as to who were the loudest: Australians, Germans, or Italian tourists enjoying their holidays to the maximum.

While working on the excavation high above the straits between Ithaka and Kefalonia, we would regularly see flotillas of yachts, like flecks of salt on the vast blue gulf, making their way from port to port during the day so they could find safe harbor at night. With one of Greece's largest and most secure harbors, Ithaka is a sailor's dream, but at almost every anchorage in the country during summer you will find dozens of sailboats lined up at night, cheek by jowl.

Can you imagine hopping from island to island on your own schedule and anchoring in tiny coves for some private swimming? Or just taking in the preternaturally cerulean water and dove-white beaches of the Aegean and mystically bluish-dun earth of the Ionian island chain from your floating berth? Long before Odysseus set sail on his ill-fated journey to Troy, the Mediterranean had been a natural home for sailors. While you may not encounter your own whirlpools of Scylla and Charybdis or have to be tied to the mast to avoid throwing yourself into the sea after hearing the Sirens sing their sweet and lethal song, you can enjoy this enchanting, age-old pleasure of actually sailing Homer's wine dark seas. If you're the boating type, or if you just like being out on the water and want somebody else to do all the work, there's a sailing holiday made just for you. Few things are more romantic than sailing off into the Greek sunset on your very own private yacht, so here are a few places to create the dream vacation of your life:

Aegean Blue Charters

If you like the idea of hoisting sails and taking a turn at the helm, sign up for a spin on the forty-seven-foot yacht Excordis. With more than forty years of experience in the waters of the Argo-Saronic region, ASA-certified skipper Mark Beer will take superb care of you. Mark's gleaming yacht can handle up to seven passengers and a hostess can be hired if you want somebody else to cook dinner. Thanks to a deep knowledge of the language and culture, Mark knows the best anchorages, tavernas and beaches, and is your personal guide to a memorable vacation. www.aegeanbluecharters.com

Sailing Holidays Ltd.

Winner of the British Travel Awards, Sailing Holidays Ltd. offers three levels of cruising, depending on your proficiency. Flotilla allows for "follow the leader" group sailing for those not skilled enough to skipper their own boats. Skippered cruises are available for an extra cost and bare boating is always an option for qualified sailors. Boats can be chartered for the Ionian Islands, the Sporadic Islands northwest of Athens, or the Saronic Gulf near Athens's port of Piraeus to stay close to home. Rentals are available from early May to late October. www.sailingholidays.com

Greek Sails

With thirty years of experience, Greek Sails has earned five stars on Trip Advisor. Based on the island of Poros, Greek Sails' range includes the Saronic and Argolic Gulf islands, as well as the Peloponnese and the Cycladic island chain. With fourteen different types of yachts, Greek Sails offers a wide variety of charters, as well as flotilla, bareboat, skippered (both assisted or crewed), and cabin chartered yachts for those who want to join up with another crew and help out with the sailing. www.greeksails.com

Nautilus Yachting

Nautilus Yachting offers an even wider range for sailing enthusiasts. For bare boaters, almost the entire region of Greece can be explored, including the Ionian, Saronic, Aegean, and Dodecanese Islands that cuddle up to the Turkish coast. Flotilla sailing is available for the Ionian, Kos, Skiathos, and Athens, and bare boats can be chartered out of Corfu, Lefkas, Athens, Skiathos, Poros, Kos, and Mykonos. All three companies offer the opportunity to split your vacation between a week on the water and week on terra firma for landlubbers with their stay-and-sail holidays. Their different packages include a wide variety for beach clubs, hotels, and apartments in Lefkas, Kos, the Sporades, or a villa on Poros. www.nautilusyachting.com

Moorings

Based out of Corfu, Lefkas, and Athens, the Moorings yacht charters offers excursions to the Ionian, Sporades, Dodecanese, and Cycladic island chains, as well as land packages to explore ancient ruins along with the high seas. For those fascinated with the late Jacqueline Kennedy Onassis, you can sail up to the private island of Skorpios and enjoy a swim where Jackie O and her Greek husband, shipping tycoon Aristotle Onassis, once spent their summer holidays. www.moorings.com

Sunsail USA

Sunsail USA, also based out of Corfu, Lefkas, and Athens, offers both short island hops for less skilled skippers, and open water passages for the more advanced sailor. Opportunities to drop anchor in one of hundreds of glimmering private bays for snorkeling, or docking at cozy villages for a taste of Greek cuisine await you. www.sunsail.com

78 Hiking in Greece

FOLLOWING IN THE FOOTSTEPS
OF THE GODDESSES

When you think of Greece as a vacation destination, the first thing that comes to your mind probably isn't cross-country trekking—but it should be, for Greece has some of the most scenic and challenging hiking trails around. Between the massive island of Crete and the slopes of the Pindos Mountains in northern Greece exist a number of stunning destinations where you can lace up your hiking boots, slap on a backpack and water bottles, and take some goddess-worthy epic hikes. Although Greece seems like it has an eternal summer, be aware that some hiking regions are seasonal only and not passable during certain times of year due to flooding or wintry conditions.

Let's start in Crete, home of the world famous Samaria Gorge, sometimes referred to as Greece's own Grand Canyon. The name Samaria is a contraction of Osia Maria, a tiny church located halfway through the gorge, which is dedicated to Holy Maria of Egypt. The diminutive, one-aisled church contains 14th-century murals, and is an appropriate place to stop in and ask for a blessing along your trek.

The route starts in Xyloskalo, at the northern end of Crete's White Mountains National Park. Starting at an altitude of 1,200 meters, the route slopes downhill all the way through the canyon, terminating at Agia Roumeli on the Libyan Sea. Running down the longest gorge in Europe, the path meanders through an impressive wall of rock that is 150 meters at its widest and only three meters at its narrowest, the awe-inspiring pass known as *Sideroportes*, or "Iron Doors." As you pass through this nine-foot gap, stare up at the sheer cliff faces that soar six hundred feet above you. Many battles have been fought at this unforgettable spot, including the rebellion of Daskaloyannis, when Yannis Bonatos and a force of two hundred fighters warded off a large Turkish invasion, eventually forcing them into a hasty retreat. Prehistoric settlements have been found in the gorge, along with a shrine to the god Apollo, but the canyon is also the site of the ancient settlements of Tarra and Kaino. This is where the Cretan goddess Britomartis was born, who went on to the island of Aegina to be worshipped under the name Aphaia, or the "goddess who vanishes."

Once past the towering rocks of this passageway, the remainder of the six-to-eight-hour trek culminates in the sparkling waters of the Libyan Sea on Crete's southern coast, where you can take a swim in the aquamarine sea and refresh your soul after a physically challenging but spiritually recharging journey.

Greece has not just one, but two gorges with jaw-dropping scenery. In the Pindos Mountains of Epirus near the Greek border with Albania lies the Vikos Gorge. According to the Guinness Book of World Records, Vikos is the deepest gorge in the world. Twelve miles in length, it measures 1,100 meters at one point from rim to rim and is more than nine hundred meters deep, which is almost half a mile! Created by the erosion of the River Voidomatis, the water cuts down through the soft limestone, creating many fissures and deep caves.

The gorge is part of the Vikos-Aoos National Park in Zagoria, an area of more than forty villages known collectively as the

Zagorohoria. A series of mountain paths connects the villages, where modern roads didn't exist until the 1950s. The people of the Vikos Gorge are known for their medicinal and herbal recipes, which have been handed down for generations, and the locals use St. John's Wort, lemongrass, and absinthe in their remedies to cure illness.

A popular starting point for your seven-hour trek is Monodendri, where you can peer into the gorge from the 15th-century monastery of Agia Paraskevi, whose chapel terrace was designed for maximum views of the stunning canyons beyond. Hikers can choose a number of trails through the gorge, passing through villages embedded in thickly forested mountains famous for their stonework and linked through a series of interconnected footpaths. Trails take hikers down to the refreshing Voidomatis River, said to be the cleanest in Europe.

Famous arched bridges cross the river Aoos, which also flows through the gorge. These massive stone constructions, sometimes called packhorse bridges, date to the 18th century and the most picturesque can be seen around the village of Kipi. The region is filled with a wide assortment of wildlife, including brown bears, wild cats and boars; if you can, make a stop at a taverna in one of the shaded villages and treat yourself to a bowl of wild boar stew to sustain the rest of your journey. In late summer, when the rest of Greece is perspiring under a searing sun, Vikos Gorge is already tasting the coolness of fall with beech, oak, maple, and fig trees starting to paint the ravine with a blaze of autumn color.

Just a short hop away from Athens is Kea, also known by locals as Tzia, the closest Cycladic island to the mainland. An extensive series of sign-posted trails makes the island a hiker's paradise with paths cutting through oak forests, past isolated churches and ancient towers, and culminating at secluded beaches where you can take a refreshing dip in the crisp, ultramarine waters of the Aegean

Sea. Half of the hiking paths on the island are made of cobble-stone, some lined with stone walls, and lead through the island's mountainous interior and valleys. In the springtime the island is sprinkled with wildflowers in a riot of color, and the old pathways, called *kalderimia* by the locals, are carpeted in red poppies, purple mallows, and blue lupines.

There are hundreds of other fantastic hiking destinations in Greece; these are but a few of the most well-known and popular treks. Yet virtually anywhere you choose to hike in this myth-steeped landscape, you are guaranteed an awe-inspiring, histori-cally significant, or spiritually satisfying experience around every corner, and can rest assured that the goddesses who inhabit this sacred soil are always only a few steps behind—or ahead of you—on the path.

&

79 _Scuba Diving and Snorkeling_

EXPLORE GREECE'S UNDERWATER WONDERS

From Odysseus to modern Greek shipping tycoons, the Greeks have always had an intimate relationship with the sea. With an extensive, labyrinthine coastline and more than 240 inhabited islands scattered throughout the Ionian and Aegean seas, Greece is a diver's paradise. Because Greece is a seafaring nation with a rich and deep past, there are countless wrecks to be found along the country's coasts, from ancient to modern times. The Greek waters abound in sea life, including seahorses, shrimp, eels, scorpionfish, and invertebrates, as well as the larger critters such as octopus, dolphins, and the dearly loved and protected giant loggerhead turtle, _caretta caretta_. Some of the dive destination highlights include Dragonisi Island Caverns of Mykonos, with its spectacular rock formations, monk seals, and glassfish. Off Naxos, divers can explore The Dome, a large cavern teeming with marine life and an air-filled dome that is lit with glittering turquoise light. For wreck dive enthusiasts, travel to Kefalonia to explore the HMS Perseus, a submarine sunk by a mine and now an artificial reef and home to grouper and sea bass. A German fighter plane from World War II off the coast of Crete is a great place to see eels and explore the upside-down but intact fuselage and machine guns.

Santorini Dive Center

As a dormant volcano, Santorini is a popular destination for divers to explore its massive caldera. Non-certified divers can dip their toes in the water and take introductory scuba lessons with instructors who have more than sixty years of experience. Experienced divers can take a PADI night diver course to immerse themselves in a whole new world and witness the amazing creatures that come to life in the brilliance of the dive light. Advanced open water divers can take advantage of wreck diving, test their skills at underwater photography, and try out cool toys such as underwater scooters. www.divecenter.gr

Aegean Diving College

Located on the island of Paros, Aegean Diving College is operated by Peter Nicolaides, a professional diver who has worked with Jacques Cousteau and National Geographic. In 1976, he worked with Cousteau's Calypso and excavated the famous *Antikythira* wreck as well as filming the *Britannic*, the sister ship of the *Titanic* that sank off the coast of Kea. Guests can take snorkeling lessons with expert free divers or take shallow water scuba lessons to get a feel for the sport. Snorkelers and divers alike can explore World War II wrecks as well as discover archaeological ruins that are omnipresent across Greece. www.aegeandiving.gr

Alonissos Dive Center

The tiny island of Alonissos is located in the center of the National Marine Park, a protected sanctuary for marine life. Alonissos Dive Center offers dive packages for novice divers, which includes a seven-night stay and PADI open water diver's course. Expert diver packages include a seven-night stay and ten dives, including guide and gear. The waters around the island are teeming with sea life and the dive sites include Blue Cave North, where divers can see octopus, dolphins, and damselfish, as well as Two Brothers-South, an underwater ravine and passage where moray eels hide in the shadows. bestdivingingreece.com

❧

80

The Necromanteion of Ephyra

A REAL LIFE UNDERWORLD WHERE
ANCIENTS SPOKE WITH THE DEAD

The hum of the engine, the rustle of bottle green dragonflies as they dart psychotically across the surface of the water. You are floating down a narrow river, the jadeite waters freezing to the touch. Tall grasses and weeping willows loom forebodingly along the banks, and in the distance you see the mouth of the river, emptying into the Ionian Sea. Your captain may not be the infamous Charon, ferryman across the River Styx, and your fellow passengers are very much alive, but this is no ordinary boat ride, for your old salt of a skipper is taking you to the realm of the dead. After a short ride on the sluggish waterway, the boat comes to a halt. The captain cuts the engine, leaving you to scramble up a reedy embankment. A rocky path through a cornfield leads you to your destination, a place where the ancients believed they could talk with their deceased ancestors: the Necromanteion of Ephyra.

Maybe you've read about the realm of Hades in Homer's *Odyssey*, but figured it was just a fantasy. Yet at the juncture of three rivers in Greece's northwestern province of Epirus, there is such a place, thought by some to be a real portal to the underworld. The ancient Greeks believed souls entered the underworld through cracks in the surface of the earth, and this region was physically appealing enough to resemble their idea of Hades. Beneath the soil near the ancient city of Ephyra and a confluence of rivers with a trio of woeful names, the Cocytus (River of Wailing/Lament), Acheron (River of Woe/Joyless), and Pyriphlegethon (Flaming with Fire/Burning), they constructed a series of chambers and tunnels to create an actual place for the living to come and consult with the dead.

Homer mentions the nekromanteion, or temple of the dead, in the *Odyssey*, where he described the hero Odysseus's remarkable descent into Hades to connect with his deceased mother, only to encounter numerous shades, or souls of the dead. Another mention is made when Odysseus, on Circe's advice, is encouraged to meet with Teireseus, the blind seer, in hopes of receiving an oracle to assist in his return to his beloved Ithaka. Instead, he encounters a much more lurid scene;

> *Thus solemn rites and holy vows we paid*
> *To all the phantom-nations of the dead;*
> *Then died the sheep: a purple torrent flow'd,*
> *And all the caverns smoked with streaming blood.*
> *When lo! appear'd along the dusky coasts,*
> *Thin, airy shoals of visionary ghosts:*
> *Fair, pensive youths, and soft enamour'd maids;*
>
> *And wither'd elders, pale and wrinkled shades;*
> *Ghastly with wounds the forms of warriors slain*
> *Stalk'd with majestic port, a martial train:*
> *These and a thousand more swarm'd o'er the ground,*
> *And all the dire assembly shriek'd around.*
> *Astonish'd at the sight, aghast I stood,*
> *And a cold fear ran shivering through my blood;*

Straight I command the sacrifice to haste,
Straight the flay'd victims to the flames are cast,
And mutter'd vows, and mystic song applied
To grisly Pluto, and his gloomy bride.

Pluto's gloomy bride is none other than Persephone. After being abducted by Hades (Pluto in Roman mythology) into his shadowy kingdom, Persephone ate pomegranate seeds, or food of the dead, forcing her to return annually to this realm of the departed. During this time she serves as queen of the underworld, and the Necromanteion of Ephyra is dedicated to her and her King, the "grisly Pluto."

Inhabited since the Mycenaean period, this site dates to the 14th and 13th centuries B.C., but the existing structures date to the Hellenistic period (late 4th–early 3rd centuries B.C.) Here pilgrims who wished to communicate with the dead were subjected to a series of physical and spiritual tests and fed a special diet, consisting of shellfish, such as oysters, and barley bread—most likely containing the black ergot or mold from the barley plant, which had a powerful narcotic effect.

A ritual offering of sheep, milk, and honey was performed and pilgrims would then descend through a series of underground gates and corridors, where they would chant prayers and answers to a series of questions to gain entrance to the sacred spot. After several days of preparation, magical rituals, and questioning by the temple priests, pilgrims were led down the dark narrow passageways of the underground structure. Disoriented and intoxicated, the worshippers likely underwent out-of-the-ordinary experiences in this spooky site. However, it seems that the priests employed some sleight of hand to enhance the supernatural effect of the subterranean space, making the oracle's authenticity questionable. In more recent excavations, pulley-like objects were discovered, which some believe were used to "fly" the priests around the chamber, simulating the deceased.

Hoax or not, the necromanteion is an eerie place, and the ancients went to a lot of trouble to simulate the realm of the dead. The narrow passageway will lead you to a substantial chamber carved directly into the earth and supported by fifteen stone arches. Wandering through these cold, musty corridors smelling of damp earth, you can imagine how terrifying it must have been for the pilgrims. Drugged and frightened, they submitted themselves for days to these subterranean passageways, filled with shadows from flickering lanterns, in the hopes of catching a glimpse of their deceased loved ones.

The site was destroyed by the Romans in the second century B.C., and the forbidding locale lay abandoned for centuries until the archaeological ruins were uncovered in 1958. Today archaeologists disagree as to the purpose of the site; some believe it was an agriculture fortification and that the creepy tunnels were storage facilities for grain. However, the site remains identified as a necromanteion, so if you are willing to explore the underground passages, you can decide for yourself.

If you are looking for a more conventional way to experience this mystical region, rent a kayak and paddle your own way down these frigid waters for a refreshing adventure. Make a stop in the nearby village of Parga for lunch by the seaside and take in the almost 180 species of rare birds and wildlife in the Glyki wetlands along the Acheron River. But as the sun sinks low on the horizon, keep a lookout in this numinous landscape, just in case you might catch a glimpse of an ancient soul or two still lingering at the confluence of these sorrowful rivers.

જ

81 Music and Arts Festivals

MODERN GREEK CULTURE IN AN ANCIENT LAND

We often think of Greece as the seminal birthplace of theater, both tragic and comic, not to mention music and dance. To be surrounded by all these monuments of antiquity, and the mind-reeling list of names contributing to Greece's Golden Age of arts and literature, including Aristophanes, Aeschylus, and Euripides, it's easy to forget that modern Greek culture is just as alive and well as its ancient counterpart. From May through September, Greece is bursting with festivals celebrating all manner of the arts, including music, literature, theater, dance, and cinema. The grandmother of them all, the Athens-Epidaurus Festival, focuses on theater, dance, and music, but many festivals scattered around the country offer opportunities to dip exclusively into jazz, rock, or trance realms. Here is a list of the most popular cultural festivals around the country.

The Athens-Epidaurus Festival

What could be more magical than sitting in an ancient outdoor amphitheater under the stars, hearing the wind whistle through the pines and listening to your favorite recording artist perform live? In years past, performers such as Sting, Yanni, Montserrat Caballe, Liza Minnelli, Elton John, Placido Domingo, and Diana Ross have taken the ancient stage at the Herod Atticus Theater in Athens. This most legendary of all arts festivals, starting in May and lasting through September, takes place in two magnificent venues, the Odeon of Herod Atticus, situated beneath the Acropolis hill, and the ancient theater of Epidaurus, located a two-and-a-half-hour drive from Athens near Nafplion in the Peloponnese, and offers performances of all art forms. Recent performances include the Martha Graham dance company, Isabella Rossellini's screening of her short film about animal sexuality, *Green Porno*, and multiple showcases for both ancient and modern Greek theater, music and dance. greekfestival.gr/en

Sani Festival

For more than two decades, this celebration has gathered the world's biggest jazz names at the northern Greek resort town of Halkidiki, located five hours from Athens. On a sensual green hill topped with a medieval tower, past spectators have taken in the evocative vocals of such artists as Cassandra Wilson and Cesaria Evora while simultaneously gazing at the crystalline turquoise waters of the northern Aegean. Greek legends Stavros Xarchahos and Dionysis Savvopoulos have also graced the Sani stage. www.sanifestival.gr

Kastoria River Party at Nestoria

There is a theme here: in a country where the weather is picture perfect during the spring, summer and fall, it's not surprising that outdoor venues for arts festivals abound. But when you're not gathering in ancient amphitheaters or on medieval hilltops, how about a celebration that attracts 50,000 people to the banks of a river? For five days this festival alongside the Aliakmonas River in western Greece offers visitors the opportunity to camp alongside the four different stages set up along the river's edge. Paintballing, bungee jumping, and trampolining set to music is what this youth-oriented celebration is all about, evoking the bygone days of Woodstock. Voted one of the twelve Best European Festivals, Kastoria River Party invites you to pack your tent and swimsuit and settle in for a marathon of the best Greek and international music in early August. riverparty.org

Festival of the Aegean

Founded in 2005 by Peter Tiboris, the International Festival of the Aegean takes place annually in July on the Cycladic island of Syros. Performances of opera, chorale music, jazz and liederabend abound at the island's own Apollo Theater venue, called the Picolla Scala. Recent programs have included music by Dimitri Vassilakis Jazz Quartet, Verdi's Rigoletto, and choral masterworks by Faure, Offenbach, and Debussy. This gem of an island with its capital of Ermoupoulis, called the Queen of the Cyclades, offers a delightful venue to explore the many neoclassical mansions, churches, and marble-paved streets between performances. www.festivaloftheaegean.com

Kalamata Dance Festival

Funded by the Ministry of Culture and Municipality of Kalamata, this festival was created in 1995 to showcase the work of Greek and international dancers and choreographers. In a recent article, artistic director Vicky Marangopouloy remarked, "Since it was conceived nineteen years ago, the Kalamata International Dance Festival has showcased the most important choreographers in dance. These choreographers are now part of the history of contemporary dance." Performance venues are spread about this olive capital of Greece, including the Kalamata Castle Amphitheater, the Dance Megaron and the Municipal Regional Theater. Recent performers in this annual July festival have included the Netherlands Dance Theater and a contemporary dance workshop with Marta Coronado. www.kalamatadancefestival.gr/index_en.php

International Film Festival Thessaloniki

If you're in Greece in November, it's worth a stop in Greece's second city to see some of the latest indie cinema. As with all art forms, Greeks love their movies, and the red carpet rolls out for some top-notch directors who are included in this annual gathering. Founded in 1992, prestigious names such as Oliver Stone, Jasmina Zbanic, John Malkovich, David Cronenberg, Akira Kurosawa, Sara Driver, and Werner Herzog have participated in this internationally acclaimed event. www.filmfestival.gr/default.aspx?lang=en-US&page=448

82

Writer's Workshops

LITERARY RETREATS IN THE LAND OF HOMER

After excavating on Ithaka more than twenty years ago, I was delighted to see a writers retreat was being offered on the island, giving me the opportunity to combine my love of the island with my love of writing. After attending the Homeric Writers Retreat I am a convert to the idea of spending my days soaking in the utter beauty of Greece as well as immersing myself in the intense inspiration that is imbedded in this magical landscape. Now you, too, can let the muse of epic poetry and eloquence, Kalliope, stir your creative juices, not only on Ithaka, but also at a host of unforgettable settings throughout the country.

Homeric Writers Retreat

Start your day with an uncomplicated breakfast of yogurt and honey, chamomile tea and biscuits, and then move out to a tented patio on the pool deck, laptop in tow. Gather around a table with a frappe and settle into a chair for a morning of intense instruction on the publishing market. Our session focused on how to market and sell our writing projects to agents and publishers, and participants worked on honing, streamlining, and practicing pitches, and learning the ins and outs of the publishing industry with a New York literary agent. We also learned how to build author platforms and how to make the most of social media to publicize and sell projects. When not sitting poolside for intensive daily sessions, guests have opportunities for escorted field trips to the archaeological site known as the School of Homer, a ride to the dizzying heights of the Kathara Monastery overlooking the entire island, and a two-night festival of dance, music, and food held in the pastoral village of Stavros. Author and musician Jessica Bell is your host for this motivating and unforgettable experience. Be sure to check the website, as this retreat is not offered annually. www.homericwriters.com

Olivewood and Laurel

In 1987, writer Suzanne Harris first traveled to the Mani region of Greece, and when she returned to her native Canada, she couldn't shake the lure of this magical country. Twenty years later, she returned to this southernmost tip of the Peloponnese to realize her dream: hosting a literary retreat in the country that had captured her heart two decades before. As a writer, editor, and writing coach, Suzanne offers a fully escorted, comprehensive two-week program that allows writers to unlock their creative potential. Participants start their journey in Athens and tour the Acropolis as well as enjoy a dinner with live music, and then travel to Kardamyli, a village with roots in Homer's *Iliad*. There they have one-on-one coaching sessions and lots of quiet time to write in the sybaritic setting. Off hours can be spent exploring the mountain village of St. Sophia, day trips deep into the Mani, and opportunities for wine tasting. Located five hours from the hustle and bustle of Athens, this tranquil setting "offers us the glittering sea, endless sky, fragrant hills, simple delicious food, and the glorious freedom of no demands. We are both inside and outside of time. Like Odysseus's crew in the land of the lotus eaters, we could easily forget to go home." www.olivewoodandlaurel.com

Women Reading Aloud

Julie Mahoney, director of Women Reading Aloud, leads this ten-day workshop on the secluded and serene island of Alonnisos, where your accommodations overlook the Aegean Sea. Daily morning workshops are held, following the Amherst Writers and Artists Method, and afternoons are free to take yoga classes, get a hot stone or Thai massage, and explore the island via hiking, kayaking, or just taking a bracing swim off the pension's beach. Past participant Priscilla Orr raves about the experience: "In this glorious piece of paradise, I was able to move deeply into my own work and share that with amazingly talented and generous women. The structure of the retreat as led by Julie (Maloney), the exquisite beauty of Alonnisos, and the companionship of the other writers create an alchemy—a kind of mystical experience—unlike any other writer's retreat I've attended. It was transformative." www.womenreadingaloud.org/greece-retreat.html

Limnisa

Limnisa, located in a secluded bay on the peninsula of Methana on the eastern Peloponnese and overlooking the Saronic Gulf, offers retreats in the spring, summer, and fall. In addition to personal workshops by writing instructors, Limnisa offers retreat options that afford the gift of time in an unscheduled environment for writers to focus on a personal project. As the director of the retreat, Mariel Hacking, states, "Primarily, Limnisa is intended as a place that enables writers to concentrate on their work. Most people arrive with a project and leave satisfied with the work they have accomplished while they stayed with us." Retreat guests can stay for any length of time, but a minimum of seven nights is suggested to get the most benefit. There is a daily optional yoga class followed by an al fresco breakfast. The mornings are silent. The food is vegetarian and prepared with fresh local produce. Limnisa has its own beach and organizes excursions, silent walks and sunset meditations. Past participant Alison sums up Limnisa's unique character: "Sometimes a writer (translator) gets tired of words and needs a place where she can rediscover their beauty, not to mention the time and tranquility, and nurturing hospitality, that can restore faith in inspiration and creativity. Limnisa is such a place and this week has been balm for the soul and the mind, from all aspects—the landscape, the marvelous food, the company, the quiet, the sea." www.limnisa.com

83 Language Classes

IT'S ALL GREEK TO ME

Thelo frouta. These are the first words I learned in Greek: *I would like some fruit.* I know, it's not anything profound or philosophical, but it sure was empowering for me to able to speak these words the first time I went to a street market. Soon I was able to not only buy fruit, but I was able to order dishes in a restaurant, have basic conversations with people, and feel comfortable traveling around Greece on my own. While Greece's main industry is tourism, and most shopkeepers and hotel staff speak English, it's always fun to learn a few phrases, such as "please," "thank you"—not to mention some really important words which illustrate the heart of the Greek spirit: *kefi*, or spirit of life, *filotitia*, hospitality, and the all-important *opa*, loosely translated as "let's party!" Here are a few places where you can become conversant in a language that is as old as the gods.

Omilo

Located in the Athens suburb of Maroussi, Omilo offers eight-week classes as well as intensive one-week daily sessions, and for those who would prefer to work on their own, private tutoring. Instruction is offered for all levels, including beginners who are just learning that intimidating 24-letter alphabet, to advanced classes. If you'd like to get out of the city, sign up for classes offered at several locations around the country, including the seaside town of Nafplion in the Peloponnese, where instruction is offered during the period of Greek Easter. Students can explore the ancient nearby sites of Mycenae, Sparta, Mystra, and Epidaurus as well as participate in the Easter procession, a highlight of the Greek Orthodox calendar.

If you're in Greece during the summer and you'd like to combine learning Greek while visiting the islands, you can travel to Syros, Andros, and Lefkas. Classes take place in quaint seaside towns close to tavernas and sightseeing, so during down time you can explore beaches and archaeological sites. Some tuition includes guided walks, dance lessons, and introduction to Greek music. www.omilo.com

The Athens Centre

The Athens Centre, located in the trendy Mets district of Athens, prides itself on having one of the most comprehensive Modern Greek language programs in the country. Attracting students from all over the world, the Centre serves diplomats, business people working in Athens, EU translators and interpreters, and émigrés living abroad in Greece. Courses are offered in affiliation with American and Canadian universities on semester and quarter programs to accommodate students studying abroad. Shorter Maymester, January terms, and summer programs are also offered. Small classes of four to eight students allow for maximum student-teacher ratio and combine parallel instruction in reading, writing, and comprehension skills. Instructors are Greek nationals who take pride in their cultural history and combine a love of their country's language and history to supply a well-rounded approach to learning Greek. The Centre also sponsors lectures and past speakers have included Princeton historian Edmund Keeley, translator and philosopher Philip Sherrard, and inventor and poet Buckminster Fuller. athenscentre.gr

Lexis Centre

Want to get out of the city to learn Greek? How about Crete? Greece's biggest island, Crete is almost a country unto itself with its own unique dialect and cultural traditions. Located in the harbor town of Chania, along Crete's northern coast, students can learn their Alphas, Betas, and Gammas in small groups of three to seven people for as short as two weeks and as long as twenty-four week sessions. Private tutoring is offered as well, and students who quality can take the Proficiency in the Greek Language Examination of the Aristotle University of Thessaloniki. Courses are also offered in Greek literature as well as Ancient Greek language. Lexis Centre is located in Splantzia Square, a few minutes from the city center and the Venetian harbor. Lexis believes language cannot be taught without a knowledge of the cultural environment in which it is spoken, so an intensive two-week course will include museum visits, instruction in Cretan dance, watching Greek cinema and cooking a traditional Cretan meal. Pottery seminars, day trips, learning how to play a Greek folk instrument, and a visit to a local feast are extra, but the latter will give you an opportunity to put that famous Greek phrase, "Opa!" to good use! www.lexis.edu.gr/index.php

84 Getting Married in Greece

SAYING "I DO" IN THE LAND OF THE GODDESS

Lots of people spend their honeymoons in Greece, and who wouldn't want to? Romantic sunsets, secluded beaches, delicious food, and endless sunshine—it's a lovers paradise. But why just honeymoon when you can get married there? Want an intimate ceremony in a bucolic vineyard setting? How about renewing your vows in a tiny, whitewashed Greek chapel etched against an azure sky on a sun-drenched Cycladic island? Or dreaming of an all-out wedding bash set on the cliffs of Santorini with the legendary caldera and its ultramarine waters spanning as far as the eye can see? You can have it all—and while there's red tape involved for an overseas wedding, it's not an impossible feat. There are agencies in Greece that can take care of all the bureaucratic details and allow you to enjoy your dream of a lifetime wedding.

Santorini Weddings

These folks do it all—as it says on their website, they plan, execute, and organize the wedding of a lifetime. The pros at Santorini Weddings will ensure that your dreams of a destination wedding come true. All you need do is gather up the proper documentation and make sure it gets to them four weeks prior to the ceremony so they can make sure everything is in order. Translators are available so all the i's are dotted and t's are crossed. Then the fun begins:

picking the type of wedding and setting you want. You can choose from a civil wedding, a Greek church wedding, or a Catholic Church wedding. Civil wedding locations run the gamut from a full-moon beach wedding and reception at Theros Wave Beach Bar to a magical sunset wedding on the terrace at Le Ciel Santorini overlooking the magnificent caldera.

For those with more traditional tastes, an Orthodox Church wedding is a perfect choice. The ceremony includes the exchanging of rings three times by the "Koumbaro" or best man, and the ceremony of the crowning, in which the bride and groom are crowned with white wreathes. Called *stefana*, these stunning wreaths are joined by a ribbon, which represents unity, and symbolize the blessings bestowed on the couple by God. Catholic weddings take place at St. John the Baptist Cathedral in Fira. If you are feeling flush, wedding extras include Greek dancers, a live band, and fireworks—but with a setting as famous as Santorini's caldera, it's almost like gilding the lily! www.weddings-in-santorini.com

Ionian Weddings

Want to get married on Ithaka, the island known for its legendary lovers Penelope and Odysseus? Or perhaps you had another remote island in mind for that ultra private, secluded ceremony? Ionian Weddings specializes in arranging weddings on fourteen different islands across the Ionian and Aegean chains, as well as Cyprus. Couples can choose from a wide variety of settings including beaches, historic venues, gardens, vineyards, and chapels. Brides can get married barefoot on the beach, or exchange vows in a stunning, converted 17th-century monastery near Paphos, Cyprus, the birthplace of Aphrodite, the goddess of love and beauty. For those old enough to remember Jackie O's famous wedding to Aristotle Onassis, you can get married on a sailboat with views of Skorpios in the background, the private island where Jacqueline

Kennedy married her Greek shipping tycoon. While same sex marriage is not yet legal in Greece, gay couples can enjoy a same sex blessing at several destinations, including Santorini, Mykonos, Zakynthos, and Cyprus. www.ionianweddings.co.uk

Daphne Weddings

Have you seen the movie *Mamma Mia* and fantasized about getting married atop that magnificent cliff? Now you can! Daphne Weddings specializes solely on getting hitched on Skopelos, the verdant island in the Sporades where the blockbuster flick was filmed. Weddings inside the church aren't allowed, but who cares—after you climb the 200 steps to the top you won't want to be anywhere but outside admiring the jaw-dropping views!

After a career in journalism, Dutch-born Daphne Timmers moved to Greece where she married her Greek husband. After organizing her own dream wedding, Daphne fell in love with wedding planning and Daphne Weddings was born. She takes care of all the business details so that you can enjoy "the wedding of your fantasies with a Greek traditional touch."

Aside from the *Mamma Mia* church garden, you can choose from a number of other romance-soaked wedding locations, including Amarantos, a stunning outcropping of rocks that juts into the Aegean, where a sunset wedding allows you total privacy and a sense of being embraced by the cerulean sea. At Limnonari Beach, the bride can arrive via boat while her groom awaits her on a chalk-white sand beach and a backdrop of verdant pine trees that grip the coastline. Daphne can arrange an unforgettable reception right on the beach, where formally set tables meld beautifully with the rustic backdrop, allowing guests to take in the sunset over the Aegean while enjoying homemade delicacies from a traditional Greek taverna. www.daphneweddings.com

85 Skiing in Greece

SCHUSS DOWN SLOPES NAMED ANTIGONE AND APHRODITE

I know, it sounds crazy. Skiing in Greece, the land of perpetual sunshine, beaches, and sparkling seas? But it's true—Greece is also a land of mountains, and in the wintertime those at higher elevations become covered in snow and as a result, a favorite destination for both Greeks and Europeans. It seems Americans are the only ones who don't know that winter in Greece can be just as much fun as summer, as long as you know where to go! There are more than twenty ski resorts in Greece, but here is a list of the most popular, trendy, and organized destinations in the country.

Parnassos Ski Centre

Located only a two-hour drive from Athens, Parnassos is an easy trip for those wanting to get out of the city for a day of skiing. With two main locations, the resort boasts fourteen lifts and twenty slopes that range from beginner to expert level, and also offers cross-country skiing for those wishing to break away from the downhill crowd. Of course, you're in Greece, so you can choose from a number of god- and goddess-worthy runs, including Aphrodite, Pythia, Hermes, and Charioteer. Après-ski is equally popular with high-end dining as well as cozy, romantic tavernas that offer local specialties such as *hilopites*, square-shaped pasta dishes, and *formaela*, the local cheese of Arachova. This little town comes to life in the winter and is filled with exiles from the summery islands of the Cyclades, such a Mykonos, so you will have no trouble tracking down some excellent nightlife. Arachova is also the place where you can buy those fluffy handmade *flokati* rugs, so make some room in your suitcase to take one home. www.parnassos-ski.gr/eng/page.aspx?itemID=SPG1

Kalavryta Ski Resort

The second largest ski resort in Greece is located on Mount Helmos in the Peloponnese. With twelve runs ranging in difficulty from beginner to expert, the resort has seven lifts and offers a snow-boarding park, a special moguls run, and extreme games for the younger crowd. Once again, the slopes have been christened with names from Greek mythology, so you can schuss down Electra, ski through powder on Antigone, or try out night skiing on Phaedra and Danae. Après-ski activities include touring the nearby Achaia vineyards, or exploring the magical pine forest of Strofilia, a natural reserve of conifer that separates Lake Prokopos from the Ionian Sea. www.kalavrita-ski.gr

Vassilitsa Ski Resort

Vassilitsa is the place to go for fans of extreme sports, and snowboarders love the place for its half pipe and first-ever jump contest. If you don't feel like skiing or snowboarding, you can ride down the hills in a twelve-person raft. Mount Vassilitsa's height of more than 6000 feet means lots of snow and powder in the winter that cover its sixteen slopes, ranging from beginner to expert. Located in the Pindos Mountains in Greece's northern region of Macedonia, Vassilitsa offers vacationers a chance to explore the nearby village of Grevena in their off hours. Also known as the land of the mushrooms, the region is home to more than 1,300 mushroom species, which are used to make a variety of dishes, including soups, pies, sauces, and even liquors! www.gtp.gr/TDirectoryDetails.asp?ID=38026

Kaimaktsalan Ski Resort

From the top of this mountain you can see both the sea and Mount Olympus—not bad for a day of skiing in Greece! Located on Mount Voras in Macedonia, Kaimaktsalan offers skiers a choice of thirteen slopes, as well as a snowboard fun park and a snow tubing park. A three-story chalet has a restaurant that offers traditional dishes, a café-bar and full service hotel. Sit in front of the cozy fireplace and enjoy stunning views of the surrounding mountains and Mediterranean Sea. After an intense day of skiing, make a trip to the thermal springs of Loutraki at the base of Mount Voras. The spa consists of forty-eight individuals baths, six indoor pools, an enormous outdoor pool, and offers complete spa services that will soothe your sore muscles after an intense day on the slopes. www.kaimaktsalan.gr/en/home-en

❧

VI

Cooking Schools, Olive Oil Production, Agritourism, and Beekeeping

86 Melissae and The Bee Priestesses

GODDESSES AND BEES IN THE PELOPONNESE

 My sister likes to call herself a bee priestess. After all, her name, Deborah, means bee in Hebrew, something that has motivated her to collect bee-inspired jewelry from around the world. A few years ago, while traveling in Greece, we had the good fortune to visit a bee-keeping operation high in the olive-gray dusted hills overlooking the southern Peloponnese village of Stoupa. After touring the vast array of hives—white unassuming boxes overlooking a valley thickly pungent with sage, thyme and rose-mary—I was fascinated to learn more about this delicate and often misunderstood species, but my sister became obsessed. When we returned to the States, abuzz (pardon the pun!) with her new love of all things apiary, she began building her own hives and raising bees on her property in Montana.

"Look at the size of these lavender bushes!" Deb gushed as we approached a small cottage poised on a sage and thyme encrusted hillside. Getting out of the car, we were greeted by John Phipps, an English expat and editor of *Beekeeping Magazine*. Several years before, he and his wife, Val, had moved to Greece so he could start up his beekeeping business in a place without the driving rain and sunless chill of English winters. If I hadn't known we were directly in the middle of the area of Greece known as the Mani, the verdant valley overlooking the thin finger of silvery sea in the distance could have been mistaken for the Devonshire coastline. Little did I know that in Greece, the bee is an ancient symbol of fertility, associated with the cycles of the moon and nature. This fragile and endangered species thrives in a land that worshipped bee priestesses some four thousand years ago.

Since antiquity when Eros, the god of love, dipped his arrows into honey before aiming at his targets, this golden elixir has been associated with Greece. The word for honey comes from the Greek word *melissa*. The Melissae were actually a trio of bee priestesses who divined omens from nature. As prophetesses, the three, known as Daphnis, Laurel, and Melaina, were able to predict the future and taught their skills to the god Apollo.

The bee has been associated with Greek culture since Minoan times, circa 3500 B.C., whose artists fashioned exquisite jewelry representations of the insect using granulation and filigree of gold. The bee was an important part of the myths of the Eleusinian goddesses Demeter and Persephone, who was also called Melitodes, or "honeyed ones." The goddess Artemis, whose temple stood outside the precinct of Eleusis, was also closely associated with the bee. Because she was an ancient goddess of fertility, agriculture, and the moon, many artifacts representing bees have been found in sanctuaries where Artemis was worshipped.

Archaeologist Marija Gimbutas explains a passage written by the Neoplatonic philosopher Porphyry: "...we learn that Artemis is a bee, Melissa, and that both she and the bull belong to the moon. Hence both are connected with the idea of a periodic regeneration. We also learn that souls are bees and that Melissa draws souls down to be born. The idea of a 'life in death' in this singularly interesting concept is expressed by the belief that the life of the bull passed into that of the bees."

It is perhaps at Delphi where bees were most revered. Most honeys produced by bees are safely edible, but a particular kind of honey known as an entheogen—literally god-infused—was ingested by the Delphic priestesses. The oracles, who also inhaled the methane gases emitting from the earth's crust, were assisted in their prophetic roles with the help of green or unripened honey containing nectar from oleander, rhododendron, and other members of the toxic Heath family of plants.

Traditionally, the southern Peloponnese of Greece is prime real estate for beekeepers. The lush landscape, replete with herbs, chestnut trees, hyacinth, and orange, makes it the perfect environment to raise bees. Like wine, honey takes on the terroire, and each region boasts that its mellifluous nectar is the finest. John and his Greek friend, Socrates, helped us suit up in full beekeeper mufti; as we stood by, Socrates waved a metal canister emitting smoke over the hive and proceeded to reach in, bare handed, to lift out a section swarming with bees. John leaned in, pointing to the queen, which was barely discernible among the insect-encrusted slab of honey.

"The varroa mite can wreak havoc in a bee colony," John said as he inspected a tray just removed from a hive. This parasitic insect is thought to be responsible for recent bee colony collapses that have occurred worldwide. After some forty-five minutes of inspecting this fascinating species, we eventually shed our clumsy suits. Over tea—with lavender scented local honey!—and an ample serving of some of Val's famous Greek Welsh Cakes, John seemed to express hope that, given enough time, the fortunes of Melissae and their bees will improve in the future.

GREEK WELSH CAKES

Recipe courtesy of Val Phipps
Stoupa, Greece

Ingredients:
225 g. self-raising flour
110 g. butter
pinch of salt
1 teaspoon mixed spice
zest of 1/4 lemon
110 g. sugar (fine and soft brown mixed)
110 g. currants/sultanas
1 beaten egg

Method:
Rub fat into flour.
Add sugar, fruit, mixed spice, salt and lemon zest.
Mix in beaten egg.
Roll out 1/4 inch thick.
Cut into rounds.
Bake on medium heated griddle (or frying pan) until just
cooked—slightly soft in the middle.
Dust with fine sugar.
EAT AT ONCE!!

(Should you batch-cook, make double quantity, allow to cool and
freeze. Once thawed, warm, wrapped in foil in oven.

87

Olive Oil Harvest

GREEK LIQUID GOLD

Normally people wouldn't consider traveling to Greece in the off-season. After all, it's the balmy, aquamarine waters, that pellucid Greek light and the ability to sightsee in shorts and a t-shirt that brings most people to this country in the summer months. But a few years ago, I returned to Greece in November and had one of the most enjoyable experiences in all the years I've been traveling to this country. And there was a good reason for my off-season visit: olives.

That's right. Olives. After eating my fair share of Kalamata, Amphissa, and other varietals grown in Greece, I never really thought of how they were used to produce oil. Greek-Americans tote home jugs of the stuff every year. In the days before 9/11, I even brought a canister full of oil home with me by slipping it next to my upgraded seat in Business Class. But Greece produces what some epicures believe to be the best olive oil in the world, and after this trip, I have to agree.

My sister, Deb, was filming a documentary on olive oil production and I thought—Greece in November, why not? I knew that winter could bring massive rainstorms that create mini floods that course through the Athenian concrete streets. Yet on this trip we had no such deluges; every day was warm and sunny. I picked Deb up at the Athens airport and we steered the car towards Leonidio, just around the bend of the Saronic Gulf, a town dramatically situated against the sheer russet backdrop of rock from the Badron Gorge. While Leonidio is just inland, along the Dafnonas River, its sweet little sister village along the coast, Poulithra, is where our friend Susan lives. Susan's gorgeous little seaside cottage had a few acres of olive groves, and when she asked for help harvesting her trees to take to the presses, we obliged.

We arrived and two workers had already laid down the nets beneath the trees. Deb and I each grabbed a rake and, after a quick tutorial, proceeded to release a shower fall of jade and mahogany-skinned pointed olives. The linen-colored sea lapped gently at the shore and a light breeze cooled our necks, heating up from the rising sun. Once the tumble of fruit began to accumulate in the nets, I was amazed at the myriad colors that distinguish different levels of ripeness: dusky emerald, lettuce and algae green were mixed with aubergine and amethyst-colored olives, ready to burst. After clawing away at the limbs and fronds of branches with the rakes, we dragged the filled nets to the terrace. There we hunched on hands and knees to sort away leaves, stems, and branches, bagging the trimmed olives into burlap sacks and loading them onto a pickup truck.

✳ agreekisland.com

✳ www.zorbas.de/english/active/pefnos.php

The next day we drove up the coast to a little town with a working press. Outside, I watched as other trucks, vans, and cars unloaded their haul, stacking sacks of burlap bulging with olives outside the nondescript building. Inside, a Rube Goldberg assortment of machines greeted us; the sound of the press whined and screeched as we watched the conveyer belt grumble under the weight of the harvest. The multicolored array made its way up the ramp, dropping into the hopper, and then we waited until the spigot began to spit out a stream of golden liquid. Once Susan's plastic jugs were filled, they were loaded into the trunk of her car. Before we left, we treated ourselves to an impromptu snack of bread, fresh from the bakery. Standing around the open trunk, she uncapped one of the jugs and we dipped the loaf into the warm oil, feeling as though we were consuming sunshine.

A few days later, in the small town of Stoupa, a few miles to the west on another finger of the Peloponnese, we experienced the same delight. This olive press sported advanced machinery, still humming and whining away as it munched the multicolored fruit and spun out a mellifluous, silky juice. While we stood next to the spigot, our friend, Burgi, handed us slices of warm, freshly baked bread. "Just dip it in there," she urged, "it's like nothing you have ever tasted before." She was right: there is olive oil in a bottle and there is olive oil hot of the press—and there is no comparison between the two. I heartily recommend doing this once in a lifetime, as the warmth of the oil imparts an earthy terroire that will link you to this land forever.

Most harvests in Greece are accompanied by a celebration, and this was no different. Our group gathered in a small kitchen adjacent to the press and a pan of oil was put on a flame to fry potatoes, sardines dusted with flour and sticks of purple eggplant. A rough rosé was put out in jugs and a spread was placed end to end on tables crinkled with plastic tablecloths. Apart from this, all that is needed is a little rembetika music and olive oil. Dancing is optional.

There are several ways to experience the olive harvest in Greece. The traditional guesthouse Xenonas Fos ke Chroros on Kythera will take you through the harvest to press with olive groves that are more than a hundred years old. Villa Pefnos, located near Stoupa in Agios Dimitrios, offers weeklong stays during olive picking season. Guests are also offered lessons in Greek cooking and a tour of the nearby olive capital of Kalamata. At Eumelia, an organic agritourism resort near Gouves in the Peloponnese, you can participate in both wine harvest in September and October and olive harvest from November through February.

✳ www.eumelia.com

✳ www.saintbasilolivegrove.com

All parts of Greece claim to have the best oil and folks on the island of Crete are no different. Saint Basil Olive Grove in northwest Crete alleges to have the finest you have ever tasted. Their late November olive picking holidays offer side trips, such as hiking in the White Mountains and clay pigeon shooting, and your down time can be spent in one of four private villas, each with its own swimming pool.

☙

88 Cooking Schools and Agritourism

MOUSSAKA, BAKLAVA, MASTIC, AND MORE

At first it seemed daunting: those endless sheets of phyllo dough, paper-thin, impossible to handle without tearing, and drying out almost immediately before I had a chance to fit them into the pan. *Baklava, tiropitta, spanakopitta*: all of these delectable treats have phyllo as their key ingredient, and it felt like I would never get the hang of it. But after enough tries, slaving away in my own kitchen, I finally conquered this famously finicky ingredient. Now you can too, as well as master myriad other delectable Greek treats, with a fabulous twist—learning how in the home of the gods and goddesses! Come along as we sample a few of Greece's best and most popular cooking schools. And how better to master this iconic Mediterranean cuisine than by doing so in the place where the olives, rosemary, as well as unusual ingredients such as mastic, grow, not to mention sipping the local vintage while marinating your soul in the most sybaritic of sceneries?

Diane Kochilas

One of the most famous names in Greek cuisine is Diane Kochilas. Born in New York, Diane's family hails from Ikaria, the famed island featured in Dan Beuttner's Blue Zones, where the extraordinary good health and longevity of its inhabitants has put this unique destination on the map. The author of eighteen cookbooks, including *Ikaria: Lessons on Food, Life, and Longevity from the Island Where People Forget to Die*, Diane works with Harvard, Yale, and other universities to consult on healthy eating options for student dining services and is the collaborating chef at Molyvos Restaurant in New York City.

Now you can sample some of that healthy cuisine by signing up for one of Diane's cooking classes. Daily three-to-four-hour cooking instruction is organized around a full meal, which can include anything from making phyllo dough from scratch to grilling octopus. Meals are served to all participants outdoors in the garden beneath 150-year-old vines overlooking the coast of Ikaria. Outside the kitchen, excursions include visiting a local shepherd to milk goats and learn the secrets of making *kathoura*, Ikaria's local cheese. Guests will take nature hikes and learn to identify indigenous herbs and sample local honey, wines, and olives. Dancing lessons, a night out at a local taverna to sample island delicacies and a dip at Therma, the local hot springs round out your stay on Ikaria.

"The best thing any guest ever said to us was that we don't just create an experience," Diane notes, "we create memories. I think people deeply yearn for connecting to a place that is real, a real village, where life is still agri-central. They can feel the sense of community that runs deep on Ikaria." She goes on to add, "People should expect to get a taste of village life on a small Greek island, to taste amazingly fresh food and to learn to cook simple, delicious dishes they can make anywhere in the world. They should expect to relax and let go of the clock for a week, the way we do on Ikaria all year round." www.dianekochilas.com

Kea Artinasal

Kea, a small island in the northern Cyclades, is the pastoral location for the cooking school of renowned cookbook author and self-proclaimed "passionate cook" Aglaia Kremezi. A journalist trained in art, graphic design, and photography, Aglaia turned her attention to food and has published three cookbooks as well as articles for *Epicurious* and *The Atlantic* magazines. Aglaia's six-day cooking classes include making (and eating!) fig-leaf-wrapped charcoal-grilled fish, *amygdalota*, traditional almond cookies, stuffed and fried zucchini blossoms (heaven on earth!) peppered with hikes to the Karthaea archaeological site, sunset drinks and meze at Xyla Beach and preparing the ricotta-like *mizithra* cheese from local milk. Aglaia is proud of how her program differs from typical cooking schools. "Our participants cook and eat with us in our home, not in a restaurant kitchen. We treat them exactly as we would our family and friends. People bring us gifts, and they feel so grateful, as if they were invited, and not our 'clients'—they understand how much we, too, enjoy the programs!" www.keartisanal.com

Masticulture

Located in the village of Mesta on the Aegean island of Chios is an unusual agritourism agency that offers a variety of cultural experiences to explore this gorgeous island. Chios is one of the largest producers of mastic, a plant resin made from a small evergreen tree, and Mesta lies in the heart of this region. Often referred to as "tears of Chios," mastic is used in spoon sweets, desserts, cheese, and breads, but the most well-known use is in the licorice tasting liqueur known as *mastiha*.

As food writer and blogger Alexis Adams says, "The owners of Masticulture, Vassilis and Roula, are truly wonderful people. They often set up culinary-related tours and, in fact, always include a culinary theme in their *mastiha* tours." As an agritourism agency, Masticulture offers a hands-on experience on the production of local mastic, wine and olives. Guests can use traditional tools to harvest mastic, forage for wild mushrooms and greens known as *horta,* and participate in cultural classes and workshops such as pottery, dance, and trekking. Plan to pre-book for any of the themed experiential activities that are offered from April through November. www.masticulture.com/english-homepage.php

Ambelonas Corfu

Author of *Corfiot Cuisine—In Search of the Origins,* Vasiliki Karounou invites you not to just a cooking class, but to a full day immersion into the food, culture, and history of Corfu. This Italianate island, the northernmost of the Ionian chain, is a product of its rich Venetian heritage and is a paradise for food lovers. As Vasiliki says, "We're passionate about Corfiot tradition and we're firm believers that truly loving this island and everything it has to offer—from ruins to impressive Venetian-influenced architecture; from beautiful landscapes to food with tastes and flavors that have been melded in the Corfiot tradition by people of different cultures who lived in the island; from warm hospitality to folklore events—comes with a serious responsibility." She goes on to say, "Ambelonas Corfu is a simple and flexible space, combining wine and olive oil culture with gastronomy, situated in a wild natural setting with panoramic views of central Corfu."

Guests start a typical experience at this sprawling, family-owned estate with an herbal soft drink, such as lemon verbena or lavender, or cold red wine with citrus, and tour the olive oil production facility and vineyard. A food photography introduction is offered and then participants engage in preparation of a five-course meal, using the estate's own fresh ingredients, which is served al fresco in Ambelonas's pastoral setting along with local wines. Traditional Greek music accompanies the meal, and those with enough energy after such a massive feast can work off the calories with dancing lessons! In addition to lessons in Corfiot cuisine, Ambelonas also offers instruction in traditional techniques for preserving foods, wild herbs, and vegetables. realcorfu.com/ambelonas

Crete's Culinary Sanctuaries

Nikki Rose, founder and director of this multi-dimensional curriculum located in north-central Crete, sums up her program's focus on culture, traditional cuisine, and sustainable organic agriculture: "The Mediterranean Diet concept that originated in Crete is not a diet—it is a way of life. Preservation of traditional foodways also protects our safe food sources and environment. Participating in educational travel programs that protect and celebrate cultural and natural heritage can be a wonderful experience with good company and cuisine." Nikki refers to the island as feminine, and reminds visitors that the ancient inhabitants of this landscape, the Minoans, worshipped Gaia, or Mother Earth. Her program offers participants the opportunity to spend time with locals in rural communities working to preserve their traditional trades. Botanical hikes are offered to explore the countryside and harvest indigenous plants used in ancient and modern medicines as well as cuisines. Visits to organic farmers, fishermen, and artisan food producers will yield the freshest produce, seafood, cheeses, legumes, wines, breads, and olive oil for use in meal preparation. Nikki, the author of *Crete: The Roots of the Mediterranean Diet*, organizes her unique seminars around a seasonal calendar. Visitors can roast pork and chestnuts over an indoor fire during winter, prepare lamb on the spit for Easter, savor grilled smelts, heirloom tomatoes, and wax peppers in summer, and in the autumn, prepare raki, a rough brandy, that can be sipped alongside seafood soups, ember-baked potatoes, and pomegranates. www.cookingincrete.com/index.html

VII

Additional Islands, Beaches, Resorts and Goddess-Worthy Sites

89

Skyros

WHERE THETIS GAVE BIRTH TO ACHILLES

When I visited Skyros, I had no idea of the wide variety of pleasures this tiny, wasp-waisted island held for visitors. Located to the northwest of the Greek mainland, Skyros is easily reached via ferry from the town of Kimi, located on Greece's second largest island, Evia. Considered part of the Sporades islands, some purists believe Skyros, at the southernmost end of the chain, actually belongs to the Cycladic island group because of its similar nest-like, boxy architecture. As the least visited island in the group, Skyros's isolation has preserved its unique character. Foreigners are not allowed to purchase land and locals, while very welcoming, remain staunchly determined to keep the flow of tourism from overtaking their own quiet paradise. And when the ferry draws near to shore, you can see why.

Arriving in Skyros town, the first thing that greets you is the soaring crag of burnished rock rising sharply above the blindingly white cubist stacks of houses clotting the hillside. The Castle of Lykomedes sits atop the bluff and is the site of an ancient acropolis, as well as the current Venetian fortress that stands today. If you climb to the summit you will be rewarded with a breathtaking panorama of the glimmering waters of the Aegean and views to the north and the Sporades Marine Park, home to a vast array of wildlife including dolphins, Cory's shearwaters, and Eleonora's falcons.

The word *nisoi* in Greek means islands, and in antiquity each island had its own divinity. The *nisoi* were primal gods, or mountains cast into the sea by the god Poseidon. Philostratos the Younger had words of praise for the goddess of Skyros in his work, *Imagines*,

> *The heroine crossed with reeds—for doubtless you see the female figure at the foot of the mountain, sturdy of form and dressed in blue—is the island of Skyros, my boy, which the divine Sophocles called "wind-swept." She has a branch of olive in her hands and a spray of vine.*

The goddess Thetis also has a connection to this island. A Nereid, or goddess of the sea, Thetis is the mother of the hero Achilles, one of the main players in the Trojan War. Against his father's wishes, Thetis hid the boy as a girl on the island of Skyros until she could complete her plan to make him immortal by passing him through the fire and rubbing him with ambrosia. Hyginus, a 2nd-century Latin mythograper, states in his work, *Fabulae*,

> *When Thetis the Nereis knew that Achilles, the son she had borne to Peleus, would die if he went to attack Troy, she sent him to the island of Skyros, entrusting him to King Lycomedes.*

When exploring Skyros, keep in mind the island is divided into two distinctly different sections: the northern end is lush and coated in emerald conifer, while the dun-colored southern end is drier, more barren, and prone to strong winds coming in off the Aegean. If you're looking to do some sunbathing, it's probably better to choose another island. Although we enjoyed the small beach of Linaria, most all the beaches of Skyros, such as the lovely slices of white sand and rippling sapphire waters that characterize Molos and Magazia, are also exposed to the prevailing winds off the Aegean.

One of the delightful surprises unique to Skyros is its legendary herd of ponies—a pint-sized breed that has run free across the island's vast plains for centuries. These ponies are likely those depicted on the Parthenon frieze, in which the riders appear large by comparison to their mounts. This was not done to emphasize the prominence of the soldier but instead reflected the choice of the Skyrian breed as a desired mount. It is said that Achilles rode off to the Trojan War on a chestnut-colored Skyrian pony, further emphasizing the stamina and bravery of the breed.

❇ www.aroundskyros.com

These handsome creatures, with their dappled as well as deep chestnut coats and long shaggy manes, have unfortunately become an endangered species. Until recently, ponies were communally owned, used for summer threshing and left to graze the remaining months of the year. A decline in local agriculture and cross breeding has diminished the herds and efforts are underway by a variety of groups to preserve the species from extinction. The best place to view the ponies is the Skyrian Pony Center near the pine-fringed beach of Atsitsa Bay.

Skyros is well known for its diverse crafts and folk art. To see intricate traditional embroidery, rare books, and photographs, make a stop in the Faltaits Museum. Housed in a traditional whitewashed, converted two-level residence in Skyros Town, it was opened in 1964 by family descendent Manos Faltaits. Visitors can revel in Skyros's rich cultural and ancient heritage thanks to local craftsmen, influenced over the centuries by the island's eclectic heritage, including Byzantine, Venetian, and Ottoman occupations. Local crafts such as ceramics, woodcarving, and embroidery have been raised to a higher level of art due to a wealthy ruling class that championed and supported the artists. Everyday objects, such as traditional furniture, copper kitchen items, carpets, and paintings reflect the cultural life and social structure of the local Skyrian people, and are well worth a stop.

If you are on Skyros during the Lenten period, usually late February or early March, you might encounter the strange and wonderful Goat Festival, which is held during this period, and has its roots in pagan tradition. If you've ever seen the M. Night Shyamalan film, *The Village*, you might recall (spoiler alert!) the horrific costume kept under lock and key used to scare the inhabitants from roaming into the surrounding forests for fear of coming upon an evil, goat-faced beast. On Skyros, this beast comes alive annually. Author John Cuthbert Lawson describes the costume: "The mask for the face is made of the skin of some small animal such as a weasel, of which the hind legs and tail are attached to the hood, while the head and forelegs hang down to the breast of the wearer; eye holes are cut in these as in the other forms of mask."

The goat mask dancer is only one of the characters in this festival that has its roots in the ancient celebrations of Dionysus, the god of wine. Two distinct roles appear in the festival: the *geroi*, or old men, who wear the goat masks and black hoods and load themselves down with heavy bells; and the *korela*, who are distinctly female. Men dress up as women, wearing the traditional Skyrian women's clothing, covering their faces in cloth. Their job is to clear the way for the *geroi* through the crowded streets and entertain and sing to them when they tire.

The party continues over a full two drinking- and feasting-infused days and has roots in the story of Persephone, goddess of the Underworld, in which torch-bearing men wildly wave their lights to celebrate Persephone's release from Hades. The Skyrian festival offers an unusual spin on this well-known Greek myth; the purpose of local men wearing goatskins and pounds of goat bells whirling around in a frenzy is to release Persephone from her Underworld prison so that spring can once again warm the earth.

❧

90 *Sifnos*

THE GOLDEN ISLAND

In antiquity, Sifnos was the Fort Knox of Greece. This tiny island, surrounded by a peppering of its sibling isles in the Cycladic Chain, was known for its rich veins of gold, silver, and iron, which were mined as early as the third millennium B.C. Sifnos was so renowned for its stores of gold that visitors to the sacred site of Delphi will discover one of the small temples dedicated to the Oracle, known as the Siphnian Treasury, was erected by the islanders and is one of the richest at the site.

As you arrive in the port town of Kamares, you will notice that Sifnos appears greener than your average Cycladic island. The center is mountainous, with the main peak, Profitis Ilias, erupting dramatically almost three thousand feet above sea level. Curiously, the main towns, named after the twin gods Apollo and Artemis, are also located on this central spine of the island, and a twenty-minute bus ride to Apollonia is worth the effort. Near the town's main *plateia* or central square is the Museum of Popular Arts and Folklore, where you can admire local crafts such as embroideries and the island's famous pottery.

✳ www.visitgreece.gr/en/greek_islands/cyclades/sifnos

This hilly central spine is also home to Apollo's sister town Artemonas, named after Apollo's twin, Artemis. The village is like an outdoor museum with its array of Venetian and neoclassical mansions and elegant churches; two miles east along the path below is the town of Kastro, which served as the island's capital in both ancient and medieval times. Some of its walls are formed from Venetian houses, and the town offers a stunning view of the Aegean. A short hike will bring you to Artemis's ancient temple site, which is now occupied by the church of the Virgin Mary of Konchi with its multi-domed roof.

The island is an iconic example of Cycladic lusciousness with its strips of sandy white beaches, unusual for Greece with its preponderance of pebbled shores. Terraces of tiny, box-like ivory houses race up the verdant and dun-patched hillsides that are perforated with bell towers, dovecotes, windmills, and emerald arborvitae piercing the lapis lazuli skies.

Sadly, Sifnos's mines are emptied today. One can see the many mine shifts that were used in antiquity scattered around the island. Legend has it that locals offered up an annual sacrifice of a solid golden egg in honor of Apollo. Yet when the gold mines were close to being exhausted, the locals thought they could fool the god by offering up a gold-painted stone instead. Bad idea, as we all know, for trying to fool the gods results in revenge. Apollo was so angered he sent a tyrant to raid the remaining precious metals and the mines were flooded.

During their height of affluence, the Siphnians asked the Delphic oracle if their riches would last, and they received this reply from the Pythia,

When the council chamber in Sifnos shines white
And white too is the forehead of the market place
Then is there heed of a man of foresight to beware
Danger threatens from a wooden host and a scarlet messenger.

The wooden host and scarlet messenger came in the form of pirates from the island of Samos. They raided Sifnos, taking any remaining wealth and left the island, once one of the richest in Greece, destitute. The moral of the story: don't consult the Delphic Oracle unless you want an honest answer.

When my husband and I visited some years ago, the coastal area of Plati Yialos was not as built up as today, but this is still considered the nicest beach on the island. During our stay there was only one restaurant, and our evening regimen consisted of going to Nikos's, the area's lone taverna. The night before we left, I was checking under our bed for any stray items and found a wad of cash encased in a clot of dust bunnies, which made me wonder if a little of Sifnos's old affluence might still be hovering in the air.

There are many monasteries in Greece, but near the town of Faros is the Nunnery of Chyrssopigi (Virgin of the Golden Spring), built in 1550 by Bavarians on the site of a former church. The Nunnery occupies the most gorgeous spot on a tiny islet, connected to the island by a bridge; the searing white structure jutting out onto the cerulean sea is a must photo op. If you are feeling monastic, guests are able to stay and enjoy the nearby beaches and abundant fresh island fish. As in many parts of Greece, some believe the icon of the Virgin here has healing powers, so bring along your most pressing questions to petition the BVM.

There is some debate as to how Sifnos got its name. Some say it is the name of the first settler who was the son of a hero named Sounio, others state it means "empty," referring to the stripping of the island's natural resources in antiquity. If you like the idea of a verdant island coated in snow-white cubist dwellings, a different church to visit every day of the year, and some old-fashioned peace and quiet, then Sifnos isn't empty at all; in fact, it may be just the place for you.

❧

91 Nafplion

HERA'S VIRGINITY RESTORING SPRING

Many years ago I was planning a trip to Ithaka with my friend and fellow hellenophile, Mary Lou Roussel. We had worked together on an excavation on the legendary island, and in spite of never uncovering the Palace of Odysseus, we continued to return every other year or so because we had fallen in love with the place. However, this time she recommended we stop along the way at Nafplion, a seaside town tucked between the fingers of the Peloponnese that extend into the Aegean, just south of the ancient settlements of Mycenae and Epidaurus. I was slightly annoyed at having to veer off course and sacrifice my sacred few days on my beloved island, but Mary Lou was determined. "I've heard Nafplion is gorgeous," she assured me, having done her homework. "Trust me toots, you won't be disappointed."

As we drove across the arid, khaki-colored Argolid plain, I noticed a change in the environment as we approached this coastal town. The atmosphere appeared lighter, clearer, the dust being replaced by a salty sharpness in the air. Pulling the car up to the hotel, I was mesmerized by the sheer beauty of the harbor and the water, thick and silver, reflecting the afternoon sun, lapping against the town's tidal walls. As I got out of the car I turned around and was struck by the sight of a castle, soaring hundreds of feet into the air, a mass of dove-gray rock braced against the robin's egg blue sky. I was no longer annoyed at Mary Lou—Nafplion was clearly well worth a detour. Getting there is easy. You can take a bus or rent a car, and the drive along the Saronic Gulf into the heart of the Peloponnese will take you four hours. If a sea journey is your choice, hop on a hydrofoil from the port of Piraeus that will get you there in the same amount of time.

Meandering through the narrow streets, we savored the heady aroma of local dishes that permeated the air: *keftedes me menta* (meatballs in mint), marinated anchovies, and thickly pungent and salty grilled *sardelles* (sardines). One evening we gathered along the shoreline for an impromptu dinner with some locals we chatted up and feasted upon a banquet of *fasolia me tomata* (fresh green beans sautéed in tomato and onion), spit-roasted pork loin, and broiled bream in lemon and olive oil. Several copper pitchers of *krasi mavra* (literally, black wine) fueled a spirited conversation that rang out over the harbor, the evening water the color of diorite and reflecting a rising full moon, shimmering miasmically in the wake left from fishing boats.

The goddess Hera, the long-suffering consort of her philandering husband, Zeus, visited Nafplion annually for a curious treatment: by bathing in the gentle waters of a local spring, she supposedly restored her virginity. Perhaps Hera thought this might entice her hubby to stop chasing other goddesses and impregnating mortals, but to no avail. She was also known as a fertility goddess, so perhaps her efforts at the very least kept her sense of youth and vigor alive and refreshed. Unfortunately, it doesn't look like this trick works for us mere mortals!

Mythology tells us that the town's namesake, Nafplio, was the son of the sea god Poseidon and Danaus, and plays a role in several ancient dramas. It is supposedly where Helen and Menelaus's ship pulled to shore many years after her fateful abduction to Troy, and is also where they discovered that their sister-in-law, Clytemnestra, had been murdered by their nephew, Orestes. Located just down the road from Mycenae and another important Mycenaean site, Tiryns, this is a likely port for these ancient kingdoms.

As in Athens, Nafplion's main *plateia* is named Syntagma, or Constitution Square. Pull up a chair at one of the cafés surrounding this sleek, paving-stoned plaza and nurse a café *megala metrio* (coffee with milk and medium sugar) and nibble on a *kataifi*, a singularly memorable Greek dessert resembling shredded wheat, that is a heavenly confection of honey, walnuts, and flaky pastry. The central square of any Greek town is where the action is, and in the evening the entertainment is supplied by Greek life at its best: families gathered around tables laden with food and wine, and kids on bikes, tricycles, and strollers. Greeks dote on their children and I have often watched in amazement as they stay up until all hours of the night, running between impromptu soccer games, riding coin operated horses and occasionally stopping by their parents' table, being fork-fed French fries, ice creams, and Pepsi.

We enjoyed wandering down the gleaming, parquet stone streets to window shop. Local women, smartly dressed in elegant wool and linen suits, passed by in pairs, carrying their purchases of produce and bakery goods. Blood red, velvety purple, and dazzlingly white bougainvillea twisted and trailed over the neoclassical mansions that lined the streets. Turkish fountains and mosques attest to the region's Ottoman occupation and recall the Greek war of Independence, when Nafplion was named the country's first capital between 1823 and 1834.

Take a caique out onto the Argolic Gulf and stop at the tiny islet of Agio Therodori. Once a fortification during the Venetian period, this fortress, known as Bourtzi, is not only the most photographed place in Nafplion, but it offers a breathtaking view of the city, offering up a layer cake of turquoise water, reflecting the shimmering harbor lights in the evenings, and the towering heights of the castle of Palamidi hovering hundreds of feet above the shore.

✳ www.greeka.com/peloponnese/nafplion/nafplion-excursions
/nafplion-palamidi-castle.htm

If you are feeling energetic, it's only 999 steps to the top. This is where modern revolutionary Theodore Kolokotronis was imprisoned, but the echoes of ancient warriors such as Themistocles, Epaminondas, Achilles, and Leonidias still can be heard among these ancient battlements. The view is worth the climb in itself; you will be treated to a panorama of the sparkling Argolic Gulf in one direction and the vast Argolid plain as far as the eye can see in the other.

On our last day, Mary Lou and I treated ourselves to dinner at a restaurant perched on a cliff high above the city. As the summer sun dissolved into the syrupy sea, we toasted each other over a tangy retsina, crunchy kalamari dusted with sea salt, and *salata horiatiki*, village salads of blood red tomatoes, cucumber, crescents of red onion, and salty feta cheese. Even though it delayed my arrival to our ultimate destination, I have since become a solid fan of Nafplion. For those who wish to dive deep into this stunning region of the Peloponnese—or perhaps are curious to dip into those springs where Hera annually restored her virginity—put this stunning gem by the sea on a priority list to visit.

✻

92 *Sounion*

WHERE LORD BYRON LEFT HIS MARK

If your idea of romance is to experience sunset by the sea with a Greek temple in the background, this is the place to go. The remains of this Doric temple, with its elegant, fingerlike tapered columns rising seventy-three meters above the sea, provides the perfect backdrop for anyone wanting the best "*Wish you were here*" shot for the folks back home. At Sounion, this temple, dedicated to the sea god Poseidon, is the main attraction.

You may recall that a battle between Athena and Poseidon is depicted on the pediment sculptures on the Parthenon of Athens, with Athena claiming victory and naming rights for the city below. Poseidon, in a show of bravado, thrust his trident into the earth, causing a gush of seawater to flow out in a burst. Athena's gift to the city was the planting of an olive tree. In *The Greek Myths*, mythologist Robert Graves explains why one's gift was more precious than the other's:

> *Poseidon is greedy of earthly kingdoms, and once claimed possession of Attica by thrusting his trident into the acropolis at Athens, where a well of sea-water immediately gushed out and is still to be seen; when the South Wind blows you may hear the sound of the surf far below. Later, during the reign of Cecrops, Athene came and took possession in a gentler manner, by*

*planting the first olive-tree beside the well. Poseidon, in a fury, challenged
her to a single combat, and Athene would have accepted had not Zeus
interposed and ordered them to submit the dispute to arbitration. Presently,
then, they appeared before a divine court, consisting of their supernatural
fellow-deities, who called on Cecrops to give evidence. Zeus himself expressed
no opinion, but while all the other gods supported Poseidon, all the goddesses
supported Athene. Thus, by a majority of one, the court ruled that Athene
had the better right to the land, because she had given it the better gift.*

*Greatly vexed, Poseidon sent huge waves to flood the Thriasian Plain, where
Athene's city of Athenae stood, whereupon she took up her above in Athens
instead, and called that too after herself. However, to appease Poseidon's
wrath, the women of Athens were deprived of their vote, and the men forbidden to bear their mother's names as hitherto.*

Poseidon was also appeased by the erection of the temple at
Sounion. Built in the 5th century B.C. on the site of an older
shrine, the temple is situated exquisitely on the rocky cape extend-
ing out into the sea. The area was prized by ancients not only for
its silver mines beneath the surface, but the fact that it would be the
first landmark sighted by ships sailing to Athens's port of Piraeus.
Sailors from all over would visit the sanctuary and give thanks for
such a valuable signpost, and ask Poseidon for safe passage on their
sea voyages. And visitors with a major league pitcher's arm can try
their hand (or arm) at chucking a stone from the heights and try
to land it in the sea—some have actually achieved this feat! On a
clear day, you can see the islands of Kea, Kythnos, and the edge of
the Peloponnese in the distance, floating like massive, motionless
turtles in the mercury-smooth sea.

Of the original thirty-four columns, sixteen are still standing today. Most columns have twenty grooves, but these have only
sixteen, accentuating the more elongated, runway-model-thin

pillars. While inscribing graffiti on ancient remains is a taboo subject among archaeologists, there are noteworthy names etched on one of the pillars from travelers visiting the site in the 18th and 19th centuries, among them Lord Byron, (although it was possibly left by an admirer.) Enamored of all things Greek, Byron had high praise for the glorious sites of Sounion,

> *Place me on Sunium's marble steep—*
> *Where nothing, save the waves and I,*
> *May hear our mutual murmurs sweep:*
> *There, swan-like, let me sing and die;*
> *A land of slaves shall ne'er be mine—*
> *Dash down yon cup of Samian wine!*

In ancient times, the southern boundary of the Athenian city-state extended to this tip of the Attic peninsula, some forty-three miles from the city. There the Athenians not only built a sanctuary with shrines dedicated to Poseidon, but also to the goddess Athena, patroness of their city. In antiquity, Athena was worshipped here too; unfortunately, her temple is not as well preserved at Poseidon's.

On a flat plain beneath the rocky rise where Poseidon's temple sits are the remains of the goddess's shrine. Almost as romantic as taking a shot of the setting sun with the backlit cape and temple is the experience of wandering through the bare outline of stones delineating Athena's temple. Less imposing, perhaps by choice to please both gods, the goddess's temple was hidden from view of the sea so as not to incur Poseidon's wrath. The gods' dispute was not limited to the ruling of Athens. During Odysseus's long journey home from the Trojan War, Athena was dedicated to helping the flawed hero, while Poseidon, in retribution for the killing of his son the Cyclops, took every opportunity to block Odysseus's return to his beloved Ithaka. Poseidon raped a beautiful young Medusa in

Athena's temple and her revenge was to turn the young woman into a fearsome, serpentine-headed monster.

After the sun sets in a blur of eggplant, cerulean, and tangerine, be sure to stop on your way back to Athens for a dinner at Mikrolimani. This tony marina (its name means little harbor) is the anchorage for billionaires' yachts and the home to many upscale fish restaurants, most notably Varoulkos (Akti Koumoundourou 52, Piraeus). It is thought by some to be one of the best restaurants in the Athens region, and Chef Lefteris Lazarou will take good care of you with his exquisitely presented platings of marinated sea bass with *stamnagathi* (greens), mussels *saganaki*, grilled octopus from the nearby island of Kalymnos, and steamed clams with Lemnian wine. As the last light of day fades into the molten Aegean Sea, lift your glass of smoky Robola to the sky and make a toast to Athena. She may not have the biggest temple at Sounion, but she won the ultimate battle of the sexes.

᷍

93

The Mani

WHERE WOMEN AND MEN FOUGHT SIDE BY SIDE

If you visualize the Peloponnesian peninsula of Greece as a hand with digits flaring out into the blue Aegean below, think of the Mani as the middle finger. For over the past centuries, due to wars, invasions, and unwanted outsiders, the people of this harsh and remote region of Greece have carved out their own stubbornly independent existence, and continue to do so today.

On a recent drive through the upper part of the Mani, my sister and I were in awe of this barren and scrubby landscape, mostly treeless except for the hardy groves of olive clinging to the rocky soil and bent over like old women tilling the fields. We traversed the peninsula from the town of Gytheio, a port town with ferries running from the island of Kythira, to Aeropolis, a little town on the western shore. Driving through a thunderstorm that blackened the sky, we pulled off the road to take shots of lightning bolts being tossed like Poseidon's tridents from masses of gray clouds and striking the jadeite colored seas below.

The inner Mani is laced with stone roads that wind up the mountains towards tidy, sparsely populated villages, making this region a difficult one to traverse. The road rises over the mountainous ridge south of the Taygetos range and empties out on the Gulf of Messenia. As we headed south towards Gerolimenas, the road wound along the sea, turquoise water lapping against mounds of elephant gray rock, seemingly becoming narrower and narrower, giving the feeling that we were headed to the ends of the world.

And in some ways, The Mani is the end of the world. Legend has it that the tip of the Mani peninsula is the mythical entrance to the Underworld. Its inhabitants, the Maniots, are a people with a rugged and oftentimes violent history of vendetta, war, and invasion. The region's occupation dates back to the Neolithic period, and the current inhabitants trace their ancestry to the Spartans. During the Christianizing period, the locals clung to their pagan beliefs, setting the trend for a staunch and fierce sense of independence that has lasted to the present day.

✳ www.maniguide.info

Successions of generations have fought off invader after invader to preserve their self-sufficient way of life, from the Franks in the 10th and 11th centuries through the Byzantines, Venetians, and Ottoman Turks. These indigenous families cultivated a feudal society during the 14th century in which people lived in tribal villages and developed Hatfield and McCoy-like vendettas that became the stuff of legends. Like spikes being driven into the sky, the region is peppered with stone fortresses, for which the Mani is known. Many were built by the Nyklians, a family that rose up to dominate the region, and about eight hundred are known to exist. Square in shape, the towers vary between fifty and eighty feet in height, and the larger the tower meant the more powerful the family. The structures have few windows, but are pocked with peepholes and apertures just large enough to thrust a dagger through an invader's body. Each has several floors, and three to four rooms crannied with a series of trapdoors and ladders, making hasty retreats possible whenever necessary.

When families weren't busy killing rival clans, Maniot men and women fought side to by side to ward off the Turks. In 1770, an invading Ottoman army of eight thousand battled its way through the Peloponnese, ultimately torturing and killing the chieftain John Mavromichalis. To avenge his death, a group of five thousand Maniot men and women attacked the enemy camp and emerged with only thirty-nine fatalities. In another legendary fight, the wife of leader Constantine Kolokotronis donned battle gear and, holding her infant, Theodore, fought alongside one hundred and fifty men and women against an army of 16,000 Turks. The valiant group ultimately succumbed after twelve fierce days of battle, but Theodore Kolokotronis survived, thanks to his mother's valiant efforts, and went on to become the famed commander of the Greek War of Independence.

In general, during these blood feuds, women were off limits to attackers as men only killed men. Women's roles instead were largely to resupply food and ammunition, and during harvest season, truces were called so that crops could be gathered for the winter. The writer Patrick Leigh Fermor, who traveled here in the 1950s before the advent of paved roads, has written a wonderful account of the region in his book, *The Mani*. If you're a fan of churches, there are hundreds in this region to explore. But don't expect the whitewashed structures with sky blue domes. These Maniot churches, like the populace, are rudimentary and down-to-business, recognizable by their simple stone hewn exteriors and red tiled roofs.

94 *Meteora*

WHERE BOND GIRL CAROLE BOUQUET
HANGS FROM A CLIFF

Bond. James Bond.

If you're old enough to remember the old Bond—and I'm not talking about Pierce Brosnan, I'm referring to Roger Moore—you'll remember his diorite-haired, sloe-eyed love interest in the film *For Your Eyes Only*. The French film star Carole Bouquet swims with Bond through an underwater Greek temple, dodges bullets sprayed from the evil Ari Kristatos's seaplane, but her most spectacular feat is rappelling from the edge of one of the most stunning physical landmarks in Greece: the monastery of Meteora.

Meteora, a series of sandstone pillars ringed by mountains in the distance, rises up on the fertile Thessalian plain like monolithic clusters of tweed-colored pins in a Cyclopean bowling alley. I still get vertigo when I watch the scenes of Bouquet clinging to the vertical rock, along with the preternaturally coiffed Moore scaling the sheer face of these cliffs to smoke out Ari; for it's not only a great place for bad guys to hide, it's an even better place for good guys to get close to God.

Second only to Mount Athos, the monasteries of Meteora remain some of the most important in Greek orthodoxy. The name, which means "suspended in air," is an apt description of these otherworldly peaks that dominate this part of Thessaly in north-central Greece. While there are pathways and even roads in some cases, the only way the earliest occupants were able to access the death-defying heights of these rock pillars was via a system of ladders, pulleys, and baskets. Mountain peaks have traditionally been places where pilgrims have tread to be close to God, and in the 11th century, Byzantine hermits claimed these pillars for themselves. During the 14th and 15th centuries the present monasteries were built atop these monstrous, elephant-leg-like rock formations, and by the year 1500 there were twenty-four. Today only four remain active.

✳ whc.unesco.org/en/list/455

As is typical, almost all the monasteries are male only, except for one: Saint Stephanos. This sole nunnery has a fantastic view of the valley towards Kalambaka, the nearest city, in the distance. Its church, built in 1798 and dedicated to Saint Haralambos, has the relic of the saint's skull, given to the nuns by Prince Vladislav of Wallachia. The nuns believe the skull has the powers to cure illness, and visitors from all over make a pilgrimage to the church to be healed.

Nearby Saint Nikolaos Anapafsas Monastery, built in the 14th century, is more easily accessible, and its interior is decorated with frescoes by Cretan artist Theophanis the Monk. The most famous monastery of the group, the Great Meteoran Monastery, has a large church with a twelve-sided dome and today is used as a museum.

The Aghia Triada, or Holy Trinity Monastery, was used in the Bond film. It was founded by the Monk Dometius and is spectacularly positioned at the apex of a needle-like pillar of rock. Visitors need to be ready for a sweaty climb, for this monastery is accessed only by climbing 140 extremely steep steps. Be sure to take a peek into the Church of St. John the Baptist with its paintings dating to 1682 on your way up.

Two brothers founded the Roussanou Monastery in 1545. To admire its wall paintings and wooden iconostasis, the non-faint of heart will need to cross a narrow bridge between this and another peak. Varlaam Monastery was first established by an ascetic who built a tiny chapel on this rocky peak in the 14th century. After the monk's death, the site fell into disrepair until the arrival of two rich priests from the city of Ioannina. Legend has it they first had to scare off a monster that inhabited a cave at the site before they established a church dedicated to all the saints. Supposedly it took them twenty-two years using baskets and pulleys to lift all the building materials to the summit, but only twenty days to actually build the structure.

Don't forget to bring a scarf or wear a long skirt or pants, as visitors are expected to cover legs and shoulders out of respect. Bring a camera and plan to spend the whole day at the site: climbing up and down the stairs and pathways will take your breath away, but, then again, so will the views.

❧

95 *Mount Olympus*

HOME OF THE MYTHOLOGICAL GODS
AND GODDESSES

I picture them they way they are depicted in bas relief and in paintings, side by side, some twisted in conversation, and some just looking regal, as they follow in procession, robes flowing, carrying the attributes of each: Zeus with his thunderbolt, Hera and her

scepter, Poseidon carrying his trident, Athena, her helmet and owl, Demeter holding her sheaf of wheat, Artemis with her bow and quiver, Apollo strumming his lyre, Ares with his helmet spear, a veiled Aphrodite, Hermes wearing his winged cap, and Hephaestus with his staff. As the throne of Zeus and the home of the twelve major Greek mythological deities, Mount Olympus was considered an idealized place, and there are multiple peaks in Greece, Turkey, and Cyprus called Olympus. But the massif of mountains located one hundred kilometers southwest of Greece's second city, Thessalonika, is thought by most to be the original location for the mythological Olympus.

At just under 10,000 feet, Mytikas (the nose), the tallest of this series of jagged peaks, is the highest mountain in Greece and the second highest in the Balkan region. Etched against the eternally cobalt skies, copper tinged in the summer and sprinkled with white in winter, Mytikas was called *pantheon by* the ancient Greeks, the name associated with the twelve major gods of Greece. The mountains are engraved by a series of Alpine ravines that Homer dubbed "mysterious folds," where the gods were thought to convene and consort among the valleys' holly, ash, yew, and cherry plum trees.

This region, dusted with snow in winter for seven months and carpeted in a riot of flowers in summertime, was made into a national park in 1938. Because of the abundance of flora and fauna in the park, UNESCO additionally declared the area a biosphere preserve. *The Iliad* describes Olympus as "magnificent, long, glorious and full of trees," and today is no exception. The park's meadows and gorges are filled with multiple species of oak, bay laurel, and cedar along with groves of European Black and Bosnian pine scattered over four floral zones thanks to differing microclimates.

Olympus is a hiker's paradise. The more adventurous visitor may want to set out and climb the highest peak, which was only conquered one hundred years ago by a Greek, Christos Kakalos, and two Frenchmen, Frederic Boissonas and Daniel Baud-Bovy. July and August are the best months, but also the most popular, so you may want to book a hotel in advance. Summiting is possible without climbing equipment; rugged shoes, comfortable clothes, and a backpack with provisions and enough water are sufficient. The trip will take two days for most, but longer for those with a more leisurely itinerary.

As you keep one eye on the peaks above you, be on the lookout for various critters that live among the trees and forest floor, including the red fox and neon splotched salamanders scattering across the forest floor and disappearing under rocks. Various types of eagles, storks, and even vultures can clot the skies and Olympus is well known for its butterflies. All in all, more than 1,700 species call Olympus home, including twenty-three rare varietals not found anywhere else, making it one of the richest ecological areas in Greece.

The main event is, of course, the gods and goddesses. The king of the gods, Zeus, solely occupied the peak known as Stefani. During high summer today, thunderstorms are prevalent in the region and you can visualize Zeus in all his glory, tossing thunderbolts from his throne. Whereas Zeus was known for his vengeance as well as endless flings with paramours both divine and mortal, his wife, Hera (and sister!), kept close watch on him and regularly avenged herself on the poor objects of Zeus's seduction. The remaining immortals include Hera, who was the youngest daughter of Titans Cronus and Rhea, and her other siblings, Demeter, Poseidon, Hades, and Hestia. As god of the sea, earthquakes, and tsunamis, Poseidon carried his iconic trident and was known, like brother Zeus, for his violent outbursts and multiple love affairs. Demeter is the eternal middle child and wanted everyone to get along; as goddess of fertility her attributes include the pig, wheat, and poppy. As goddess of war and wisdom, Athena was born, fully formed, from the forehead of her father Zeus, and her symbols are the owl and the olive tree, sacred to Athens, her namesake city. Ares is the god of war and carries his spear with him. He is married to Aphrodite, goddess of love and beauty, and their children are the result of the dubious union of love and war: Phobos (Panic), and Demos (Fear).

At the foot of Olympus lies the site of Dion. Before departing on his many campaigns to the East, Alexander the Great made sacrifices to the gods here, and there is a small archaeological museum to visit. Zeus's prolific fling with the Titanide Mnemosyne produced the nine Muses, who are said to inhabit the northern slope. They include Euterpe (music), Cleo (history), Calliope (epic poetry), Erato (love poetry), Terpsichore (dance), Melpomene (tragedy), Polyhymnia (hymns), Thalia (comedy), and Urania (astronomy). So if lightning and Zeus's thunder raining down from above isn't enough supernatural excitement when visiting Mount Olympus, keep your eyes open on your trek to the summit, for you just might spy nine of his daughters cavorting amongst the poppy and lavender-filled valleys or skipping along the snowy peaks.

96 *Kosmas*

A PELOPONNESIAN VILLAGE ABOVE THE CLOUDS

Zeus had torn open the sky and a cascade of hail had rained down upon our car, collecting like snow on the wipers and hood—if I hadn't known we were in Greece, I would have thought we were in the Alps instead. Yet after the slow, slippery climb up the side of a mountain to reach this tiny town, the drive to Kosmas was worth it. Located in the Parnonas mountains above the coastal town of Leonidio, this picturesque, terracotta-studded hillside village in the southern Peloponnese is a little slice of heaven.

It was early November when my sister Deb and I visited, so the winter weather wasn't unusual. We parked the car and took a stroll, hoping to have lunch at one of the tavernas lining Kosmas's main square. Built in a semicircle, the balconied fronts of rustic stone buildings face a gray and white stone village church, dedicated to the Saints Anargyroi, Cosmas, and Damian. Twin siblings who lived during the third century A.D., the brothers were physicians and early Christian martyrs who accepted no payment for their services, earning the name *anargyroi*, or "holy unmercenaries." Most impressive were the towering chestnut trees that ringed the church and shaded the square, each encircled with a cobbled planter of the same grayish white stone. The trees undoubtedly provide a haven of shade in the summer, but in winter they loomed like colossal,

twisted monuments, their branches sprawling and reaching forebodingly towards the sky.

With the aerial views to the valley below, the trees burnished in
claret and ginger, you feel as though you are in a Bavarian mountain village until you sample the local cuisine. This is a meat-eating
town, especially in the winter, and instead of schnitzel and sauer-
braten, the fragrance of oregano-dusted, roasted lamb permeates
the crisp air. The usual menu items prevail, with chicken, *souvlaki*
and lamb chops, but you can try some grilled pies stuffed with veg-
gies called *saitia,* and even a dish you would never find in the U.S.:
kokoretsi. Sweetbreads are diced and compacted, sausage-like, into
casings (sometimes lamb or goat intestine are cleaned and serve as
useful sausage containers). The resulting concoction is laced with
string to hold it together, bathed in olive oil, lemon, and salt and
put on the spit. If you are adventurous, it's worth a taste—wash it
down with a local wine *apo bareli* (literally from the barrel).

In the fall, the region is known for its chestnuts, which vendors
roast in copper braziers, but visitors can sample other local delicacies. According to Matt Barrett, "The specialties of the village are
yida, a goat soup that is eaten in the winter, *gkougkes,* which is a local
thick pasta with cheese, and *pitaroudia,* the local horta or spinach pie
which is fried, grilled, or sautéed instead of baked. They have an
excellent local rosé, more tan than pink and almost like sherry."

My sister and I opted to do some shopping and found this ethereal, cloud-dusted community to be artistic as well. On one end
of the square we wandered into a pottery workshop called Kosmas
Arcadias, run by Evangelos Stathakis. My eyes were immediately
drawn to a row of small, bright red vessels that lined a shelf. I was
delighted to find they were candleholders, whimsically formed into
pomegranate shapes. Lighting a tiny votive, the sales girl placed it
inside, allowing the candlelight to stream through the perforated
container, dappling the ceiling with animated golden beams.

On the other side of the square, we stopped into a tiny dry goods shop jammed with metal buckets, nails, and garden tools. I turned a corner and spied a shelf full of goat bells, their hammered copper surfaces gleaming in the darkened shop. When I picked one up, the metallic clang resonated throughout the shop and out the door, its eerie peal echoing across the flagstones of the square and pricking the ears of a sleeping dog.

Lost in the mists of Arcadia, Kosmas seems to hover above it all. Nowadays, whenever I want to return to thoughts of this diminutive village at the top of the mountains above Leonidio, I pick up the bell and give it a shake. The lonely sounds of goats in the valleys and slopes beneath Kosmas are brought back, as is my longing to return one day to this enchanting Greek Brigadoon.

⁂

97 Zakynthos and Shipwreck Beach

ONE OF GREECE'S MOST STUNNING SHORES

I have a confession to make: I have a debilitating fear of heights. That's why, when I heard about the towering cliffs that loom above the forebodingly named Shipwreck Beach on Zakynthos, I was afraid to visit this stunning, yet petrifying place. However, as I read more about this remote island in the Ionian Island chain, my curiosity got the better of me, and ultimately, I summoned the courage to go. It was well worth the effort.

Located off the western coast of the Greek mainland, Zakynthos was known in antiquity for its pine forests, which were used to construct ships. Today's Zakynthos is still wooded with vast swaths of conifer, and is also known for its dried sweet seedless grapes. The next time you're in the grocery store and see those red canisters of raisins in the produce section, look in the middle of the label for the word "Zante," which is the Greek name for the island.

Lured by the exceptionally soft sand beaches of the popular resort of Laganas, Zakynthos is where the great loggerhead turtles come ashore during the summer to dig holes for their nests and lay their eggs. Known as *caretta-caretta*, Zakynthos islanders have become increasingly protective of the these magnificent creatures, and in order to preserve their habitat from beach-goers, the Greek Protection Society has set up watches at night. Hatchlings are drawn by the moon's light to the sea, and property owners along the southern beaches of the island are asked to turn off their lights at night to protect them from being distracted by the artificial light and lured in the wrong direction.

❄ www.zakynthos.net.gr

It's well worth renting a car if you come to the island, which you can easily circumnavigate in a day. Your starting point, the main port of Zakynthos town, was completely rebuilt in 1953 after a massive earthquake leveled almost the entire island. From the quaint arcaded street that runs parallel to the waterfront, you can watch fishing boats come in and unload their catch, then stop afterwards at one of the small tavernas along the wharf to sample the local seafood, including sardines, red mullet, and silver sea bream.

Another Zakynthian culinary specialty is the dubiously named spatchcocked chicken. Split along the backbone and laid out flat, the chicken is seasoned with salt, pepper, and olive oil, put directly on a barbeque grill and topped with a foil-wrapped brick to weigh it down. The bird cooks more evenly this way and the barbequing renders it with a deliciously smoky flavor.

According to Homer, the island was settled around 1500 B.C. by Prince Zakynthos, the son of King Dardanos of Troy. Legend tells us that the goddess of the moon, Artemis, hunted in the famous pine forests of Zakynthos, and that a cult to this famous tomboy deity was established on the island by the Arcadians in the first century B.C. Some sources claim that Christianity was established here when Mary Magdalene stopped on the island in 34 A.D., and a festival in the village of Maries is held annually to commemorate this event. In the 15th century, Zakynthos came under Venetian rule, and as the Flower of the East, or *Il Fiori di Levante*, the island underwent a renaissance, producing many poets and writers, including the Greek National Poet, Dionysios Solomos.

Aside from pine forests, spatchcocked birds, raisins and turtles, my main reason for coming to Zakynthos was to see one of Greece's ten most extraordinary beaches. Legend has it that a boat carrying contraband cigarettes was shipwrecked in a storm and washed ashore on Navagio Bay, a remote stretch of sand on the north of the island. Inaccessible by land, it is surrounded by soaring, 600-foot chalk-white cliffs, and the location is so famous that Anthony Bourdain even filmed an episode of his TV show, *No Reservations*, in this photogenic spot.

Instead of taking the approach from sea, I had heard that a road led up to the cliffs at the tip of the island at Cape Skinari, allowing you to view the beach from above. In my small rental car, I made my way up the spine of the island, past the 16th century monastery of the Virgin Mary of Anafonitrias, where the island's patron saint, Dionysios, spent the last years of his life as an abbot. Downshifting around hairpin turns and near-aerial views of the sea, the road coiled its way through fields of lavender and sage. Climbing up towards the tiny mountain villages of Volime and Korithi, the car punctured a low-lying cloud cover, and as the wisps of cotton candy mist blew past the window it felt as though I had arrived at the gates of heaven.

Past Korithi the road came to a dead end, emptying into a small parking area on a cliff-like plateau. Cutting the engine, I got out of the car and was hit by a stiff wind. A group of people was walking in the distance, followed by a German shepherd who ranged nervously around the rocky outcrop. Hurrying to catch up with them, I hiked up a slight rise from the parking lot. Suddenly I heard a low roaring sound and watched as a couple, a dozen yards ahead of me, held hands and knelt down on the ground. As I got closer, I realized, a petrifying sixty-story drop below them was the beach. A Danish tourist offered to hold my hand and I leaned over, my heart in my mouth, just a little bit more. A sheer drop, hundreds of feet below,

I could see the hulk of the broken ship. Sitting like a burnt insect on the pristine sand, it looked like a toy from this height.

A gust of wind slapped me in the face and I grasped the Dane's hand harder. He pulled me back and, gingerly, I backed away from the edge. Incredibly, there was no guardrail around the site, only a set of ropes tied loosely to posts driven into the ground. Standing on the cliff, I felt like I was on the edge of the world. The sea, a layered parfait of turquoise, emerald, and indigo, pounded and crashed below, the waves echoing up the cliffs. I watched the ultramarine water spanning out for miles, the sun igniting the surface with blinding light.

After a few moments of astonishment, I realized where I was standing, and my sense of awe quickly reverted to terror. Carefully making my way down the slope, I returned to my car; sitting in the front seat, I needed a moment to catch my breath.

Although I wasn't able to see them from this height, I knew a series of caves had been worn into the cliffs from the relentless action of the sea, and you can take a boat to enjoy the surreally aquamarine water from these grottoes beneath Cape Skinari. Next time, I promised myself. While I was happy I was brave enough to witness this unparalleled sight, I vowed that any future visit to this stunning island would remain at sea level. My poor acrophobic heart couldn't take another peek over the edge.

※

98 *Costa Navarino*

AN ECOLOGICALLY FRIENDLY LUXURY RESORT IN MESSENIA

Freeze frame: Julie Delpy, the ethereally beautiful French actress, is sitting at a table by the edge of the sea. The syrupy waves of the Ionian lap at her feet as she sips her glass of ouzo. Sooner or later her husband, played by Ethan Hawke, shows up to confront the underlying issues in their marriage. I won't give away the ending, but let's just say their choice of location for a vacation certainly doesn't hurt. If you've seen *Before Midnight*, the latest in the series of movies by Richard Linklater and starring Ethan Hawke and Julie Delpy, then you know this place: the gorgeous, thoroughly decadent, and thoroughly green resort, Costa Navarino, is straight out of a movie.

Ever since the 13th century B.C., when King Nestor welcomed Telemachus to his palace in search of his father Odysseus, the region of Messenia in the southwestern Peloponnese has been a center of art, culture and luxury, welcoming guests from all over the world. Yet it appears the ancients were not the only ones to find this landscape beckoning them to construct palace-like structures. Near the coastline, construction continues on one of the largest resort complexes to be built in Greek history. The luxury hotels, restaurants, spa, and two championship golf courses of the Costa

Navarino resort complex are being developed a short distance from the archaeological site of Nestor's palace, situated to command the same view of Homer's legendary sea.

The Costa Navarino resort extends over three thousand acres of gently sloping land overlooking one kilometer of sandy beach along the Ionian Sea. The use of local limestone and green building methods have resulted in a series of buildings that blend into the landscape, not taking away from but adding to it. This hotel is definitely on the upper end, but you get what you pay for. Many rooms have their own swimming pool, beautifully overlooking the Ionian. You can sit out on your own patio, order a bottle of local wine from room service and toast the sunset overlooking the gleaming sea.

The resort is family friendly and offers children the opportunity to do arts projects and go on nature hikes. Adults can opt for a massage in the facility's world-class spa and go snorkeling or scuba diving in the area's vibrant waters with a PADI certified instructor. Take a day trip to visit the ruins of the Palace of Nestor, or the local shuttle will take you to have dinner in the nearby, Italianate village of Pylos. In-home cooking classes are offered, and guests can learn the regional recipes of Messenia from the local women's association. In the fall, visitors are treated to vineyard and wine-tasting tours to sample the local vintage, as well as participate in the local harvest. Twelve restaurants offer diners a wide variety of organically grown ingredients, and award-winning chefs serve an extensive range of Greek, fusion, and continental cuisines based on the rich flavors of the Messenian region.

According to spokesperson Marina Papatsoni, the resort has taken the best interests of the region to heart, "As Messenia is one of the regions with the highest biodiversity in Europe, its preservation and the protection of ecologically important habitats surrounding Costa Navarino is a key element of the development," she reports.

The resort's architectural design is based on principles of bio-climatic architecture safeguarding the integrity of the landscape and horizon. Roofs are planted and buildings are earth-sheltered to enhance biodiversity and habitat protection. The building foot-print will end up being less than half the percentage permitted and more than 90 percent of the total land area will be dedicated to natural and planted landscape.

❋ www.costanavarino.com/

"An extensive recycling program for paper, plastics, glass, used oil, batteries, and organic waste has been set in motion, resulting in a significant reduction of the amount of waste ending up in landfills," Papatsoni says. Part of the waste management system is the operation of a large-scale wastewater treatment facility within the premises of Costa Navarino. In addition, the resort has started a project—the biggest ever attempted in Europe—to uproot on site olive and other fruit bearing trees and replant them on site. Of an estimated total of twenty-four thousand olive and citrus trees, more than eight thousand trees have been replanted so far with an almost one hundred percent success rate.

Messenia, apart from being one of the most archaeologically rich regions of Greece, also contains a large area of natural wet-lands, which are home to a number of bird species, some of them endangered. Costa Navarino and the Hellenic Ornithological Service work in concert to upgrade the wetlands by removing non-native plant species that burden the river's ecosystem. The Gialova lagoon is Greece's southernmost major wetland supporting hun-dreds of bird species in Greece as well as the African chameleon. Costa Navarino has sponsored programs to protect these habitats as well as a project that will map the nests of the loggerhead sea turtle (*caretta caretta*) in cooperation with Archelon, the Sea Turtle Protection Society of Greece. Resort lighting close to beaches is installed with special covers and uses low intensity bulbs to avoid disturbing turtle nests during hatching season.

Those who have yet to visit Messenia are in for a delightful surprise. In a landscape where ancient treasures are still being discovered and modern landmarks are being erected, be prepared to travel in time over a span of 5,000 years. With so many sites to choose from: archaeological treasures, exotic natural habitats and one of the worlds' most luxurious resorts along this legendary coastline, the region is as historically rich and opulently welcoming as it was in Nestor's time.

❧

99 *Kandylakia of Greece*

ROADSIDE SHRINES AND THE GODDESSES
WHO TEND THEM

Some of my favorite things to see along the roads of Greece are the myriad shrines that dot the winding switchbacks as you drive through the countryside. These tiny memorials, known as *kandylakia*, exist all over Greece, and every region and island has its own collection. Sometimes propped up on spindly metal stilts, sometimes firmly secured on brick pillars, their existence is often to observe a death, and this is something I try to keep in mind. Over the years as I've crisscrossed this country by bus, train, car, and on foot, I've kept a mental journal of these tiny places of worship.

On Ithaka these shrines literally line the only road that serpentines above the silver Ionian between the main town of Vathy and the north of the island. When I first arrived on Ithaka in the mid-1980s, the roads were unpaved and the gravel, rocky surface made travel even more difficult—and dangerous—than it is today. Some places along the route are edged in steep cliffs hovering three hundred feet above the gleaming straits of Kefalonia, so you need a pair of steady hands at the wheel.

Today this spectacular drive is smoothly asphalted, but even improved road conditions can't stop reckless young drivers who like to roar around these hairpin turns on their motorcycles. When I lived here, one of my friends actually went over a cliff on his motorcycle—and survived. Every time an accident happens, one of these shrines is erected, either to thank God for saving the life of an individual or to mourn and honor the life of someone who perished on that spot.

Along the roads in the southeastern Peloponnese, from Poulithra to Leonidio, over the mountains to Kosmas and down to Gythion are some of the most remarkable examples of these shrines. On one particular drive along a winding series of switch-backs, my sister and I were mesmerized by the slate-gray Aegean pounding below as storm clouds gathered in an angry gray-green confusion, spitting out Zeus-worthy bolts of lightning. As the sun broke through the tempest, the golden rays streamed down, illuminating one particularly beautiful memorial on the edge of a cliff. Erected on a sturdy stone base, its crucifix slightly askew on the top, its freshly painted sapphire door and whitewashed exterior gleamed in the late afternoon sun, sharply contrasted against a jadeite miasma of sea.

Take some time to pull off the road and examine these shrines. Most of them resemble tiny chapels, but I have seen elaborate, white multilayered wedding cake structures, detailed to dollhouse perfection, as well as models with bell towers and terracotta roofs, brightly trimmed in shades of blue, red, and yellow. Peek inside to see a variety of contents: fat beeswax candles, gold-rimmed icons of saints, and bottles of oil for lamps. Most contain a scattering of ex-votos atop a lining of foil, but on occasion I have seen some unusual contents: a can of beer, a bottle of ouzo, and a pack of cigarettes. The strangest I came upon was a board, positioned atop a metal feta canister, by the side of the road. On top sat an unopened bottle of beer, next to a votive candle and a can of Heineken. A bouquet of flowers, long since dried, lay nearby, the desiccated blooms shuddering in a stiff breeze. Who had left this strange assemblage? Like Hestia, who guarded the ancient family hearth, I wondered: what modern goddess tends to these evocative memorials?

One afternoon, driving down the Saronic coast to the town of Leonidio, I happened to catch sight of an old widow, cloaked in black, approaching a shrine. Assiduously, she removed the small melted candles, replacing them with fresh ones from her small bag, and lit them. I watched, respectfully, from a distance, until she finished her work. Climbing onto her donkey sidesaddle, she gave the beast a slap with a switch and began up a steep dirt path. Was the shrine for a husband who had passed away? Or a son in one of those motorcycle accidents? I'll never know, but as I watched her disappear behind a veil of crimson bougainvillea into the upper reaches of the cliff, I realized that, in Greece, the goddess manifests herself in a multitude of ways.

❧

VIII

One of Greece's
Great Scenic Drives

100 *A Drive to Remember on Ithaka*

FROM VATHY TO KIONI ON ODYSSEUS'S ISLAND

I have driven this road so often that I sometimes feel I could do so blindfolded. But I wouldn't dare; with the occasional sheer cliff along the road that drops straight off the edge to the gleaming, mercury-colored Ionian hundreds of feet below, it's not a good idea, and besides—I'd miss the unparalleled views. No matter what mode of transportation, or how often I traverse it, I will never tire of this epic drive from the main town of Vathy to the village of Kioni in the north of the island.

By most standards, Ithaka is a small island. Shaped like a bulbous ant with a bisected waist, it sits like a chubby baby in the lap of neighboring Kefalonia, a giant of an island just to the west in the Ionian island chain. Ithaka is the island Odysseus spent twenty years trying to return to, and this longing—called *nostos* in Greek—is shared by many who have also been smitten by this legendary landscape. As evoked by Constantine Cavafy's *Ithaka*, a poem beloved by Jacqueline Kennedy Onassis, it is a place that inspires journeys, both physical and psychological.

Keep Ithaka always in your mind.
Arriving there is what you are destined for.
But do not hurry the journey at all.

Better if it lasts for years,
so you are old by the time you reach the island,
wealthy with all you have gained on the way,
not expecting Ithaka to make you rich.

These prophetic words have moved me since I first stepped foot on this legendary soil, and it is the drive that winds up its coiled, serpentine roads that mesmerizes me the most. Once you arrive in Vathy, the island's capital, hire a taxi, or if you can, rent a car from one of the local agencies. Make sure to grab your camera, bikini and some sunscreen and follow the signs out of town to experience an unforgettable day trip.

Stop Number One: At the top of the hill just above the village, park the car on the dirt road leading up to the millhouses and take in the view overlooking expansive Vathy harbor. Famous for being the home of Odysseus, the island is also known for having the largest natural harbor in Greece, measuring one mile from the two large promontories of rock at the entrance of the harbor to Vathy town. Admire the candy-colored buildings that grip the harbor below, and watch the day sailors come and go, tacking back and forth across the water like confused moths. By the way, that tiny island in the middle of Vathy harbor bristling with windblown conifers surrounding a miniature chapel was once used to quarantine lepers.

Stop Number Two: Just around the corner is Dexia Bay. Homer tells us this marks the spot where Odysseus returned to his beloved island under cover of darkness and in disguise, hoping to evade the nasty suitors badgering his beleaguered wife, Penelope, who waited twenty years for her beloved husband to return from the Trojan War. Tiny Rabbit Island floats like a beauty mark on the placid bay and Mount Neriton looms beyond, rising precipitously from the water's edge.

The road continues north, winding around a bay known in ancient times as Rheitron. Seen from certain angles, this long and narrow body of water does resemble a river, which it was referred to in antiquity. Swing beneath the five hundred meter peak of Aetos, the small mountain that marks the center of the island. As you look across the water, you will see a strip of road winding its way up a sharp slope—this is where the fun begins, so make sure your seatbelt is fastened tight!

As you climb the slope, take a moment at each switchback to marvel at the view below: the turquoise waters span as far as the eye can see, studded with islands that appear to dissolve into an amethyst haze. Just before you reach the summit, you will pass an area where, for a brief moment, you will be able to see both sides of the island at once, then, like a door snapping shut, the view to the right will abruptly be cut off. The massive island of Kefalonia will appear across an expanse of mirrored water, looming like a battleship to your west, where land meets water in a miasmic ribbon of sea and earth.

Stop Number Three: Take the cutoff to the monastery of Kathara, which sits at the top of Mount Neriton. The road becomes increasingly steep and narrow, and at this dizzying elevation, it will feel like you're on an airplane. In Homer's *Odyssey*, Odysseus describes the grandeur of his beloved island:

> *I live in clearly-seen Ithaca, where there is an imposing mountain, Neriton with its trembling foliage.*

Pull the car onto the curb and take lots of photos, as the view down to Vathy harbor is heart stopping. From this pinnacle you can see both Vathy and Dexia Bay, as well as Mount Aetos. Look out to the east and you will see a series of tiny islands and the mainland melting away into the silvery Ionian.

Stop Number Four: After you've made your way back down to the main road (mind you, this drive is not for the fainthearted) continue past tiny villages clinging to the cliffs and wind your way around the final turn into Stavros. This small, shaded village overlooking generous Polis Bay is where a delightful, two-night festival is held every August, attracting folks all the way from the mainland. Souvlaki, freshly fried *loukomades* (doughnuts) and bottomless cups of rough local wine are on the menu, as well as nonstop music and dancing that literally fills the town square in the front of the church. Pay homage to a statue of Odysseus that overlooks Polis Bay, where twelve ancient tripods and a dedication to Odysseus were found in a submerged cave.

Stop Number Five: Just past Stavros, take the right fork in the road and wind your way down to Frikes. This tiny fishing hamlet with its aquamarine pebbled shores is a refreshing place to stop for a drink, or lunch if you don't feel like driving all the way to Kioni. Watch the ferry come in from Lefkas and admire the colorful sailboats bobbing offshore.

Stop Number Six: The final leg of the journey takes you around a series of three beaches, called Kravoulia One, Two, and Three, all reachable with staircases leading down from the road. I personally love Kravoulia Two, with its egg-sized smooth stones and parfait of turquoise, lavender, and silver waters. After warming up in the sun, I could float all day in the brisk but buoyant sea, and gaze at the endlessly blue skies above. Private yachts often sneak in and out of these peaceful coves, and I enjoy watching their gleaming chrome and white hulls glide by and disappear behind the arborvitae-studded cliffs.

Stop Number Seven: As you arrive in Kioni, relish the views along the road as it snakes high above the village before dropping down to sea level. In the distance you can see three windmills that dot the headland protecting the bay, and the sapphire waters popping in and out of view between the cypress trees spiking the cliffs along the road. As you arrive at the bottom of the hill, park the car and walk to the water. Several quaint tavernas line the shoreline—pick any one and pull up a chair along the harbor's edge. As you admire the snow-white houses and their terracotta roofs nestled amidst the conifer-encrusted hillside, order a plate of grilled octopus, a *horiatiki* salad of cherry-red tomatoes, crisp cukes, topped with an oregano-dusted slab of salty feta, and toast your epic drive with a bottle of ice-cold Mythos beer. After lunch, walk along the wharf and listen to the wind whistle through the riggings of sailboats anchored along the shoreline.

The road comes to an end in Kioni, but no worries! All you need do is turn the car around and retrace your steps back to Vathy. I can guarantee you won't be disappointed to have to do it twice—for experiencing this stunning drive in reverse will surely fill you with *nostos* for this beautiful island, and remind you, as echoed in Cavafy's timeless poem, that's it's all about the journey.

> *Ithaka gave you the marvelous journey.*
> *Without her you would not have set out.*
> *She has nothing left to give you now.*
> *And if you find her poor, Ithaka won't have fooled you.*
> *Wise as you will have become, so full of experience,*
> *you will have understood by then what these Ithakas mean.*

Books for Further Reading

Andrews, Kevin. *The Flight of Ikaros: Travels in Greece During a Civil War.* Middlesex: Penguin, 1984.

Burn, A.R. *The Pelican History of Greece.* Middlesex: Penguin, 1965.

Campbell, Joseph. *Goddesses: Mysteries of the Feminine Divine.* Novato: New World Library, 2013.

Cavafy, C.P. *Collected Poems.* Ed. George Savidis. Trans. Edmund Keeley and Philip Sherrard. Princeton: Princeton University Press, 1975.

Cosmopoulos, Michael. *Bronze Age Eleusis and the Origins of the Eleusinian Mysteries.* New York: Cambridge University Press, 2015.

Cosmopoulos, Michael, ed. *Greek Mysteries: The Archaeology and Ritual of Ancient Greek Secret Cults.* London: Routledge, 2003.

Durrell, Lawrence. *Prospero's Cell: A Guide to the Landscape and Manners of the Island of Corfu.* New York: Marlowe and Company, 1945.

Durrell, Lawrence. *The Greek Islands.* New York: The Viking Press, 1978.

Fiada, Alexandra. *The Xenophobe's Guide to the Greeks.* Horsham: Ravette Publishing, 1994.

Fowles, John. *The Magus.* New York: Dell Publishing, 1965.

Frazer, Sir James George. *The Golden Bough.* New York: MacMillan Publishing Company, 1922.

Gage, Eleni N. *North of Ithaka: A Granddaughter Returns to Greece and Discovers Her Roots.* New York: St. Martin's Griffin, 2004.

Gage, Nicholas. *Eleni.* New York: Ballantine Books, 1983.

Gage, Nicholas. *Hellas, A Portrait of Greece.* New York: Villard Books, 1987.

Graves, Robert. *The Greek Myths*, volumes I & II. Middlesex: Penguin, 1955.

Habegger, Larry, Sean O'Reilly and Brian Alexander, eds. *Travelers' Tales Greece: True Stories.* Palo Alto: Travelers' Tales, Inc., 2003.

Hall, Manly. *The Secret Teachings of all Ages.* New York: Jeremy P. Tarcher/Penguin, 2003.

Homer. *The Odyssey*. Trans. Richmond Lattimore. New York: Harper and Row, 1967.

Homer. *The Odyssey*. Trans. Robert Fagles. New York: Viking Penguin, 1996.

Kaltsas, Nikolaos and Shapiro, Alan, eds. *Worshiping Women: Ritual and Reality in Classical Athens*. New York: Alexander S. Onassis Public Benefit Foundation, 2008.

Kazantzakis, Nikos. *Zorba the Greek*. Trans. Carl Wildman. New York: Simon and Schuster, 1953.

Luce, J.V. *Celebrating Homer's Landscapes: Troy and Ithaca Revisited*. New Haven: Yale University Press, 1998.

McCabe, Robert A. *Greece: Images of an Enchanted Land*. New York: The Quantuck Lane Press, 2005.

Mylonas, George E. *Eleusis and the Eleusinian Mysteries*. Princeton: University Press, 1962.

Orso, Ethelyn, G. *Modern Greek Humor: A Collection of Jokes and Ribald Tales*. Bloomington: Indiana University Press, 1979.

Pomeroy, Sarah. Goddesses, *Whores, Wives and Slaves: Women in Classical Antiquity*. New York: Schocken Books, 1975.

Porter, Eliot. *The Greek World*. New York: Arch Cape Press, 1980.

Raeburn, Nancy. *Mykonos: A Memoir by Nancy Raeburn*. Minneapolis: New Rivers Press, 1992.

Renault, Mary. *Fire From Heaven*. Middlesex: Penguin, 1970.

Rotroff, Susan I. and Lamberton, Robert D. *Women in the Athenian Agora*. Athens: American School of Classical Studies, 2006.

Simmons, Jane, ed. *The Greek Islands*. New York: DK Publishing, 1997.

Stone, Tom. *The Summer of my Greek Taverna*. New York: Simon and Schuster, 2002.

Wasson, R. Gordon, Hofmann, Albert and Ruck, Carl A. P. *The Road to Eleusis: Unveiling the Secret of the Mysteries*. Berkeley: North Atlantic Books, 2008.

Acknowledgments

Without the help of many fellow hellenophiles, I could not have whittled down my massive list of places to go in Greece to just a mere one hundred.

First of all, my thanks to Larry Habegger and James O'Reilly for giving me this amazing opportunity, and for believing in my ability to deliver Greece in one hundred chapters. Your kindness, patience and unbelievable ease to work with have been a blessing.

My love to Amy Summer, Deborah Summer Muth, and Gael Summer for accompanying me on multiple journeys to Greece— thank you for these rich and memorable odysseys of sisterhood!

Poli agape to Mary Lou Roussel: my beloved fellow Greek traveler for so many years.

Hugs and kisses to Einat Bronstein, Cindy Florin, and Rita Rivera Fox for their treasured friendship and unwavering support throughout the writing of this book and always.

To the loveliest of Greek goddesses (and a few Greek gods!) who guided me, inspired me and informed me with their unique expertise, advice, and counsel: Jessica Bell, Erika Bach, Demetri Vlassopoulos, Diana Farr Louis, Diane Kochilas, Tina Kyriakis, Susan Rotroff, Mary Carpenter, Susan Beer, Mark Beer, Dinos Michaelidis, Maria Michaelidis, Alex Waugh, Vassilis Ballas, Roula Ballas, Alexis Adams, Aglaia Kremezi, Burgi Blauel, Fritz Blauel, Shelley Sarver, Angeliki Fotopoulo, Ariana Ferentinou, Costis

Karavia, Kathleen Pepper, June Field, Nikki Rose, Mariel Hacking, Penny Marinou, and Costas Moraitis.

A shout out to authors who over the decades have inspired me with their writings about Greece: John Fowles, Lawrence Durrell, Constantine Cavafy, Mary Renault, Nicholas Gage, Eleni Gage, Ethelyn G. Orso, Alexandra Fiada, Nikos Kazantzakis, Robert Graves, J.V. Luce, and Homer (translated by both Robert Fagles and Richmond Lattimore.)

To my old Study in Greece pals, with whom I explored the country so many decades ago: Paula Mirk, Georgia Norris, and Paki Donaldson Spears.

Hilia efharisto to Deborah Ruscillo Cosmopoulos and Michael Cosmopoulos for reading many chapters and making sure my references to dates, historical fact, and archaeological detail were accurate and well presented.

A grateful nod to my 100 Places sisters, Susan Van Allen and Marcia DeSanctis, for their kindness and expert guidance as I negotiated the intricacies of this book, and for welcoming me into their club. Deep gratitude as well to Rita Golden Gelman and Eleni Gage for reading my manuscript and taking the time to share their valuable edits and comments.

I thank Katharine Butterworth for showing me the depths of Greece, and for her commitment to drop kick her students through the goal posts of life.

To David Damick (aka Costas) for his generous guidance and expert counsel. May there be a Greek island with a garden to tend in your near future!

Love and thanks to my parents, Jim and Maudie Summer, for inspiring in me the love of travel and for taking me on my first trip to Greece.

A deeply heartfelt *efharisto* to the people of Greece, who never fail to amaze me, amuse me, and impress me with their boundless ability to overcome obstacles and celebrate the richness of life.

To my children, Elena and Alec, who have traveled and worked with me on excavations in Greece—I love you both so very dearly. And love as well to my son-in-law, Alex—I hope our entire family can travel to Greece together some day soon!

Last, but far from least, to my husband, Phil Slavin. Your patience, attention to detail, and loving care in editing this manuscript, as well as your unwavering support, have been invaluable to me—thank you for being there always. I love you, *agape mou*. My favorite journeys have all been—and will be—with you.

Index

About the Author

Amanda Summer is an archaeologist and award-winning writer whose work has appeared in *The New York Times, Islands, Archaeology, Odyssey,* and *The Best Travel Writing.* For the past thirty years she has returned to the Greek island of Ithaka, where she searched for the palace of Odysseus starting in 1984 with a team from Washington University in St. Louis. Currently she is on staff with the Iklaina Archaeological Project in Pylos, Greece. Even though she has traced the odyssey of history's most famous male adventurer, she has a passion for stories about women who have found transformation through travel.